WORKING LONGER

New Strategies for Managing, Training, and Retaining Older Employees

William J. Rothwell, Ph.D.

Harvey L. Sterns, Ph.D.

Diane Spokus, Ph.D.

Joel M. Reaser, Ph.D.

HarperCollins
LEADERSHIP

AN IMPRINT OF HarperCollins

Working Longer

© 2008 William J. Rothwell, Harvey Sterns, Diane Spokus, Joel Reaser

Published by HarperCollins Leadership, an imprint of HarperCollins Focus LLC.

Bulk discounts available. For details visit:
www.harpercollinsleadership.com/bulkquotes
Email: customercare@harpercollins.com

ISBN 978-0-8144-7392-4 [TP]

Printed in the United States of America

ADVISORY BOARD

EDITORIAL BOARD

DEDICATION

William J. Rothwell dedicates this book to his wife *Marcelina*, his daughter *Candice*, his son *Froilan*, and his grandson *Aden*.

Harvey Sterns dedicates this book to his wife *Ronni*, children *Anthony*, *Randy*, and *George*, and grandchildren *Alastair*, *Sarah*, *Sabrina*, and *Noah*.

Diane Spokus dedicates this book to her parents and brother, *Amil*, *Mamie*, and *Mark Bielarski* and to her four children, *Jennifer*, *Kelly*, *David*, and *Emilee*, and to her grandmother, *Paranka Kostyrka Bobonich* and her granddaughter, *Isabella*.

Joel Reaser dedicates this book to his wife *Susan* and to his 99-year-old father *Rev. Paul Reaser*, who is still working part-time and living full-time.

CONTENTS

Foreword   xi

Preface   xv

Acknowledgments   xxiii

Advance Organizer for This Book   xxv

Part I Introduction   1

Chapter 1
Older Adult Workers in Today's Work World   3
  Defining Adult and Older Adult Workers   6
  Self-Management   9
  Organizational Issues   13
  Working Longer   15
  Changes in the Work Environment   16
  Challenges to Be Faced   18
  Work in the Same Organization or Move?   21
  Careers in Later Life   23
  Support from Employers   29
  Decision Making and Work Opportunities   32
  Midlife Changes   33
  Summary   35

Chapter 2
Adapting the Workplace to Accommodate Physiological Age-Related Changes in Older Adults   36
  Aging: A Global View   40
  Biological Aging   40
  Psychological Aging   50
  Social Aging   52

vii

Older Adults Continuing to Work   53
Designing the Workplace for Older Americans   54
Stereotypes About Aging   56
The Americans With Disabilities Act   57
Minorities in the Workplace   63
Work Issues   66
Active Older Workers   66
Adapting the Workplace for Older Adults   67
Summary   68

Chapter 3
**How to Train Older Adults: Aging Influences
on Cognitive Tasks**   69
Translating What We Know into Adult and Older Worker Training   72
Summary   80

Part II Design   83

Chapter 4
Instructional Design for Training Older Workers   85
ADDIE Model   85
Individual Differences   98
Training   99
The Value of Training Older Workers   101
How Older Adults Learn Best   104
Guidelines for Training Older Adults   105
Transferring Training Results   105
Training Modalities   106
Older Adults as Learners   107
Diversity Training   109
Summary   110

Chapter 5
Improving Learning Performance   112
Workplace Learning Competence and Its Importance   112
Workplace Learning Competence and Workplace
    Learning Climate   113
Learner Characteristics of Older Versus Younger Adults   116
Implications of Learning Principles for Training Older Adults   117
Summary   126

Chapter 6
Career Development for Adults and Older Workers   127
Self-Management: Career and Retirement   127
Obstacles to Self-Management   144
Models of Career Development   146

Looking to the Future   151
Recommendations   155
Future Directions   157
Summary   158

Part III Managing Organizational Knowledge 167

Chapter 7
What Employers Can Do to Plan
for an Aging Workforce   169
The Evolving Workplace   169
Getting Ahead of the Trends   172
Action Steps for Preparing for the Workforce of the Future   197
Summary   200

Appendix: Resources List   201

Notes   214

About the Authors   234

Index   239

FOREWORD

As noted in the Foreword to the first book in this series—*AMA Innovations in Adult Learning: Theory into Practice,* published by the American Management Association's AMACOM division—it is AMA's hope that this new series will enable adults, and those who support their learning, to expand their thinking and find creative solutions to tough challenges at work.

ABOUT THIS NEW SERIES

Books in this series are grounded in the lessons of theory, practice, and research. The authors hope to equip readers with a solid understanding of the know-why of issues, the know-what of options, and the know-how of experience in order to best inform effective solutions and action.

This new series offers insights into how adults can effectively learn in today's workplace and how organizations can better support and use that learning to power their performance. We hope to bring people together across interdisciplinary, professional, geographic, or cultural boundaries to provide readers with solutions to learning challenges. Books will present findings from cutting-edge research, theory, and practice. Authors will synthesize relevant research or present the results of new, original research that links theory and practice. They will identify and provide relevant resources and practical tools for application, In short, these books bridge the academic, professional, and work worlds by focusing on theory-to-practice and practice-to-theory.

ABOUT THIS BOOK

This book in the new series pushes at the boundaries of the way that society, organizations, and adults themselves think about a phenomenon that is predicted to be ground shaking.

The anticipated tsunami of retiring baby boomers in the United States has set off a flurry of studies, reports, and planning to address the many and varied consequences, some of them dire, of predicted massive, en-masse retirements among this group of workers. Coming at a time when birth rates are shrinking, the United States might well experience what many countries in Europe have already begun to grapple with—a critical shortage of talent, knowledge, skills, and experience in jobs in businesses and all other sectors. Coming at a time of intense global competition—from rapidly growing economies such as Brazil, Russia, India, and China—and growing political unrest, businesses and organizations of all kinds in the United States face this challenge at a time of unique vulnerability.

Working Longer will be a valuable addition to the resources used by businesses and organizations of different kinds as they plan ways to address this quantitative and qualitative shift in the workforce. The authors reframe the problem of the baby boomer mass eligibility for retirement. Rather than think about this as a problem, they suggest that "baby boomers might also be the solution to the problem—if they remain in, or return to, the workforce."

Grounded in solid research, insight into best practice, and the experience of the authors and their colleagues, this book will inform readers about what organizations can do to attract and best utilize baby boomer talent in ways that will mitigate critical talent shortages. Part One of the book synthesizes information about adult development and how this affects learning and performance capabilities at work and examines implications for how organizations might alter the physical environment and organizational conditions to make working longer a desirable option for older adults.

Part Two provides answers to the issues raised in Part One. It answers questions such as: How should training and learning initiatives change to best help older adults learn? Which training modalities might best suit older adults who, like younger adults, are also individuals with unique learning styles and preferences? How should classic training and career development models be modified or changed so that they reflect and meet the real needs of aging workers when, and if, those needs differ from younger adults in the workforce?

Part Three enables organizations to be proactive in getting ahead of the trends. Sound advice is encoded in checklists—one each for small, mid-size, and large businesses—to use in preparing for the workforce of the future.

Working Longer includes a wealth of practical tips, templates, and tools, beginning with an advance organizer and ending with the checklist for preparing for the future. There are additional resources in the Appendices, including a list of websites for learning more about the aging population and how to meet their needs when recruiting, training, and supporting them in the workplace.

AN INVITATION

We invite you to enjoy this book! But, as you do so, we also encourage you to think about other needs that professionals like you in this field may have. If you have a topic or issue that you believe deserves treatment in the series, we welcome you to contact us. We also encourage you to visit the website that accompanies this book series.

Victoria J. Marsick
Columbia University, Teachers College
New York, New York

Andrea Ellinger
University of Illinois
Champaign-Urbana, IL

PREFACE

The United States, and indeed the world, faces an employment crisis because of changing demographics. As is well known, millions in the baby boom generation are now eligible to retire—or soon will be. This could create a global talent crisis, which has prompted many organizations to launch succession planning or talent management programs.

But, ironically, although their retirement may cause the talent shortage, baby boomers may also be the solution to the problem—if they remain in, or return to, the workforce. If employers and individuals alike would retire traditional notions of retirement and revisit their stereotypes of older workers, then it might be possible to recruit, retain, and develop or train older workers more effectively. Such a reassessment of talent could be mutually beneficial to, and help meet the needs of, employers and individuals alike.

SOURCES OF INFORMATION

As we began writing this book, we decided to explore state-of-the-art practices in recruiting, retaining, and developing older workers. We consulted several major sources of information:

1. *A tailor-made survey.* In 2006–2007 we surveyed HRM professionals about practices with older workers and also asked those employers to provide a parallel survey to older workers. Selected survey results, which were compiled in January 2007, are published

in this book for the first time. While the response rate to this survey was disappointing, the results do provide interesting information. This survey is described more completely at the end of this Preface.

2. *Web searches.* We examined what resources could be found on the World Wide Web relating to important topics in this book.

3. *A literature search.* We conducted an exhaustive literature review on best practices and common business practices in recruiting, retaining, and developing older workers. We also looked for case-study descriptions of what organizations have been doing to recruit, retain, and develop older workers.

4. *Firsthand in-house work experience.* All four authors of this book qualify as members of the "older worker" category. Our own opinions and firsthand experiences are thus valuable.

5. *Extensive external consulting and public speaking.* The authors have spoken to many people around the world about the topics raised in this book. The thinking in this book does not represent a U.S.-based opinion alone. Instead, thoughts of people from many cultures are reflected here. And, indeed, those opinions are worth knowing about, since the world—not just the United States—is experiencing an aging crisis and a pending talent shortage.

The purpose for using these sources was to ensure that this book provides a comprehensive and up-to-date treatment of typical *and* best-in-class practices in recruiting, retaining, and developing older workers.

THE SCHEME OF THIS BOOK

Working Longer: New Strategies for Managing, Training, and Retaining Older Employees—Theory into Practice is written for managers, trainers, and human resource managers who wish to establish, revitalize, and review programs designed to improve the utilization of older workers in workplace settings. It is geared to meet the needs of human resource management (HRM) and workplace learning and performance (WLP) executives, managers, and professionals. It also contains useful information for chief executive officers, chief operating officers, general managers, university faculty members who do consulting, management development specialists who are looking for a detailed treatment of the subject as a foundation for their own efforts, and others bearing major responsibilities for talent management and development in or for organizations. Finally, the book may also be useful to older workers who are themselves contemplating how to preserve a vital outlook during pre-retirement and post-retirement career planning.

The book is organized in three major parts. Part One, Chapters 1–3, introduces the book. Chapter 1 is entitled "Older Adult Workers in Today's Work World." It defines adult and adult workers, discusses the importance of self-management, reviews organizational issues associated with older workers, describes the implications of *working longer*—the title of the book—and reviews some important physical changes that affect workers as they age.

Chapter 2 is entitled "Adapting the Workplace to Accommodate Physiological Age-Related Changes in Older Adults." It describes biological aging, psychological aging, social aging, and what is meant by aging globally. It explains issues associated with older workers continuing to work, summarizes why it is important to consider ways to design the workplace to be friendly to older workers, reviews unfortunate stereotypes associated with aging, discusses the implication of the Americans with Disabilities Act as it affects the changing workplace in the United States, and explains what it takes to help older workers remain active.

Chapter 3, the final chapter in Part One, discusses how to train older adults. It focuses on the influence of cognitive tasks on training and learning among older workers.

Part Two focuses on the design of learning and development programs geared to older workers. It examines instructional design and learning-oriented issues for older workers. It also examines career planning for older workers.

Chapter 4 is entitled "Instructional Design for Training Older Workers." It reviews the traditional steps in the instructional systems design (ISD) model and how it should be modified to address unique issues affecting older workers.

Chapter 5 is entitled "Improving Learning Performance." It summarizes workplace competence and its importance, reviews research on workplace learning competence and learning climate, summarizes what is known about learner characteristics of older versus younger adults, and discusses the implications of learning principles for training older adults. Chapter 6 focuses on "Career Development for Adults and Older Workers." It describes key issues associated with self-management: obstacles to it and models of career development as they apply to older workers. Paying attention to career issues for older workers is one key to retaining them.

Part Three provides advice for employers on taking action to recruit, retain and develop older workers. It consists of only one chapter—Chapter 7—which is entitled "What Employers Can Do to Plan for an Aging Workforce." It offers pointed advice to employers in small, mid-size, and large businesses for creating work settings that are older-worker friendly.

RESEARCH CONDUCTED BY THE AUTHORS

Currently, employers are challenged with how to recruit, train, and retain older workers. Consequently, they struggle to develop and implement creative and innovative human resource practices that contribute to a productive workplace that is also welcoming to older workers. As a result, the authors conducted a survey research study to determine what was being done in the workplace among employers and also asked older workers about current or desirable employment practices for older workers.

The data from this study are important in formulating workplace policies related to recruiting, training, and retaining older workers while taking into account individual differences.

Instrumentation

The authors used a quantitative descriptive research method to conduct this study. The data collection was done through a web-based survey instrument. Descriptive statistics were used because they describe data of the sample in a simple, straightforward way. Survey research generally involves interviews or questionnaires.

Strategies and approaches to potential retention of older workers in the workplace were assessed using this online survey developed and delivered through Survey Monkey using a combination of open-ended questions as well as Likert-type response scales.

Target Population and Sample

As part of the project for the book, we conducted a survey of employers. The purpose of the survey was to assess employers' perspectives on older workers. The survey was posted online. E-Mail invitations were sent to 9,079 individuals on the American Management Association's mailing list. That list includes executives, human resource professionals, and line managers. Of those, 208 responded to the survey, which yields confidence levels of ± 6.7 percent.

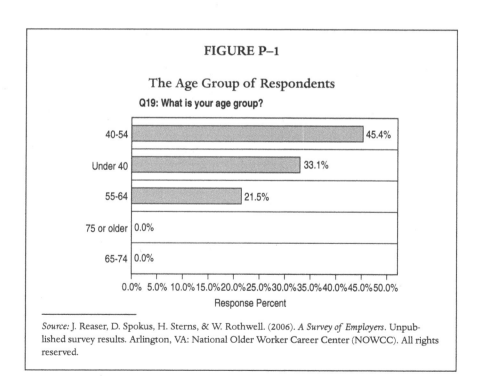

FIGURE P–1

The Age Group of Respondents

Q19: What is your age group?

Source: J. Reaser, D. Spokus, H. Sterns, & W. Rothwell. (2006). *A Survey of Employers.* Unpublished survey results. Arlington, VA: National Older Worker Career Center (NOWCC). All rights reserved.

Of those 130 that provided detailed demographic information, the profile of respondents included:

- A third (34.6 percent) had 5000 or more employees; 13.8 percent had 2000–4999; 41.6 percent had 100–1999; and 10 percent had fewer than 100 employees.
- Half were HR managers; a third (31.5 percent) were line mangers; and, 18.5 percent were executives.
- One-third were under 40 years of age; not quite half (45.4 percent) were ages 40–54, and the remainder (21.5 percent) were between 55 and 64 years of age.

Questions were designed to accommodate the diverse employment issues that affect older workers. Half of the respondents worked in HR management, 31.5 percent were line managers, and 18.5 percent were executives. Figures P–1, P–2, P–3 illustrate the age

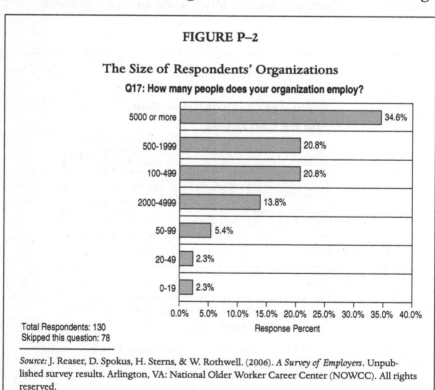

FIGURE P–2

The Size of Respondents' Organizations

Q17: How many people does your organization employ?

Category	Response Percent
5000 or more	34.6%
500-1999	20.8%
100-499	20.8%
2000-4999	13.8%
50-99	5.4%
20-49	2.3%
0-19	2.3%

Total Respondents: 130
Skipped this question: 78

Response Percent

Source: J. Reaser, D. Spokus, H. Sterns, & W. Rothwell. (2006). *A Survey of Employers.* Unpublished survey results. Arlington, VA: National Older Worker Career Center (NOWCC). All rights reserved.

FIGURE P–3

The Industry Categories of Survey Respondents

Q16: In what business sector is your organization?

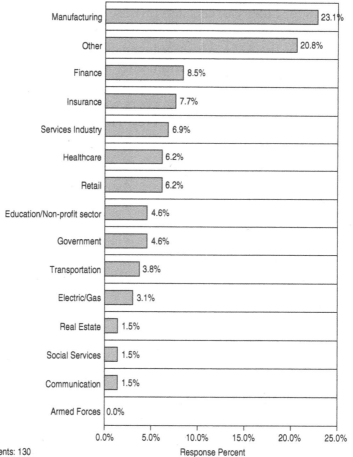

Manufacturing 23.1%
Other 20.8%
Finance 8.5%
Insurance 7.7%
Services Industry 6.9%
Healthcare 6.2%
Retail 6.2%
Education/Non-profit sector 4.6%
Government 4.6%
Transportation 3.8%
Electric/Gas 3.1%
Real Estate 1.5%
Social Services 1.5%
Communication 1.5%
Armed Forces 0.0%

Total Respondents: 130
Skipped this question: 78

Response Percent

Source: J. Reaser, D. Spokus, H. Sterns, & W. Rothwell. (2006). *A Survey of Employers*. Unpublished survey results. Arlington, VA: National Older Worker Career Center (NOWCC). All rights reserved.

groups of survey respondents, the size of the organizations represented by the respondents, and the industry types represented by the respondents.

While the response rate of the survey was disappointing, it does provide some information to raise questions about employment practices for older workers and provide a simple straw poll of what is happening in some organizations. Initially, a letter was sent to members of the AMA who employed older workers asking them to complete the survey. In addition, after several days, a reminder letter was sent as a follow-up to the employers' survey.

A second survey of older workers was distributed by employers who were respondents to the survey. That much smaller group consisted of only 23 individuals, far too few to draw conclusions or generalize to a larger population.

The results of both surveys are spread throughout the book to support what the authors have to say about recruiting, retaining, and developing workers.

William J. Rothwell, Ph.D., SPHR
University Park, Pennsylvania

Harvey L. Sterns, Ph.D.
Akron, Ohio

Diane M. Spokus, Ph.D. Candidate
University Park, Pennsylvania

Joel M. Reaser, Ph.D.
Arlington, Virginia

ACKNOWLEDGMENTS

Writing a book can be difficult. It demands much more effort and commitment than most people care to admit. And that was certainly true of this book. Completing this project required the dedication of the authors, the patience of editor Jacqueline Flynn of AMACOM, and the effort to secure copyright permissions of Ms. Lin Gao, Dr. Rothwell's dedicated graduate research assistant at Penn State.

As colleagues, we would therefore like to extend our thanks to Dr. William Rothwell for his executive guidance, encouragement, patience, and continued support in writing this book. He was, of course, also a contributing author.

Harvey Sterns would like to thank his graduate assistant Yoshie Nakai for her very helpful assistance.

Diane Spokus would also like to acknowledge the help of her colleagues, Dr. William Rothwell, Dr. Harvey Sterns, and Dr. Joel Reaser, who provided feedback on specific chapters, helped develop survey questions, analyzed survey results, and supported her while she worked on her doctoral dissertation. She would also like to acknowledge the support and enthusiasm she received from Dr. Harry Bobonich, who shares her lifelong passion for learning. Last, she would also like to acknowledge her grandmother, Pauline Kostyrka Bobonich. It was through this close relationship that she developed a compassion and admiration for working with older adults.

ADVANCE ORGANIZER FOR THIS BOOK

Complete the following assessment before you read this book. Use it to help you assess your own knowledge about recruiting, developing, and retaining older workers. You may also use it to refer directly to topics in the book that are of special importance to you now.

Directions: Read each item below. Circle **Y** (yes), **N/A** (not applicable), or **N** (no) in the left column next to each item. Spend about 15 minutes on this. Think of the climate for older workers in your organization as you believe it is and not as you think it should be. When you finish, score and interpret the results using the instructions at the end of this Advance Organizer. Then be prepared to share your responses with others in your organization as a starting point for planning improvements to the climate for older workers. If you would like to learn more about any item, refer to the number in the right column to find the chapter in this book that discusses the subject.

Circle your response in the lefthand column for each response below.

			Has your organization:	*Chapter*
Y	N/A	N	1. Clarified why older workers are important to the organization and how their talent may be tapped?	1
Y	N/A	N	2. Clarified what physical and psychological changes typify the human aging process?	2

				Has your organization:	*Chapter*
Y	N/A	N	3.	Clarified what cognitive changes occur in adults as they age?	3
Y	N/A	N	4.	Examined the process of training design used in the organization to ensure that it yields results appropriate to older workers?	4
Y	N/A	N	5.	Reviewed what is known about individual learning competence and how it applies to older workers?	5
Y	N/A	N	6.	Reviewed what is known about adult learning principles and how they may be applied to the unique issues affecting older workers?	5
Y	N/A	N	7.	Summarized what is known about career planning as it applies to older workers?	6
Y	N/A	N	8.	Summarized best practices in recruiting older workers?	7
Y	N/A	N	9.	Summarized best practices in retaining older workers?	7
Y	N/A	N	10.	Summarized best practices in training older workers?	7

_____   **Total**

SCORING AND INTERPRETING THE ADVANCE ORGANIZER

Give your organization 1 point for each Y and a 0 for each N or N/A. Total the points and place the sum in the line next to the word TOTAL above.

Then interpret your score as follows:

10   Your organization is apparently using effective methods of recruiting, retaining, and training older workers.

8 to 9   Improvements could be made to how your organization manages older workers. On the whole, however, the organization is proceeding on the right track.

6 to 7   Older worker management practices in your organization do not appear to be as effective as they should be. Significant improvements should be made.

5 or less   Managing older workers is not effective in your organization. Take immediate corrective action.

I | INTRODUCTION

1 | OLDER ADULT WORKERS IN TODAY'S WORK WORLD

We are in the midst of a huge shift in population and workforce demographics. One of the numbers that dramatizes just how much things will be changing over the next ten years is that twice as many workers 55+ will be added to the workforce than there will be workers in the traditional core group of 25- to 54-years-olds—*twice as many.* That's 10 million older workers and 5 million in the traditional core group. Employers will see their share of those 10 million both in their existing workforces as they age in place and in the form of older workers applying for jobs.[1]

The dramatic increase in the number of middle-aged and older workers in the U.S. national labor force is transforming the world of work. People are exploring working longer, new career and employment options, and the use of experience in new and challenging ways. There is a need to rethink how we see middle and older adulthood.[2,3] And depending upon the sector of an employer's business, employers may soon find themselves having to create new strategies to attract older workers just to maintain productivity levels.

One of the other ramifications of the demographic shift is that we are running short of workers in the United States. The Government Accounting Office (GAO) forecasts a shortfall of 10 million workers by the end of the decade. Figure 1–1 shows the trends in the economy and the trends in the workforce.[4]

The middle line shows the growth in the Gross Domestic Product (GDP). Who is going to do the work? The line at the bottom is the

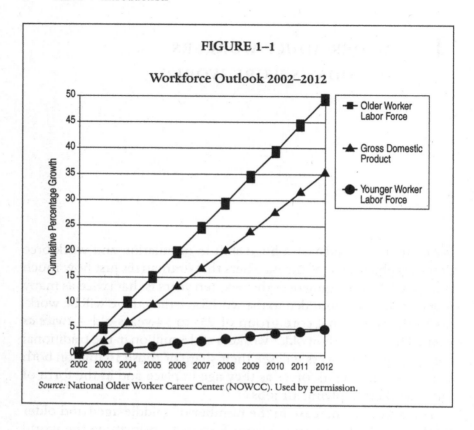

FIGURE 1–1

Workforce Outlook 2002–2012

Source: National Older Worker Career Center (NOWCC). Used by permission.

increase in the number of workers in the traditional core age group of 25- to 54-year-olds. It is clear that the economy will have to depend on the greater contribution of those ages 55 and above.

Other independent research provides the same forecast. The Pension Research Council at the Wharton School forecasts an 8.9 million worker shortfall, assuming a 1.5 percent annual increase in productivity. Only if productivity increases by 2.44 percent does the labor supply meet the demand. Annual increases of 2.66 percent were achieved in the 1950s and 1960s, but the overall average for the last three decades was 1.5 percent annually.[5]

Certain industries are already beginning to feel the pinch. Some of these include energy, education, manufacturing, healthcare, aerospace, defense, and federal and state civil service.

This is the situation for nursing:

- The average age of RNs is more than twice that of U.S. workers generally.
- In 1980, the majority of RNs (52.9 percent) were under age 40; by 2000, more than two-thirds (68.3 percent) were over age 40.
- 419,000 RNs under the age of 30 were working in 1983; fifteen years later, this number had fallen to 246,000.
- By 2010 approximately 40 percent of all working RNs will be more than 50 years old.[6,7]

One of the issues for the energy sector is the projected shortage of overhead linemen. In a soon-to-be-released study of the power industry reported on National Public Radio and conducted by Mike Ashworth of Carnegie Mellon University, it was found that of the 400,000 workers in the industry, half will be eligible for retirement within five years. The average retirement age for linesman is 50 years. The real crunch will be in those jobs that are physically demanding, such as overhead lineman. The Bureau of Labor Statistics estimates over 100,000 workers in this category. Both labor and business are very concerned about their ability to replace retirees.[8]

Another very important area of concern is the lost knowledge issue. In a new book called *Lost Knowledge: Confronting the Threat of an Aging Workforce*, author David Delong[9] begins by describing the achievements of NASA in the 1960s and 1970s in putting a man on the moon and exploring space. Last year when the president proposed sending a man to the moon again, few people mentioned the simple and startling fact that the U.S. space agency has forgotten how to get there. That's because in the 1990s NASA underwent a period of cost-cutting and downsizing that encouraged the engineers who designed the space program to take early retirement.

Is it time to panic? It is only if we approach hiring, management, retention, and retirement as if we were doing business in 1900. The 55+ worker of today in many ways may be comparable to the 40-somethings, even the 30-somethings, of previous eras.

Most organizations are not really prepared. In a survey conducted by the Society for Human Resource Management (SHRM) in collaboration with the National Older Worker Career Center (NOWCC) and the Committee for Economic Development (CED),[10] it was found that:

- 59 percent of companies do not recruit older workers.
- 65 percent of companies have no retention practices.
- 71 percent of companies have no specific provisions or benefits for older workers.

As Comptroller General David Walker points out,[11] older workers are an increasingly important human resource for the national economy:

- U.S. workers are living longer, healthier lives.
- Opinion polls suggest that some older workers want to extend their careers.
- Evidence shows that staying mentally and physically active can increase life spans.
- Older workers have experience, key skills that are not always quickly replaced, leaving potential for occupational bottlenecks.
- Projected slow workforce growth and long-range fiscal imbalances serve to reinforce the need to provide individual opportunities for older workers.
- Meeting policy challenges of extending employment lives of older workers can lead to budgetary, economic, and other benefits for this nation and others.
- We need to review and reconsider existing incentives and barriers both in the public and private sectors.

DEFINING ADULT AND OLDER ADULT WORKERS

In defining the adult and the older adult worker, Sterns and Dover-spike[12] suggested five general approaches: chronological/legal, functional, psychosocial, organizational, and life-span orientation.

By the *chronological/legal approach*, the distinction between older and younger workers is most frequently chronological age. Although little theoretical justification is offered for the age range criterion, it seems to follow the legal definition of age. The Age Discrimination in Employment Act (ADEA) of 1967, amended in 1978 and 1986, protects workers over the age of 40. In recommending such a law, President Johnson stated that approximately half of all private job openings were barred to applicants over 55, and a quarter were closed to applicants over 45. Another commonly used cutoff point comes from the Job Training Partnership Act and the Older Americans Act. Both recognize people aged 55 and older as adult and older adult workers.[13]

The *functional approach* is a performance-based definition of age and recognizes that there are many individual variations in abilities and functioning at all ages. As chronological age increases, individuals go through various biological and psychological changes, including declines, as well as gain increased experience, wisdom, and judgment. Individuals can be identified as "younger" or "older" than their chronological age, based on objective measures of their performance. The concept of functional age has been criticized from a number of perspectives, including the definitional, research design, and statistical points of view. Major problems are the use of a single index and the typical assumption of decline. Despite these criticisms of the concept, different approaches and definitions of functional age continue to exert their influence on the field. Alternative approaches propose a more traditional methodology drawn from industrial psychology that emphasizes appropriate assessment strategies and the design of measures that assess attributes directly related to job performance.

Psychosocial definitions of adult and older adult workers are based on social perceptions, including age-typing of occupations, perceptions of the adult and older adult worker, and the aging of knowledge, skill, and ability sets. The individual's self-perception is also considered. How individuals perceive themselves and their careers at a given age may be congruent or incongruent with the societal image of age. Relatively little research has addressed the quite basic question of how we know when workers will perceive themselves to be identified by others as old. Figure 1–2 shows one way to define who is an older worker.

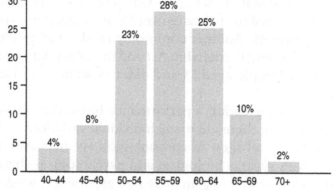

FIGURE 1–2

Age at Which Employees Considered to Be Older Workers

Source: Nancy Lockwood, *The Aging Workforce: The Reality of the Impact of Older Workers and Eldercare in the Workplace.* Arlington, VA: Society for Human Resource Management, 2003, p. 3. Used with permission of SHRM.

The *organizational view* of adult and older adult workers recognizes that the effects of age and tenure are necessarily related and that individuals age in both jobs and organizations. An adult and older adult worker often has spent substantial time in a job and substantially more time in an organization. A definition of adult and older adult workers based on the aging of individuals in organizational roles is more commonly discussed under the topics of seniority and tenure. The effects of aging often may be confounded by the effects of tenure and vice versa. Organizations age, too. Indeed, an organization may be perceived as old because of the average age of its members. As the average age of its members increases, new demands are placed on the organizational subsystems such as human resources.

Finally, the *life-span approach* borrows from a number of the previously described approaches but adds its unique emphasis. It advances the possibility for behavioral change at any point in the life cycle. Substantial individual differences in aging are recognized as critical in examining adult career patterns.

Three sets of factors are seen as affecting behavioral change during the life cycle. The first set includes normative, age-graded, biological, and/or environmental determinants. These bear a strong relationship to chronological age. The second set of factors is normative, history-graded influences that affect most members of a cohort/generation in similar ways. The third set of events is non-normative. This set includes unique career and life changes, as well as individual health and stress-inducing events. The unique status of the individual is the result of the joint impact of these factors. According to this approach, there are more individual differences as people grow older.[14]

SELF-MANAGEMENT

In fast-changing organizational and professional environments, self-management of careers has become a major issue. Responsibility for maintaining and updating knowledge, skills, and abilities rests with the individual. Douglas Hall and Phillip Mirvis in *The Career Is Dead—Long Live the Career*[15] have captured this theme in their discussion of the protean career, which stresses continuous learning and self-direction of both one's life and career. Among the challenges to staying vital in one's work is finding the right balance between work, leisure, family, and other personal interests. How to stay fresh and involved in one's work is critical to staying competitive and useful to the organization or as an active professional.[16]

Older workers have been singled out in downsizing efforts on the basis of stereotypic beliefs and as being unsuitable for retraining or being unable to perform in fast-paced work environments. Depending on the age of the career entry, middle-aged and older workers have been more likely to occupy mid-level management positions that have been the focus of downsizing and restructuring strategies. Those who have survived find themselves in the most demanding situations in their work lives. A person may be working for the same company but now may be valued only as long as there is a need for his or her skills and performance. Or one needs to be prepared to take one's skills to a new setting where they are needed.[17]

A protean career is directed by the individual rather than the employing organization. The individual becomes personally responsible for directing his or her own learning, skill mastery, and reskilling. A person has to be knowledgeable in the current professional trends. One needs to compare essential skills to one's own competencies and take action to acquire needed skills such as special statistical skills, computer programs, special techniques, design approaches, new organizational strategies, and whatever is called for by one's job or organization.

The individual with successful career self-management then may be one of the valued successful adult and older adult workers of the future. In fact, it may be more expensive to replace a knowledgeable, adaptable, and continuously learning older employee with a younger worker with less protean-type career experience. Adaptable, knowledgeable mature workers may give organizations new options for employing older workers. This new careerism has led to employees being more critical in self-analysis, more assertive in seeking feedback, and more likely to refuse transfers and promotions that subvert career goals as they envision them.[18]

A decade ago, Willis and Dubin, in *Maintaining Professional Competence*,[19] raised this important issue of maintaining currency in one's work. Job characteristics that have been found to be relevant to updating work behavior and experience include task diversity, complex and challenging work, and participation in decision making.

One major aspect of professional competence involves effective functioning on essential tasks within a given profession. Professional competence involves developing and maintaining proficiencies, including (1) the discipline-specific knowledge base, (2) essential technical skill, and (3) ability to solve profession-related problems. A second major aspect of professional competence relates to the characteristics of the individual, including intellectual ability, personality traits, motivation, attitudes, and values. These characteristics support individual development and competence.

Performance in work and professional domains is a demonstration of a person's level of professional competence. Management or supervisory personnel can assess level of competence through direct observation. Assessment procedures to evaluate competence can include tests and simulation tasks. Such assessments can be used for licensure, recertification, or self-assessment. What is essential here is the recognition that the person is in a constant learning mode.

In *New Opportunities for Older Workers*[20] (a statement by the Research and Policy Committee of the Committee for Economic Development), a strong call was made for companies to pay attention to aging boomers as workers and to provide a supportive environment for capable able older workers to continue. There is clear support for upper management to carefully reconsider the value of capable and talented older workers; "managers and other employees exhibiting age bias are allowing misplaced stereotypes to overrule sound business decisions" (p. 35).

BOX 1–1

Ageism—Or "the Gray Ceiling"

Many companies circumvent the ADEA by using the Older Workers Benefit Protection Act (OWBPA). As explained in the August 2003 issue of *HR Magazine*, "most companies inoculate themselves against age complaints by asking dismissed older workers to sign releases and confidentiality agreements in exchange for retirement with incentives, severance and buyouts." As a result, many older workers' issues are not brought to the surface.

Ageism, sometimes called "the gray ceiling," is one of the major barriers for older workers (see below). According to the Education Resources Information Center, older workers have a greater fear of discrimination than fear of change.

As pointed out in *Update on the Older Worker: 2002*, age discrimination in the workplace is a reality. Although exact figures of age discrimination are not available, age is a significant barrier for many older men and women, as evidenced by the longer time required to find employment, the lower salaries many older workers experience, and the amounts awarded by courts to victims of age discrimination. Furthermore, according to research published in the *Industrial & Labor Relations Review*, access to jobs for older workers is even more challenging due to the entry barriers associated with occupations with pension benefits, steep wage profiles, and computer usage.

Source: Nancy Lockwood, *The Aging Workforce: The Reality of the Impact of Older Workers and Eldercare in the Workplace.* Arlington, VA: Society for Human Resource Management, 2003, p. 3. Used with permission of SHRM.

Empirical research does not support the common perception that an older worker performs more poorly on the job than a younger worker. Age is weakly (positively) related to job performance. The older worker is generally at a disadvantage relative to a younger worker in training situations. However, an older worker is able to learn training materials to the extent required to perform a job successfully. In terms of positive stereotypes, the research supports the belief that an older worker is less likely to be voluntarily absent from work than a younger worker. The age of a worker was unrelated to voluntary turnover. Counter to common beliefs, an older worker is neither more nor less likely to voluntarily leave a job than a younger worker. Additionally, weak positive relations are found between age and work-related attitudes. The older worker seems to have only slightly more positive feelings toward the organization and work.[21]

Stereotypes do not generalize to all older workers and may potentially impact workers in two ways. First, to the extent an older worker includes these perceptions in his or her self-concept, the worker may unnecessarily limit his or her options. In terms of career self-management, the worker may limit avenues of exploration or not pursue certain opportunities. Alternately, the worker may not even engage in self-management activities. Second, to the extent that organizational decision makers act on these perceptions, the older worker's employment or career opportunities may be inappropriately limited. The most appropriate conclusion, however, is that each individual, regardless of age, should be evaluated (or self-evaluated) based on his or her own merits, skills, abilities, and motivation, and not on the stereotypical characteristics of a particular age group with which the individual happens to be associated.[22]

One of the most important determinants of remaining in the work force is feeling valued, appreciated, and respected within the company. A major part of good management in the near future will be nurturing existing employees and attracting new employees with the protean career orientation who are maintaining professional competence.[23]

Sterns, in his model of career development and training, sees the option of full- or part-time retirement as part of the decision to no longer be actively involved in career development and work activities. Decisions regarding career and updating are based on many factors. However, individuals can move in or out of the work role.[24]

ORGANIZATIONAL ISSUES

Organizations are currently facing rapid demographic changes with more aging workers and greater diversity. Organizations need to consider the different cohort/generation characteristics of their employees that can result in different expectations,[25] attitudes, degrees of commitment, and levels of satisfaction in current work situations. From the individual perspective, employees at various points in their career can assess their present situations and develop personal and professional expectations. This can lead to decisions to update, add new skills, and maintain professional competence. Organizations that have this more dynamic view of adult and older adult workers can better understand the characteristics of their current workforce and provide an environment to support individual career development.[26]

Adult and older workers are competitive when they have higher levels of expertise or experiences, motivation on given jobs, as well as job flexibility and managerial support. Thus, performance should be individually examined and not based on age; rather, it needs to be based on the individual's capabilities.

Several individual factors have been suggested in the context of career development, including personality, organizational commitment, attitudes toward mobility, self-management capacity, and family-related and work-related relationships. Personality variables such as locus of control, self-efficacy, organization-based self-esteem, and general self-esteem have been identified as influencing an individual's career development. Attitudes toward mobility may not be related to chronological age and may be influenced by various factors such as career stage, growth need, fear of stagnation, and perceived self-marketability.[27] This will be discussed in detail in Chapter 6.

A person's capability to self-manage may be independent of age, guided by norms that are evolving and not fully understood. Relationships at the workplace (supervisors, co-workers, and subordinates) may provide current norms to guide a worker's own career

BOX 1–2

How Does Your Organization Rate for Being Older Worker Friendly?

Directions: Use this simple questionnaire to rate how older-worker-friendly your organization is now. For each item listed in the left column below, check "yes" or "no" in the right column. It would be interesting to administer this questionnaire to a group of your senior managers and then separately select and administer the questionnaire to a group of your older workers. Then compare the differences to see where opinions vary.

Would you say that this organization:	Yes ✓	No ✓
1. Provides training programs for older workers to maintain their skills and abilities?	☐	☐
2. Includes a segment on the management of older workers in diversity training programs for managers?	☐	☐
3. Provides life and retirement education for workers as they approach retirement age?	☐	☐
4. Provides a range of options for phased retirement?	☐	☐
5. Revises pension plans to eliminate penalties or disincentives for extended working careers?	☐	☐
6. Offers pro-rated employee benefits?	☐	☐
7. Provides a retention bonus payable after a fixed additional period?	☐	☐
TOTAL	_____	

Scoring
For each item you check "yes" to above, give your organization 1 point. For each item you check "no" above, give your organization 0 point. Add up the 7 items and place the total score on the line above.

Interpreting the Score
If your organization scores 6–7, your organization is doing an excellent job in creating an older-worker-friendly work environment. If your organization scores below that, then establish an action plan for improvement.

Source: Working Beyond the Traditional Retirement Age. Downloaded on 11 March 2007 from www.van.umn.edu/options/2b6_workbeyond.asp

decisions. Other factors that may influence self-management include responsibilities to family and caregiving issues (childcare, eldercare) that can vary at different life stages.[28]

Organizational factors supportive of worker growth include training opportunities, flexibility at the workplace, a reward system, and the organizational culture. Often in the past, training was not made available to older adult workers. This placed the responsibility on the individual worker to maintain and add to his or her skills in order to remain competitive. Organizations need to support self-growth aspirations. Organizational support is a key element for individual workers' success and development and may play an important role in the person's choosing to work longer.

The field of adult and older adult training can evolve in many important ways with the life-span approach. The considerations of age-related and non-age-specific factors as well as contextual factors may provide organizations with a new level of understanding of aging and work. This approach offers a better understanding of the current aging workforce and fulfills the promise of an industrial gerontology that started close to fifty years ago.[29]

WORKING LONGER

The decision to retire or to continue working reflects a complex array of factors including economic well-being, personal preference, subjective health, attitudes regarding leisure, and the desire to continue work. In response to changing social and organizational environments, self-management has emerged as a major theme. With workers changing employers, occupations, or jobs within their current company, individual responsibility is required for maintaining and updating knowledge, skills, and abilities. Similar to work, retirement has moved into the realm of self-management. The transition from work to retirement can take many forms, including bridge jobs, part-time work, or new careers.[30]

Satisfaction and ability to work reflect normative aging, generational differences, and unique life events of the adult and older adult worker. Intervention in the workplace in such areas as wellness promotion, training and retraining, and human resources management may make work life extension a more frequent choice. The ultimate responsibility for maintaining professional competence rests on the individual employee, however. At the same time, an organization can foster competence by providing updating opportunities, challenging work assignments, and interaction with co-workers and management.

Another aspect is that an individual may have to work longer than planned, or he or she may have to accept an early buyout package rather than risk being laid off or fired at a later date. Individual characteristics and work-related factors impact work and retirement choices. These factors influence anticipatory retirement planning and decision processes.[31]

CHANGES IN THE WORK ENVIRONMENT

The Age Discrimination and Employment Act (1967, 1978, 1986) over a period of years has in general eliminated mandatory retirement in the United States. Our ideas about retirement have undergone an evolution over the last forty years; a major theme of the 1971 White House Conference on Aging was to convince people that retirement was a good thing and that people deserved a period of rest and relaxation at the end of the life span. Yet there were people who chose to work longer. Ideas about mandatory retirement were pervasive. The ADEA legislation of 1967 created a protected class of people age 40+ but maintained mandatory retirement at age 65. In the revisions of 1978, mandatory retirement was raised to age 70, and there was an uncapping of federal workers. In the 1986 revisions, there was uncapping of mandatory retirement with the exception of commercial airline pilots, air traffic controllers, age authenticity in actors, military, diplomatic corps, and individuals in key leadership positions with pensions greater than $44,000 per year.[32]

Some theories emphasize the awareness of health issues and personal death as a crucial "marker" of midlife and older adulthood, an awareness that is not based on the actual nearness of death so much as the recognition that underlying biological changes are occurring. Biological changes become central when they are diseases, many of which emerge in midlife and have the potential to dramatically redirect the course of life.[33]

Generally, middle-aged persons are perceived as potentially better workers because they have a more complex, holistic view of issues and are more attuned to their own contributions to both problems and solutions. On the other hand, the increased focus on self-determination may lead individuals to withdraw investment in career building in favor of greater attention to family, friends, or self-development. This clearly conflicts with current expectations that all workers remain engaged, ambitious, eager to update, and flexible in meeting the changing demands of their workplace.[34]

Organizational changes are also altering the nature of the relationships between organizations and employees. Employers' commitment to employees may last only as long as there is a need for their skills and performance. Similarly, employees' commitment to the employer may last only as long as their expectations are being met. These changes place greater emphasis on employees' adaptability and abilities in learning to learn.

Older workers, however, may also be at a disadvantage in terms of moving toward greater career self-management. Transitioning from a typical, organizational-driven career to a self-managed career may be a rather challenging task, particularly if an individual initially entered the workforce with a one career–one employer ideal. Additionally, stereotypic beliefs about older workers may lead to the underutilization of this group as new relationships emerge between organizations and employees.[35]

Age effects as outcomes within an organization can be attributed to the age of employees. Chronological age and age distributions impact age norms. Age distributions are the actual age distributions in the organization, whereas the age norms are shared perceptions of the normal ages with an organization or role. Individual age expectations are also important, as they reflect the degree to which the individual applies the social norm to him or herself. Age norms are likely to occur when the range of perceived ages is narrow and agreement on typical ages is high. Organizational tenure is expected to increase recognition of age group distinctions because individuals of roughly the same age and organizational tenure will have shared history and experience. These age norms may provide a context that influences judgments about individuals.[36]

One can look to parents and peers for models, but each person's circumstances, feelings, and situations may be very different. Uncertainty regarding what present and future employment will offer is real for individuals who presently have job security, stable working conditions, and choices about their retirement. This can change quickly with corporate buyouts, new public policies, and changing attitudes on the part of workers themselves. The possibility of losing one's job, being faced with an early buyout, or uncertainty regarding future prospects are all part of the current world of work. At the same time, there are capable people continuing in fairly traditional careers. Others may lose jobs but are re-entering the job search, finding that it is a major challenge to find a new position at the same or better salary. Often the person has to settle for reduced salary and benefits, if any. It appears that 20 percent of older adults want to work beyond traditional retirement age, and this number will continue to grow dramatically.[37] In any case, it is important to focus on individuals who will continue to work. People may not only wish to work longer, they may have to. All of these individuals, regardless of their health and disability status, it is believed, will feel the financial pressure to continue working.[38]

CHALLENGES TO BE FACED

Many people now ranging in age from the 40s to the mid-60s have felt that they would have a choice about working after the normal retirement age. This belief was based on the expectation of an expanding economy and a strong economic climate. Many middle-aged and older workers are surprised that the large numbers of early buyouts, layoffs, and the general trend of downsizing have continued, even by successful companies, and most recently economic forces have diminished investments, leading to changes in plans for early retirements. It is apparent that the relationship between employer and employees no longer promises life-long employment. This places middle-aged and older workers in the position of having to be responsible for their own careers, maximizing the employment opportunities presented to them and competing with people of all ages in finding new employment.[39]

People will have to fight harder to remain in the work force longer. The present 50- and 60-year-olds were hired at a time when they could choose among jobs. They were a part of the workforce when there was accelerated growth and numerous promotions. They had to deal with the slower promotions and salary increases of the 1980s but still expected that they would have control over how long they worked and when they exited the work force. At the peak of their careers, they now have much less control or no control at all.[40]

Employment benefits, especially retirement benefits, have changed from defined benefit programs to defined contribution. Many employees were told that they would receive the same level of benefit with these conversions, but this has definitely turned out to not be the case. Individuals now pay or co-pay into pension and health benefit programs both before and after retirement. This has been devastating for many individuals who had 401K plans or equivalent and/or stock portfolios, resulting in fewer discretionary resources in retirement and the need on the part of many individuals to return to full-time work.

As a result, baby boomers may need or desire to supplement their pension or benefits. Kenneth Dychtwald[41] proposes that the baby boomers are more likely "to do their own thing" and will be comfortable breaking the retirement norm. A new trend toward more cyclic lifestyles (multiple periods of training, work, and leisure) is, and will continue to become, more common. The increasing pressures of changing technology and the need for continuous training to remain competitive in the job market are the forces that will drive multiple-cycle careers.

Older adults have many different reasons for staying longer in the workforce. They want to earn money and have health insurance, and they seek other intrinsic benefits, such as developing new skills, using time productively, and feeling useful and needed. Work allows people to stay in touch with current developments; it provides structure to older people and helps them retain a sense of doing something worthwhile.

People who enjoy work will want to continue to maintain the social interactions and relationships they enjoyed with co-workers, and they will want to continue to participate in meaningful activity. The work one does contributes to identity and a sense of self. An increasing concern for health and youthfulness may also contribute to longer career patterns. Being retired may conflict with a person's youthful image, leading him or her to postpone retirement. Many women, having entered the work force in midlife, may want to work longer for many of the same reasons as mentioned above. They may need to work longer to receive benefits in retirement. A majority of older adults are women, and 60 percent of women 45 to 60 are employed. Women's participation varies by industry. It is now estimated that 75 percent of women were in the workforce by the year 2000. Women have become a major component of the workforce and will become a larger component in the next decade.

Middle-aged and older workers of today are have to reconsider their plans based on recent economic events. Clearly, people are trying to make meaningful decisions about their futures. The decision to continue to work, modify work, or retire is influenced by many factors. Time left (at work or in the labor force) is part of a decision process influenced by eligibility for Social Security, employer pension, financial resources, and age norms. As has been described, this is extended decision making for retirement that can be observed in the changing plans and intention regarding retirement that workers entertain over time.

Sterns and Alexander[42] reviewed the issues relating to industrial gerontology by emphasizing the decisions of workers throughout the life span. They emphasize that career decisions are not limited to a specific age or stage; decisions are not age-specific.

One of the most notable social perspectives of life-course decisions was offered by Neugarten and her colleagues in their description of the power of age norms to shape behaviors in all domains. One consequence is the development of a "social clock" by which progress is charted, according to one's personal timetable and according to the one held by others in the social system. In this perspective, jobs and career progress are both governed by age norms (as well as gender norms). There are "young men's jobs" and "mid-life jobs." Neugarten described the shift in relations between generations, particularly evident in the workplaces; the shift from "apprentice" to becoming part of the "command generation" and "mentor" to the younger workers was an important marker of feeling middle aged among high-achieving adults. Neugarten later de-emphasized age norms and argued that the United Sates had become a largely "age irrelevant" society. The social role model has clear applications to the work realm, since role defines one's place in social structures. A review of the career development literature and first-person accounts make it clear that many persons who are now middle-aged and older came of age when "career ladders" were anticipated, and expectations of progress were tied to age. By age 35 to 40, men "knew" whether they were likely to be promoted in their line of work or sidelined, and this awareness had significant repercussions. Personal identity was heavily invested in the work role, and the degree of competence, authority, and power implied in titles (such as journeyman, master craftsman, assistant vice president, Lt. Col., CEO) was an important element. In addition, social relationships within the workplace and even in the wider community were governed by work role status. In the current era, when adults are likely to change careers several times, organizational structures are less hierarchical, and promotion is based more on expertise than tenure, the previous notions of "appropriate work roles for middle age" have been challenged. The models developed on earlier realities may not fit in the future.[43]

WORK IN THE SAME ORGANIZATION OR MOVE?

Over the past two decades, employees' attitudes toward working have become increasingly more important to organizations in their efforts to predict worker behavior. General attitudes about work contribute to a desire to continue to work and to maintain the skills required to excel. The work environment itself also influences employees' attitudes about their job performance and whether they want to continue to work.

The desire to continue working in an organization has been researched under the topic of organizational commitment. John Meyer and Natalie Allen[44] distinguish between two dimensions of organizational commitment that affect work attitudes in different ways.

The first, *continuance commitment*, is the employee's perceived cost of leaving or a perceived lack of alternatives to make up for investments in the benefits of the current job. Individuals remain at work because they are not willing to risk loss of salary, health benefits, or pension investment. This aspect of organizational commitment is especially relevant to older adults. As workers increase their tenure with an organization, they may feel increasing continuance commitment because they have established a home and friendships in the area, have become specialized in a skill that they feel cannot be transferred, or believe that they could not get the same salary or benefits if they moved to a new organization.

Affective commitment, the second dimension of organizational commitment, refers to the employee's affective, or emotional, orientation to the organization. Affective commitment is concerned with the individuals' interest in the work and loyalty to the organization and its goals. This emotional tie to the organization motivates them to remain, not because they cannot afford to leave, but because they feel a sense of contribution and growth by staying with the organization. Other things being equal, an organization that encourages maintenance at one's job, provides challenging work, and offers opportunities to inject new ideas will not only be more likely to stay ahead of competitors but will also reduce turnover and retain more productive employees.

An organization can measure the success of its efforts to improve the work environment by examining organization-based self-esteem. This kind of self-esteem is measured by the degree to which organization members believe they are valuable, worthwhile, and effectual employees.

Evidence is mounting that the intrinsic rewards of work—satisfaction, relationships with co-workers, and a sense of participating in meaningful activity—become more important as an individual ages. The abolishment of the mandatory retirement age allows working older adults to continue to participate in these benefits until they feel that they have the financial resources and personal network outside the workplace to retire. Contemporary research has established that financial incentives influence retirement behavior, although the relative importance of economic factors compared to affective and social factors is undergoing change. There is considerable disagreement about the effect of economic factors.

Job satisfaction shows consistently that work-related attitudes are more positive with increasing age in surveys of employed adults. Older adults may have a different perspective on work than younger adults. For older workers, survival needs are less likely to be urgent because they will probably have reached a maximum income for their jobs. Desire for more control over the job is still strong. However, older workers have seen less evidence that hard work leads to promotions, salary increases, or other rewards. Goals may not change with age but expectations of achieving these outcomes can diminish.[45]

CAREERS IN LATER LIFE

The life span approach to older workers advances the possibility for behavioral change at any point in the life cycle. Substantial individual differences in aging are recognized as vital in examining adult career patterns. These differences create difficulty in developing theories that adequately address the broad range of differences. Late careers are often more difficult to study than early careers because there is less consistency in the developmental tasks.[46] For example, in an early career, individuals must choose a career. In a late career, a person may continue a career, start a new career, modify a career, or retire.

Lydia Bronte[47] interviewed individuals who had long careers into their 80s and 90s. The participants are proof that it is possible to continue being creative and productive past age 65. They present a positive view of what can be accomplished late in one's career or even early in a career started late in life. While it was not a rigorously designed study, it provides portraits of individuals who break the stereotypes of older adult careers.

While Bronte found a great deal of variety in careers, she identified three basic career patterns. The "homesteaders" are individuals who stay in the same job or profession for their entire careers. Many of these individuals are in artistic or scientific fields. They are still

BOX 1–3

Age Is the Recipe for Success
By Elizabeth Eyre

When was the last time you went to McDonald's and were served a Quarter-Pounder with Cheese meal, with a Cream Egg McFluny on the side, to eat in, by your gran?

No, I can't remember the last time it happened to me either (I don't think either of my grandmothers ever set foot inside a McDonald's restaurant in their lives) but the fast-food chain that's famous the world over for employing spotty, attitudinal teenagers lacking the social skills demanded by a paper round, has more than 500 employees aged over 60 in the UK alone.

And the company says that the "grandparental role" adopted by these older workers within its restaurants—offering their younger colleagues support, advice and the benefit of their many years of working experience—is a main ingredient of its recipe for success.

McDonald's has 1,200 restaurants and employs 67,000 people in the UK; it is the biggest employer of students in the country. It claims to have "probably the most diverse workforce in the UK," and is currently investing a lot of money trying to explode the myth of the Mcjob, in an advertising campaign highlighting the flexibility it offers employees, and the training and promotion opportunities that make working in McDonald's more than just a temporary job for students needing beer money.

The latest advertisement features 65-year-old judo coach Fred Turner, who came out of retirement to work at the McDonald's restaurant in Salford. Like so many recently retired people, he found the value of his pension had fallen so much—by an eyewatering 40 percent—that he was forced to return to the labor market. He now combines shifts at McDonald's with judo coaching sessions at a local sports centre.

The advertising campaign was launched a month ago. David Fairhurst, vice president, people, for McDonald's in the UK, says: "Although it might take people by surprise to think of mature workers like Fred choosing to work at McDonald's, these employees are a very important part of our workforce. They say time and time again that our fast-paced, energetic environment keeps them feeling young.

"Our younger workers also get a lot out of having older people to look up to and ask for advice, and our customers frequently comment on the impressive quality of service delivered by mature workers in the restaurants."

Source: Elizabeth Eyre, "Age Is the Recipe for Success." *Training Journal*, October 2006, pp. 26–28. Used by permission.

This latest attempt to get people to "look beyond the Mcjob issue" was conceived very much with the new age discrimination legislation—which came into force on October 1—in view. Fairhurst told TJ: "We were conscious that the legislation was forthcoming—it was at the front of our minds. We place a high value on our strong core of employees aged over 60 and we're working hard to make sure that our procedures comply with the legislation, which they do.

"We wanted to do something disruptive with the advertising campaign. We wanted to get people to address what we stand for as an employer; we were trying to get people to look beyond the 'Mcjob' issue."

By using Turner in the campaign, Fairhurst said McDonald's was trying to demonstrate that it's a "welcoming organization for older workers." Indeed, as part of the publicity surrounding the launch of the advertisement, Turner is quoted as saying: "It's very fast-paced, but I get a real kick out of keeping up with customer demands without compromising on the quality of the burgers I prepare. The best thing is that, if I get stuck, the youngsters help me. They all call me 'Mr Fred' out of respect, as I'm a bit older than most employees. They're brilliant. And my friends think it's great, too."

Turner's not the only older employee held up by McDonald's as evidence of its age-friendly stance. Eighty-year-old Neville Green, who has come out of retirement to work three days a week at a restaurant in Southampton, and Sheila Kahn of Croydon, 77, who has been with the company since it started operating in the UK in 1974, were two of the case studies made available to the media for the advertisement's launch.

These older employees are part of an increasingly diverse McDonald's workforce. According to Fairhurst, 60 percent of the company's employees are aged under 21, and 10 percent of its operations managers are Asian. "We have probably the most diverse workforce in the UK, incorporating a broad ethnicity," he said. One of the reasons for this is that we hire purely with an 'attitude rather than aptitude' focus—if you've got the right attitude for work and for serving customers, we'll hire you.

"We consider it a strength to hire a group of people from different backgrounds and we want to send out the message that 17-year-olds work alongside 83-year-olds. We have more than 500 employees over the age of 60, but we want to do more—we want to encourage more older workers to join us."

So why should someone who has spent a lifetime in work and is now enjoying a life of leisure return to the daily grind with an organization that has an irrevocably young image? There is the obvious financial reason, of course, but McDonald's also cites its "proven track record" of offering employees flexible working arrangements: The company has recently introduced the UK's first "family contract," enabling two members of the same family working in the same restaurant to cover each other's shifts without prior notice, and it allows employees to choose the hours they want to work in advance. Parents can work during school hours, taking their holidays during school breaks, and students can work around their courses.

There is a range of employee incentives available to older employees in exactly the same way as they are to the younger ones. It includes stays at the company villas in Spain and Portugal—a way of recognizing exemplary performance—bonuses based on a mystery shopper scheme, and spot awards including vouchers, iPods, and tickets to events.

And older workers are entitled to exactly the same benefits as other employees, including being eligible for private health insurance after three years' service. This entitlement extends to the L&D opportunities offered by the "Hamburger University": a network of seven training faculties around the world providing a range of management courses.

The Hamburger University in the UK held its first course in October 1977 and, just a year later, more than 200 managers had graduated. In 1989 it relocated to McDonald's new UK head office in East Finchley, London, where it had two lecture theatres and classrooms. Twelve years later it was expanded, with more classrooms and added interpretation facilities, to allow courses to be delivered to students from across Europe.

To date, HU London has held courses for more than 22,000 students, with 3,000 managers passing through its doors in 2005 alone. Another 88,000 students have attended courses at the regional training centers in Salford, Leeds, Glasgow, Sutton Coldfield, and Woking.

HU London delivers various management courses, mainly by an in-house training team. The flagship operations and middle-management courses are in shift-management, restaurant-operation and leadership, business leadership and operations consultants. Courses are also available for support staff.

"One of the strengths of our environment is that we're relatively structured when it comes to skills development," Fairhurst said. "The Hamburger University in London costs us £14m a year to run and 17,000 people go through our programs to help employees develop and grow each year. Training and development is emphasized and encouraged for everybody, and our older workers respond enthusiastically to the training they are offered—95 percent of McDonald's workers aged over 60 say they feel motivated in their jobs.

Our structured approach to training and development means that people can move up when they are ready—there are plenty of opportunities for people to progress."

Fairhurst gives the example of a woman who joined McDonald's at the age of 65 as a cleaner. She was "talent-spotted" and promoted to a customer-care role and now, aged 70, she works six-hour shifts five days a week "We believe that training—formal and on the job—is very important," he said.

And it certainly seems to be working. Fairhurst says that 93 percent of McDonald's older workers look forward to coming to work. "We have some fantastic peoplemetrics that demonstrate a very engaged workforce. In fact, we have one of the most engaged workforces in the UK. One of the things the older workers like is the flexibility we offer them; we have older people joining us for confidence, value, money, and social reasons.

"One of the reasons we employ older workers is the wealth of experience they bring with them. They have skills from previous careers, and they tend to be very strong at customer service because they are confident and have experience of life—they are brilliant in terms of hospitality. They fulfill a grandparental role for our younger workers, too—we have a dynamic of older and younger employees working together, where younger employees look to older ones for advice and older workers say working at McDonald's is an anti-ageing treatment!

"There is a very strong family and community bond amongst McDonald's workers and that mutuality of older and younger people working together is the real recipe for success."

McDonald's in the UK can be contacted via its website—www.mcdonalds.co.uk—or its customer services hotline on 0870 524 4622.

---

deeply engaged in their careers and feel that they have more potential for growth.

The second group, the "transformers," change jobs once. Early transformers change careers shortly after starting an occupation. This process seems to be part of the trial-and-error process. In contrast, late transformers tended to be well established financially and personally, giving them the freedom to pursue another interest later in life.

The third group, the "explorers," changed careers from as few as three to as many as ten times. The reasons for the shifts were varied, as were the career paths. Bronte's book, *The Longevity Factor: The New Reality of Long Career and How It Can Lead to Richer Lives*, illustrates the variability in career pattern and ages of career peaks and contributions. Early models of career development were linear models, which assumed that individuals moved through predictable career stages and then retirement. For older adults, maintaining skills for a period of time and then declining was the predicted pattern. This notion that career stages are linked to age will lead practitioners to incorrectly develop career development opportunities that are congruent with the age and stage of various cohorts. These models ignore individual differences and the contributions that older workers make. People may be aware of norms and expectations regarding their expected retirement. At the same time, workers may have the options of part-time or full-time work in the same career or in a new career or new job in their later life.

In 1986, amendments to the Age Discrimination in Employment Act eliminated mandatory retirement policies in most occupations. However, mandatory retirement legislation is only one cause of involuntary retirement; another cause is poor health. Those forced to retire because of poor health are more likely to suffer negative consequences. Therefore, the elimination of mandatory retirement may not greatly improve retirement satisfaction. Rather, it may be the factors that influence the retirement decision, such as health, income, and pre-retirement attitudes, that will determine adjustment.

Surveys estimating the preference for continued work after retirement suggest that more than half of retirees would like to continue some part-time work rather than retire completely. Far fewer actually do so. There are several possible explanations for this. Alternative work schedules are not readily available, and individuals may be unable to find part-time work in their area of expertise. But a large variety of alternative part-time options does exist, and employers may retain highly skilled workers by providing one or more of these options.[48]

Many advantages for older employees result from these options. They can continue to earn an income and remain productive. Phased or alternative work options also enable the older person to adjust psychologically to life without constant work demands, and the shorter or flexible work hours make it possible for workers to take care of personal matters more easily. The major barriers for older employees are the Social Security earnings test, tax penalties, and pension plans that preclude working or limit hours. Additionally, job coordination may be difficult, and many of these options fail to provide benefits for the older workers.[49]

Advantages for employers include decreased absenteeism, turnover, and tardiness, increased productivity, and decreased overtime costs. Older workers have fewer voluntary absences, less turnover, fewer accidents, and they can provide ideal role models to younger employees. They can also help train younger employees and may attract older consumers. Disadvantages for employers in having older employees include supervision and scheduling difficulties and the potential for higher benefit costs.

The unemployment rate of older adults 60 and over is the lowest among all age ranges. These rates are often just estimates, though, because older discouraged workers may choose to retire rather than continue a frustrating job search. It takes an average of seven weeks longer for an older worker to find employment compared to a younger worker, and if one is a black male, a male with health problems, or one with less formal education, it takes even longer. When the number of discouraged workers are added into the unemployment rates, the rate becomes much higher, 2.9 to 4.8 percent. These rates are closer to those of younger workers.[50]

With the many recent company buyouts, layoffs, and closings and increases in technology, the number of displaced workers is dramatically increasing. Job displacement has been found to be related to decreases in income and future job status; loss of pension benefits; and increases in drug abuse, suicide, divorce, depression, illness, and homicide.

In many cases, older workers are less likely to be displaced and more likely to be recalled for employment. Yet, when additional training is required due to technological changes, older workers are more likely to be displaced. Federal employment and training programs are available for displaced or disadvantaged workers 14 years of age and over. The Senior Community Service Employment Program, under Title V of the Older Americans Act, is a program especially designed for older workers. Additionally, the Job Training Partnership Act allocates special funds for older unemployed adults. There is a great disparity, though, between the number of eligible older people and the number participating in such programs.

SUPPORT FROM EMPLOYERS

The ultimate responsibility for maintaining professional competence rests with the individual employee. At the same time, an organization can foster competence by providing updating opportunities, challenging work assignments, and interaction with co-workers and management approaches to facilitate the transition. Figure 1–3 shows information on how employers maintain contact with retirees and semi-retirees. At the same time, the United States has stood alone in its advocacy for the rights of older adult workers to continue to work if they are capable and able. This is rapidly changing around the globe. A serious question for the future is what efforts will be made to make the workplace more attractive to work life extension.

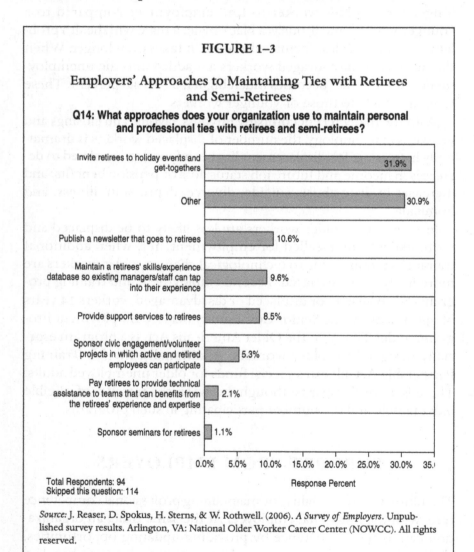

FIGURE 1–3

Employers' Approaches to Maintaining Ties with Retirees and Semi-Retirees

Q14: What approaches does your organization use to maintain personal and professional ties with retirees and semi-retirees?

Total Respondents: 94
Skipped this question: 114   Response Percent

Another consideration is the role that generational difference may play in a person's work life. Workers coming from different generations/cohorts have different social and cultural experiences that may affect attitudes regarding work and co-workers, career, leisure, and family life.

Age is not a good predictor of who can perform a job successfully. Whether changes in physical abilities are relevant to job performance depends on the characteristics of the job and level of performance needed to be successful. People stay mentally competent with normal aging. People maintain intelligence and learning abilities into late life. While declines in information processing and attention have been found in laboratory studies, these may not directly translate to actual work settings. A careful task analysis of a job will reveal the requisite skills and the minimum levels of performance required. Most jobs do not require maximal mental or physical performance and can be performed by healthy, moderately educated adults regardless of age.[51]

In terms of mental and physical capability, there are few obstacles for a large number of middle-aged adults and older adults. In the future, more older adults will be active and healthy, and we can expect them to have the capacity to work and continue to do so for as long as they choose. The drive to be productive, receive income, have social interactions, and contribute to the success of an organization will all be reasons why people will want to continue to work. Additionally, some people will need to work because they will need additional income in later life. One of the most important determinants of remaining in the workforce is one's attitude toward work. Feeling valued, appreciated, and respected within the company context is an important part of the desire to continue to work. Recent evidence supports a change from extrinsic (financial priorities) factors at age 50 to more intrinsic values with regard to work after the age of 60. Employees' attitudes apparently become increasingly important in determining whether they will work into late life.

Employers are becoming more positive about older workers but at the current time have decidedly mixed attitudes. Cost containment issues are very prominent today, which impacts negatively on more highly paid older workers. However, future policies on retirement and healthcare and a better understanding of the cost/benefit ratio associated with employing older workers should improve opportunities for middle-aged and older workers.

Physical and mental changes with age can be sensitively accommodated through the use of human factors approaches. These approaches can support the older worker through careful job design and restructuring the work environment. ADA requires that reasonable accommodations be made so that a disabled worker, young or old, can perform the job. Training can also facilitate older workers to perform in unfamiliar job situations. With normal aging and continued maintenance of skills, older workers can continue to work and be competitive. Future work opportunities will be more intellectual and less physical. Most jobs will be well within the range of older adults' skills and abilities. Capable, able, older adult workers can perform most jobs with great success. Evidence indicates that experience and knowledge make older workers competitive with workers of all ages. Nevertheless, workers will need to be proactive about maintaining their skills and updating them in order to remain competitive. They will need to be responsible for their own careers and perhaps their pension and health benefits. Most older workers can look forward to continuing involvement in work for as long they desire.

DECISION MAKING
AND WORK OPPORTUNITIES

The potential retirees of today may get a very mixed set of messages regarding continued work or retirement from their workplace, and society at large. There is much to be said in support of the importance of the anticipatory period before making a retirement decision. Extended decision making and interim preparation with a focus on people's agency is emphasized.

In the 1980s, life-cycle and life-stage theories were criticized for using data on male workers as the basis for development. It is increasingly evident that career progressions of women may be quite different from those of men, as the former juggle the roles of student, housewife, paid worker, mother, and others. Life-cycle and life-stage theoretical approaches have also been criticized for failure to test propositions adequately. Particularly lacking is longitudinal research using subjects over age 50. A criticism of life-stage and job theories is that they tend to ignore the interaction of work and non-work aspects of life.[52]

All life-span models include some attention to the middle years, of course—but not all give much detailed attention to the role of work. Virtually all of the models of male adult development put work at the center, with the assumption that how a man negotiates entry, progress, and exit from the domain of whatever the culture recognizes as work is a centrally organizing force in his development. Models that describe women's development are more varied. Most emphasize relational aspects, many include mothering and home management as a "work equivalent," and some more contemporary models examine the varying patterns of involvement in the paid labor force.

MIDLIFE CHANGES

The physical changes that occur in midlife are less dramatic than those of childhood, adolescence, and advanced old age. The wrinkles, grey hair, reduced sensory capacities, altered fat distribution, and even menopause are significant primarily because they signal to one's self and to others that one is moving along the life course. What they signify is variable. Minimally, they provide one cue to others about one's age, and to the extent that others respond to a person differently because he or she is thought to be "middle aged," the individual may be forced to acknowledge changes. Some theories emphasize the awareness of personal death as a crucial "marker" of midlife, an awareness that is not based on the actual nearness of death so much as on the recognition that underlying biological changes are occurring, unbidden, to those experiencing them. Biological changes become central when they are diseases, many of which emerge in midlife and have the potential to dramatically redirect the course of life.[53]

The challenges of the middle years are clearly influenced by cohort, a concept that assesses how the historical-cultural times shape the opportunities and assumptions of individuals who "came of age" during that time. Sheehy[54] suggested that five different generations (or cohorts) now occupy contemporary adulthood. She drew upon a unique database created from the U.S. Census Bureau data to compare what is happening at any stage to a particular cohort group over its lifetime, in terms of educational and occupational achievement, labor force status, income level, marriage, childbearing, and divorce patterns. The four generational cohorts are designated as World War II (aged 16 to 19 from 1937 to 1944), Silent (aged 16 to 19 from 1952 to 1959), Vietnam (aged 16 to 19 from 1974 to 1984), and Endangered (aged 16 to 19 from 1982 to 1989). Her analysis, supported by other researchers, indicates the ways in which the content of challenges perceived during the early 40s, for example, is strongly influenced by generation.

Erik Erikson[55] proposed that the distinctive challenge of midlife is to resist the temptation of self-absorption and become generative, capable of fighting to preserve values, traditions, and structures that will be best for the coming generations. Some believe this reassessment is linked to the awareness of personal mortality and the concern about how much time is left for them to accomplish youthful dreams and ambitions; or the signs of biological aging in appearance, reduced energy, and lessened recuperative powers. Others anchor such reappraisals to changes in social roles and the contexts in which social roles are enacted. Changes may be age-graded, to the extent that strong age norms persist about the "right age" to be promoted, to finish bearing children, or for adult children to be married.

There remains substantial disagreement whether reappraisals occur on a predictable timetable for all adults or occur only at times when individual circumstances prompt such reassessment. There is also great disagreement about whether "reappraisal" signifies "crisis." The general stance now seems to be to recognize a continuum of minimal appraisal through serious crisis, dependent upon complex interactions of individual needs and ambitions, current circumstances and options, and anticipated future outcomes.

For some in midlife, leisure time may provide opportunities for personal growth. Although there is no clear definition of leisure, generally, it involves an activity done primarily for its own sake, with an element of enjoyment, pursued during free time. Leisure may be used for meaningful activities, because they provide a sense of acceptance, appreciation, affection, achievement, and amusement, and they allow the participant to avoid feelings of fear, frustration, inferiority, and guilt. There are several patterns of later life leisure: "expanders," who add new activities throughout life; "contractors," who shed activities; and "maintainers," who continue in the same activites. During the early middle years, leisure activities are apt to be closely linked to career development, with skills and contacts nurtured during leisure pursuits contributing directly or subtly to greater success in current work or toward redirecting one's career. During later middle years, leisure may increasingly become the focus of activities that can be maintained through retirement into the later years of life.[56]

SUMMARY

The changing demographics of adult and older adult workers provide an opportunity to apply current life-span developmental and gerontological approaches to human resource management of adult and older adult workers. Employers need to find new strategies to recruit and retain older workers. The life-span approach advances the possibility of behavioral change at any point in the life cycle. Individual differences in aging are recognized as critical in examining adult and older adult career progressions. Self-management of career is a key concept, and career decisions are not age specific. Updating and training are career-long activities. The decision to retire or continue working reflects a complex array of factors. Increasing number of older adult workers are choosing to work longer.

2 | ADAPTING THE WORKPLACE TO ACCOMMODATE PHYSIOLOGICAL AGE-RELATED CHANGES IN OLDER ADULTS

Age represents the passage of time. We can be younger or older than our chronological age—biologically, psychologically, and socially. As discussed in Chapter 1, there are many intra (within) individual changes and inter (between) individual differences in persons as they age. As we grow older, we may experience many changes, and there are differences between people of the same age. At one point we may be working with a 90-year-old line dancer who is very physically fit and, on the other hand, we may have a 65-year-old who has limited mobility and needs to use a walker. Age is not the issue. What is important is the individuals' ability to meet the physical and cognitive demands of a particular job situation. Related to this, there are many baby boomers willing and able to replace boomers who choose to retire. In this chapter we will examine how to design a supportive work environment and how possible age-related changes in our capacities can be accommodated to make the workplace an adaptable environment for adult and older workers.

While there are undoubtedly age differences in how we learn, many researchers agree that these differences can be improved by providing conditions that foster, motivate, and stimulate adult learning experiences. Training issues may be the same across the lifespan as related to individual updating and optimization. For instance, when new computer software programs need to be mastered, usually everyone in the organization has to be trained, regardless of age.

It is important to provide cognitively interactive and supportive environments that are designed to aid adult and older workers.

This approach can be accomplished through adaptive devices and environmental design that help workers compensate for possible age-related changes.

As many employers in the industrialized world address challenges posed by pending retirements of baby boomers, they must fundamentally rethink how they respond to the needs of adult and older adult workers. (See Figure 2–1.)[1] There simply will not be enough young people to fill the traditional entry-level positions for which they are typically hired. This is in contrast to the thinking of the 1980s when more emphasis was placed on the preparation for the retirement years and for providing encouragement for people to retire. As a result, managers and employees have opportunities to work together to develop strategies to optimize human potential and to avoid obsolescence by taking an active role in maintaining, recruiting, and retaining older workers.

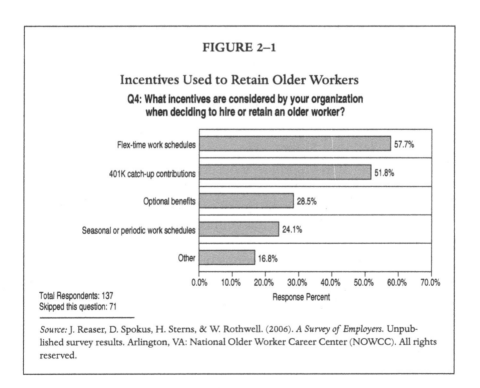

FIGURE 2–1

Incentives Used to Retain Older Workers

Q4: What incentives are considered by your organization when deciding to hire or retain an older worker?

Total Respondents: 137
Skipped this question: 71

Response Percent

Source: J. Reaser, D. Spokus, H. Sterns, & W. Rothwell. (2006). *A Survey of Employers.* Unpublished survey results. Arlington, VA: National Older Worker Career Center (NOWCC). All rights reserved.

Innovative updating of adult and older adult worker knowledge and skills may result in decreased attrition and brain drain in the workplace. However, will older adults want to continue to work past the normative age when past generations were long retired? The response to this question will depend on the individual employee. On this basis, the Alabama Older Worker Survey[2] was developed by the American Association of Retired People (AARP) for the Alabama labor force. The results of 2,049 employers participating in the survey indicate that only one in three employers has strategic plans in place for the baby boomers who will be retiring, and only one in three state that it is presently working on retention of older workers rather than having them retire. The most attractive approaches that the employers used to retain older workers were in providing opportunities for flexible work schedules, rehiring retirees as consultants, providing professional development opportunities, and offering part-time work with benefits.[3]

Census data[4] from 2000 showed an increase of 12 percent in the over 65-year-old U.S. population since 1990. Life expectancy continued its upward trend from 68 years in 1950 to almost 77 in 2000. Projected data suggest that there will be more than 40 million Americans over age 65 in 2010, and close to 60 million by 2020. In contrast, the 40- to 55-year old cohort will decline by 2020. Today, there are about 5 million people who are over age 85.[5] Consequently, the highest growth rate in the U.S. workforce will be among workers aged 55 to 64. (See Figure 2–2.) In addition, many older women are entering the workplace. Many of these women, having spent their earlier years raising their families, are now eager to return to work.

According to the U.S. Department of Labor, Women's Bureau of Statistics,[6] there were 10.3 million women employed who were above the age of 55. These women may have worked intermittently, continuously, or spent extended periods out of the workforce to raise their families, in service occupations, production, transportation, and in natural resources, construction, and maintenance occupations (789,000).[7] In addition, according to the American Association of Retired People (AARP, 2002),[8] Americans are living longer and healthier lives. Living longer is a reality.

FIGURE 2–2

Participation in the Labor Force[9]

Labor force participation rates of men age 55 and over, by age group, annual averages, 1963–2003

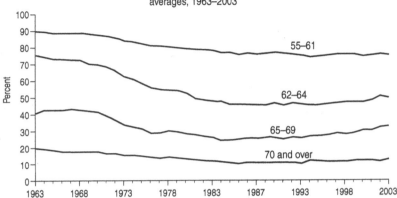

Reference population: These data refer to the civilian noninstutionalized population.
Source: Bureau of Labor Statistics, Current Population Survey.

Labor force participation rates of women age 55 and over, by age group, annual averages, 1963–2003

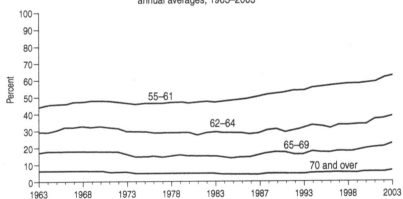

Reference population: These data refer to the civilian noninstutionalized population.
Source: Bureau of Labor Statistics, Current Population Survey

Source: Federal Interagency Forum on Aging-Related Statistics. (2004, November). *Older Americans 2004: Key Indicators of Well-Being.* Washington, DC: U.S. Government Printing Office.

AGING: A GLOBAL VIEW

Today, with downsizing and many jobs being rolled over into one position, more workers are finding themselves in stressful positions. The workplace is not what it used to be where an individual could expect to remain in one career, working for one company, with a lifetime of security. In years past that same organizational commitment brought more security than it does today. These conditions abound worldwide, and the nature of work is constantly changing and being redefined. There is increased responsibility on the part of the employee to manage his or her own career either within the same company or by moving up the ladder outside the organization.

A person's active life expectancy[10] may be measured by the number of years an individual may live without a disability. Globally, there are differences in this active life expectancy. "Switzerland rates as the highest with Australia and Canada ranking next. The population of the United States ranks in the middle"[11] (pp. 154–163). Japan leads the world at present for the number of older adults in their population. In fact, "Japan has the longest life expectancy, but lowest birth rate in the world." Its policies "aim to not only enhance the well-being of older persons, but also to help employers meet workforce needs in the face of an expected shortage of younger workers and to reduce pressure on an insufficiently funded pension system."[12] Due to birth shortages, Singapore and Korea are both encouraging women to have children and are encouraging immigration to make up for projected labor shortfalls. China will experience an enormous labor problem as the "one child per couple" policy for population control impacts future employment prospects in twenty years and less. India faces the fewest demographic-related problems of any economic powerhouse of the future, since one-third of its workers are under age 15.

BIOLOGICAL AGING

Ironically, mortality rates have been used to determine the health status of many older adults. These measures have included poor health, presence of disease, disability, or death. However, these indicators do not truly measure the ability of an individual to work and function.[13]

Aging is a process that is universal in nature and occurs over a period of time. It does not happen to us suddenly. It is only when we become aware of it through aches, pains, immobility, and other physical changes that we notice our aging. We do not, as human beings, die of old age, but our bodies' capabilities to withstand the physical, emotional, and environmental factors of everyday life may decrease our ability to function normally and adapt to change. For many of us, our bodies may be programmed at the beginning for either a long or short health span.[14] However, because of advances in technology, healthcare, and screening programs, we are not doomed by our genes. Our genes, our lifestyles, and our environment play an enormous role in shaping our biological clock. Research suggests that the environment we live and work in plays a major role in whether we remain in the workplace and take part in updating activities such as training programs. It is important to recognize that our chronological age is basically a marker, whereas our biological age is determined by the bodily changes that may occur through aging.

Variability in Aging

Another key issue in individual differences is the fact that training can increase adult optimization and possibly reverse some decrements that may be the result of nonaction. Many older workers do not participate in professional development opportunities that would help them maintain or increase their abilities through mental and physical stimulation. It is also possible that age differences among colleagues intimidate older workers' belief in their ability to learn. They may have a fear of failure, which leads to a self-fulfilling prophecy. Age is a factor that accounts for only a small amount of individual variability. There are also several sources that can be attributed to these differences, namely genetics, variations in lifestyle, disease, gender, differential rates of aging of different systems, and culture, society, and education.[15]

Maintaining Strength

An internationally well-known exercise physiologist, Dr. William J. Evans, and a medical doctor, Irwin H. Rosenberg, conducted a study[16] in the 1990s on older adults who were in their 80s and 90s. They felt that studies of aging adults should focus on human beings rather than draw conclusions based on animal studies. It was a "study of hope" for individuals who couldn't even feed themselves or take care of their Activities of Daily Living (ADLs). From this study, controllable characteristics of aging were monitored, and, despite a person's age, it was found that they could be reversed. Most individuals between the ages of 30 and 80 lose about 30 percent of their muscle mass.[17] This muscle loss leads to imbalance, falls, loss of strength, and decreased bone density. Combined, these can lead to a decrease in daily activities.

There are "ten biomarkers of vitality" that an individual can alter and that are a useful indication of health. They include "muscle mass; strength; basal metabolic rate (BMR); body fat percentage; aerobic capacity; body's blood-sugar tolerance; cholesterol/HDL ratio; blood pressure; bone density; and an individual's body ability to regulate the internal temperature."[18] Examining these factors helps us to switch gears from looking at age from the traditional chronological point of view to a view that we can reverse some age-related losses and increase muscle strength and maintain a good quality of life as we age in the workplace.

Sarcopenia[19] is a term used to describe the condition of individuals who are forced into disabilities. It describes frail individuals who really aren't suffering from any specific diagnosis, but who need assistance because of inactivity that has increased their body fat and reduced their muscle mass. This type of condition may result from sitting at a computer day in and day out, and it can have deleterious consequences.

The Evans-Rosenberg study revealed that older adults respond to exercise just as well as younger adults. In fact, the older adults benefited more from the strength training program, proving that muscle lost through inactivity is actually reversible. Some of the participants at the end of the study were stronger than they had been in the last fifteen years of their lives. The results of this study point to the myths associated with aging.[21] (See Figure 2–3.) Aging does

FIGURE 2–3

Myths About Older Workers

Myth 1: You can't teach an old dog new tricks.

Reality: Studies show only negligible loss of cognitive function of people under 70. While older workers take longer to absorb completely new material, their better study attitudes and accumulated experience lower training costs. The fastest growing group of Internet users is people over 50.

Myth 2: Training older workers is a lost investment because they will not stay on the job for long.

Reality: The future work life of an employee over 50 usually exceeds the life of new technology for which the workers are trained.

Myth 3: Older workers are not as productive as younger workers.

Reality: Overall productivity does not decline as a function of age. Productivity can actually rise due to greater worker accuracy, dependability, and capacity to make better on the spot judgments. Older workers' production rates are steadier than other age groups.

Myth 4: Older workers are less flexible and adaptable.

Reality: Older workers are just as adaptable once they understand the reason for changes. They are more likely to ask why, because they have often seen past changes in processes and procedures abandoned in midstream when they didn't bring expected rewards quickly enough.

Myth 5: Older workers are not as creative or innovative.

Reality: General intelligence levels are the same as younger workers. Eighty percent of the most workable and worthwhile new production ideas are produced by employees over 40 years old.

Myth 6: Older workers cost more than hiring younger workers.

Reality: While workers with tenure are entitled to more vacation time and pension costs related to number of years worked, replacing workers is not cost free. Aetna Insurance Company did a study of this issue and discovered these factors added 93 percent to the first year's salary of new employees.

Myth 7: Benefit and accident costs are higher for older workers.

Reality: Total sick days per year of older workers is lower than other age groups because they have fewer acute illness and sporadic sick days. While individual older workers' health, disability and life insurance costs do rise slowly with age, they are offset by lower costs due to fewer dependents. Overall, fringe benefits costs stay the same as a percentage of salary for all age groups. Older workers take fewer risks in accident prone situations and statistically have lower accident rates than other age groups.

Source: American Business and Older Employees, AARP, Washington, DC, 2000. Bureau of Labor Statistics. Downloaded from www.seniors4hire.org/myths_olderworkers.pdf

not necessarily mean frailty, but it is when we allow acute and chronic diseases to rule our lives that we begin to feel old. The frailty becomes a self-fulfilling prophecy. In other words, aging should be considered a dynamic rather than a stagnant time in our lives. This strength training study proved that no matter what a person's age is, and no matter how people have abused their bodies in the past with lack of activity, damage can be reversed through proper training. Changes in strength and sensory capacity have led to a list of myths about older adults. The sensory changes will be discussed in the next section.

The same holds true for older workers in the workplace. Instead of muscle atrophy occurring from lack of training and use, older adult workers lose their skills and may not have an opportunity to increase their knowledge if they do not participate in updated training to keep them abreast of changes in technology in the workplace.

Physical Changes That Affect the Older Adult Worker

As we age, normative changes take place with our vision and hearing.

VISION

When individuals age, their vision may become impaired. Middle-aged and older adults may need more light in order to see more clearly. Changes may also occur in vision that contribute to spatial orientation and the speed with which an individual moves. However, "scattering increases the risk of impairment from glare sources, such as that produced by reflective surfaces (e.g., glossy magazine pages under bright light)"[21] An older adult has poorer depth perception than does his or her younger counterparts. At age 40 many adults begin to read using bifocal eyeglasses. Older adults need to process two types of information, from both the near field and far field.[23]

Providing older adults with computer stations that are ergonomic is a first step in accommodating adult and older adult workers. The computer monitor should be adjusted by the individual so that it is at the correct distance and height.[23] It should be just below eye level; an individual should not be looking up at the screen. Constantly looking upward puts added strain on the eyes and neck.[24] It is also important to use the correct fonts and contrasts so that there is little glare for the older adult. In addition, perception is affected by repeated changes to an older adult's vision.[25] Therefore, in the workplace it is important to provide proper levels of lighting with reduced glare and material that has larger print with a deep contrast to help older workers adapt to changes in their vision. It might also be helpful to provide magnifiers at various workstations for individuals who have to do more detailed work.

Resources for individuals who have vision problems can be found at www.microsoft.com/enable/guides/vision.aspx and www.apple.com/disability/vision/easyaccess.html.[26]

HEARING

Losses can be experienced at almost any age. However, hearing loss may increase as we age. Men are more susceptible to hearing loss than are women. Most of us who have reached middle age may suffer from presbycusis.[27]

High-pitched sounds are harder to hear. This condition can be related to years of working with loud machinery. Therefore, in order to prevent this problem, employers should provide and insist that ear plugs or ear muffs be used.

> Hard of hearing employees often don't want to admit they have a problem. Given visual cues, they are listening and hearing. Often when they are left alone, clearly, they did not digest the information. When a pattern like this was recognized, all verbal instructions were followed up with a written backup so that the employee could respond/comment—provide feedback as necessary.[28]

Communication may be affected when the older adult worker suffers from hearing loss, and these impairments can lead to additional problems in the workplace. For instance, directions may not be followed correctly. It would be a good idea to offer yearly hearing tests to individuals so that this type of change could be compensated for early before it affects an individual's work.

Hearing losses may also lead to social problems. Older workers may shy away from meetings or taking on group responsibilities because they are aware that they have trouble distinguishing voices in a crowd. Employers would be wise to plan for these issues when preparing newsletters and monthly meetings so that individuals feel comfortable discussing their concerns and are given the resources so that they may make accommodations for such changes without feeling singled out. This workplace strategy would then enable older workers to partake in group discussions and lead groups.

Individuals who have difficulty hearing may hear soft sounds and think people are talking about them. They may appear cognitively deprived because they don't follow directions properly. This condition is so progressive that an individual may not recognize that it is happening. However, it can create problems with older adults' self-esteem and with their social interactions. They may begin to lose their social skills. People around them become frustrated and communication becomes poor.

> Resources are available to employers and older workers that provide amplification, signaling/alerting, and visual display devices that can assist a worker who has hearing difficulties. Amplification devices can be attached to a phone or worn by an individual (assistive listening device or ALD). Signaling and alerting equipment can be built in or attached to office equipment to blink or flash when a sound occurs. Workers with hearing loss should reduce distractive noise. Inform others of hearing loss to minimize miscommunication.[29]

Today, because of advanced technology, there are many digital hearing devices that fit snugly into the ear canal. They are skin colored and barely noticeable. However, the problem is that they are usually very expensive. Perhaps many older workers do not have the necessary funds to purchase proper hearing devices. Employers are encouraged to promote their use and possibly help provide these devices to workers at a minimal cost. By automatic sensor, these devices can switch from one frequency range to another by themselves without much effort on the part of the individual wearing them. Even when conventional approaches don't work, surgical implants are also available such as "bone-anchored aids for individuals with hearing problems on only one side of their bodies; and middle ear implants can be used for moderate types of deafness"[30] (p. 28). There are also "implantable devices that can be developed; cochlear implants include the implantation of electrodes inside the cochlea. This type of device converts nerve impulses which are relayed to the brain"[31] (p. 28). In addition, it is recommended to alert the hearing impaired through flashing lights, vibrations similar to our cell phones when in meetings to alert us to incoming calls, and loud sirens.[32] In the workplace it might also be helpful when communicating with someone who has hearing loss to be sure the older worker can properly read lips while people speak in a distinct tone. Make sure people face those who may experience a hearing loss. Supervisors should give directions face-to-face rather than turning around, and if possible, provide a written copy as well.

Psychometric Skills

Speed of processing is a person's ability to identify and locate visual information quickly where there might be added disruptions that take them away from the task at hand. These distractions could be noises or other workers moving in and out of cubicle workstations. These disruptions could be computer related and could distract from a learner's attention. Employers could provide workstations that give older workers more privacy with less distraction. Carpeting or other special flooring also curtails noise and provides good support for older workers who stand on their feet for prolonged periods of time. Factors associated with ergonomics affect all workers' performance, of course, not just that of older workers.

> Resources available for employers are providing ergonomic workstations that prevent discomfort experienced by those with previous injuries, poor circulation, etc. Proper seating and/or standing options are important. It is ideal to have adjustable furniture and office equipment to accommodate muscle fatigue and postural changes throughout the day. Older workers need frequent stretching or readjusting, sit/stand workstations, padded or supportive flooring and standing tools (stools to lean on when standing).[33]

Speed of processing is also a factor when discussing older driver issues such as reaction time. This is pertinent if workers must travel as part of their jobs. All these factors may play a significant part in

how older workers perform their jobs. When older workers are trying to teach themselves to learn how to use a word processor, they
may need to take between 50 percent and 100 percent extra time.[34]
Their reaction times may be slow, but they can be improved through
practice. However, through adaptation and experience, little is lost in
productivity. Despite this fact, proper training of older adult workers
is necessary when considering the importance of keeping up with rapidly changing technology because of its importance in the economy.[35]

The use of technology for many older adults is often a challenge.
Some older adults have been using computers for years, and others are
computer challenged. Some may never have used e-mail or know the
benefits of using a computer. Some problems older adults face include
using the computer mouse, hearing audio output of a computer, and
seeing computer screen images properly. Depending on where the
computer is situated, there may be glare from an opened window or
from bad lighting.

> Resources for employers and older workers include screen enlarg-
> ers; screen readers; speech recognition systems; speech synthesizers;
> refreshable Braille displays; Braille embossers; talking word proces-
> sors and large-print word processors.[36]

Older adults' motor coordination may also be affected by arthritis. This degenerative disease may increase interindividual differences
among people of the same age. These physiological changes, which
cause joint stiffness and pain, can be helped through exercise to maintain flexibility. Many times individuals wait too long to seek help,
and it is only when the problem begins to affect their quality of life
that they seek interventions through joint resurfacing or total joint
replacement.

> "I work in aviation maintenance, which requires a great deal of phys-
> ical effort. We have older workers who sometimes have difficulty bend-
> ing and squeezing into tight spaces. Our leads frequently give them job
> assignments that take this into consideration or assign them a younger
> worker who they can mentor and who can take care of the more phys-
> ical aspects of the task."[37]

Employers could work closely with physical and occupational therapists, who provide evaluations and devices that help older workers accommodate for changes that may only require a wrist brace, back support for a chair, a foot rest, or perhaps a special gel cushion for the chair. In addition, chairs that have arms make it easier for individuals to ascend and descend into a sitting or standing position. Figure 2–4[38]

FIGURE 2–4

Overview of Common Aging-Related Changes

System/Skill	Characteristic	Effects of Aging
Vision	Acuity	Diminishes
	Discriminable differences	Decrease
	Visual field	Diminishes
	Dark adaptation	Slows; more illumination required
	Color sensitivity	Reduces
Hearing	Sensitivity	Decreases, especially at high frequencies
	Frequency discrimination	Degrades
	Temporal resolution	May degrade
	Understanding in noise	Dwindles
Attention		Reduces
Short-term memory	Processing performance	Degrades Shows deficits especially when other information is processed at the same time
Long-term memory	Episodic	Performance declines
	Semantic	May slow but essentially remains
Psychomotor skills	Learning	Declines
	Reaction time	Slows
	Motion time	Slows
	Movements	Slower, less accurate, and weaker

provides an overview of the changes described in this section of the chapter. In Chapter 3 we will discuss further issues related to memory and cognitive change that may take place in adult and older adult workers.

PSYCHOLOGICAL AGING

Another point to consider is the fact that many baby boomers who are continuing to work may also be taking care of their own aging parents as well as caring for their grandchildren. It is necessary and important, therefore, to consider the context of the family when examining the older worker. Being part of the Sandwich Generation, a term used to identify older adults who care for both younger and older generations at the same time, may affect the older worker's decision to remain in the workplace. Employers could ease this situation by providing adult daycare services for older workers who have the responsibility of caring for aging parents. They may also provide more flexible work schedules to accommodate the responsibilities encountered that might affect an older worker's ability to keep a normal work schedule. When employers express concern and provide flexibility, older workers may be more committed to remaining with an organization that cares.

Case Study

Sasha spent seventeen years doing contingent work for organizations and academic institutions. She is now a woman in her mid-50s, who kept active all her life and considered herself healthy. Sasha describes her life now. She works as an adjunct instructor teaching several courses at an institution of higher learning. She is at the peak of her career, having raised four children during the seventeen years she was doing contingent work. This is a classic tale of many older adult women. She also works various subcontracting jobs as a health educator. For the past thirteen years, she has also been burning the candle on both ends as a caregiver for an aging parent and also a younger sibling who recently died. These caregiving experiences have been done at a distance where Sasha has had to travel six hours round trip every two weeks to help keep two family members at home and out of a nursing home. This traveling in all types of weather, coupled with her own immediate family needs of raising four children, the challenge of completing a graduate degree, and increased work responsibilities have classified her as part of the Sandwich Generation. However, the last several months Sasha has found herself in and out of the hospital for illnesses that have taxed her physical well-being. As a result, she had major surgery, which now requires a three- to six-month recovery period.

Ironically, Sasha's background is in aging with a focus on the importance of remaining in the workplace as long as possible in order to achieve not only job satisfaction but also life satisfaction. She is a life-long learner. Her four children are almost all independent with one younger daughter finishing college in six months.

During her acute illness Sasha was offered a position that she termed the "chance" of a lifetime. However, she had to relinquish it because she needed the time for surgery and to recuperate.

Sasha is functioning fine cognitively. However, because of her recent illness and surgery, she requires a much more ergonomically designed workstation in order to be able to sit comfortably at a computer. In addition, there is a need for more flexibility in Sasha's work schedule so that she may go for physical therapy and properly recuperate.

As depicted above, Sasha may be a co-worker or an employee. How would other people react to her special needs, considering the fact that this was an acute illness that has affected her short-term mobility? She wants to continue to be productive. Would most employers or supervisors be willing to provide an ergonomic workstation so that she is comfortable and able to fulfill her responsibilities? Would most employers be willing to be flexible with her work hours? List the steps that should be taken first.

According to the National Study of the Changing Workforce Research Highlights,[39] learning opportunities, decision making, trust, support from management, and nondiscriminatory factors are important in a supportive workplace environment. In addition, there are stressors, termed intergenerational issues, that older workers encounter when they are dealing with a younger generation in the workplace. These stressors often include educational differences,

myths, perceptions, and attitudes that create conflict and misunder-
standings between individuals of different generations. However, if
both groups are valued for their contributions, it can lead to a more
positive atmosphere where one generation learns from the experiences of the other.[40] It is important for managers in organizations to
be aware of these important issues, which can affect older worker
retention and participation in training programs. These stressors
may provide opportunities in the workplace for mentoring and
coaching. It could turn out to be a win-win situation.

As can be seen, meeting job demands and trying to fulfill multiple roles might have an impact on older adults' job satisfaction.[41] For
instance, because of caregiving responsibilities for an elderly parent,
an older worker may experience more absenteeism at various periods of time. These periods may be times when a supervisor's emotional support and shared time off from colleagues can help prevent
negative job consequences, which would result in lack of job security, loss of income, status, and self-esteem. In other words, when
individuals are faced with the inability to meet the demands in the
workplace as well as maintain their own mental and physical health,
there is a disruption in the balance between their work-family life
roles.[42] Open communication and flexibility between employers and
older workers is the key to integrating a balance between work and
family life,[43] which enables older workers to demonstrate their abilities at work while still having the ability to take charge of their work-
family life situations.

SOCIAL AGING

Older adults nearing retirement report that leading an active social
life contributes to their overall emotional and physical health.[44] However, lack of work through a premature or planned retirement may
decrease the amount of emotional and physical activity in their lives.
Consequently, the dynamics of the workplace provide workers with
a fertile environment for maintaining their social skills. Teamwork
may provide older workers with a sense of family. Working in groups
also takes the stress off individuals who do not prefer to work alone.
Each person may contribute, but the collective work of the team

provides an effective sum of the individual contributions.[45] Since many retirees are also experiencing the empty-nest syndrome, this loss of workplace activity may deprive them of a sense of community or family and affect their well-being.

Researchers have examined social support, stress, and strain, and the influence of what they have termed work interference with family (WIF) and family interference with work (FIW). These variables could have a rippling effect on work-home load, work-marital distress, and intention to leave job-marriage.[46] The results of Brotheridge and Raymond's study indicate that supervisor support was correlated with work overload, job distress, and intentions to leave their particular position in the workplace. There was a strong correlation between work overload and job distress and work interference with family. It was also found that this "stress was related to home overload and reasons to leave a marriage relationship. When an individual has little family support, there is a correlation to an overload in the home, marital problems, and the likelihood that one will leave a marriage. The conclusion to this study suggests that work interference with family had a stronger correlation than the effects of family interference with work."[47] Older workers are adaptable, and overall productivity can be maintained when workers are under stress as long as supervisors are willing to provide opportunities in the workplace that provide time for leisure, work, and professional development.

OLDER ADULTS CONTINUING TO WORK

The real question may be, "Who can afford to retire in this day and age?" Older workers may have to work despite the fact that they are ready to retire. In 1991, a study was conducted by Louis Harris and Associates with the support of the Commonwealth Fund. The audience included 3,000 older adults above the age of 55.[48] The individuals were questioned on whether they participated in paid or volunteer work. The results indicate that of "older adults over 55, 27 percent worked; 26 percent volunteered somewhere; 42 percent were helping to raise grandchildren or helping their own children, and 29 percent were caring for someone sick or caring for someone with a disability."[49] This study has been considered one of the most comprehensive studies conducted on what is called productive aging.

In the past, older workers were expected to retire at a specific age, or period in time, because it was the normative thing to do. It was expected of them regardless of whether they were ready. They have been depicted as healthy, economically secure, and self-satisfied people who spend many hours in leisure time golfing, playing tennis, traveling around the world, exercising, and soaking up the sun while lying on a lounge chair in their backyards. However, the data suggest that the baby boom generation will have the option of remaining in the workforce long past the normative age of retirement, perhaps until age 75. In contrast, people who have physically demanding, routine, and unchallenging jobs are most successful in retirement.

DESIGNING THE WORKPLACE FOR OLDER AMERICANS

When it comes to innovation, sometimes large established corporations find themselves at a disadvantage. Too often they only pay lip service to innovation and creativity as a means to revitalize their stagnant bureaucracies in preparing for the future. As a result, they encounter problems in maintaining programs that encourage new ways of thinking. In this new century, creative thinking skills will make the difference between success and failure—between those who lead and those who follow. The people who will be the most successful in the future will be creative thinkers who are flexible and can deal with rapid change.[50]

—Harry Bobonich, Ph.D.

Measuring creativity is not easy to do. It really depends on how the term is defined. However, many people believe that older adults become more creative and that artists may produce their best works as they grow older. Supervisors and managers also have a responsibility to foster a work climate that is conducive to innovation.

Managers and trainers can expect to deal with the challenge of adapting the workplace to meet the needs of aging adults. All individuals share and also differ in their abilities. Individual difference is the major concept, and individuals may experience declines at different rates. Employers know that no two people are alike in all ways. The same is true of older workers. As we have discussed, despite the declines that may take place, more older adults are continuing to work past the normative age when their ancestors were already long retired.

The normal process of aging may make our bodies and minds more susceptible to diseases that can cause immobility and disability. All these factors play a significant part in how an older worker performs his or her job or remains in the job. We may shrink a few inches in height because of spinal compression and because of years of poor posture. In addition, because of a slowing of our body's metabolism, we may also start to accumulate body fat in unwanted areas such as the abdomen. Employers that provide places for employees to walk during lunch, healthy snacks in vending machines, or fitness centers at work are providing opportunities that promote healthy lifestyles. This, in turn, may reduce many of the age-related changes that might take place for older workers.

In addition, an individual's pulmonary function may decrease and vascular insufficiencies may increase; the synovial fluids that lubricate joints may decrease, and people may experience bone spurs that cause pain when mobile. Sometimes people may wear out the warranty on their joints through a lifetime of use or abuse. In addition, several forms of arthritis, such as osteoarthritis and rheumatoid arthritis, may decrease flexibility through acute and chronic flare-ups. All of these symptoms may increase the inflammatory response, which increases pain and may cause increased immobility and loss of independence. Acute or chronic, these symptoms may have a devastating effect on older workers who are trying to maintain independence and a good quality of life while remaining in the workplace. However, providing ample time and opportunities throughout the day to get up from a workstation and move around may reduce these symptoms.

Bones are also more susceptible to osteoporosis. Bone density tests can be performed to give individuals a baseline of their bone structure and, if they are at risk of fractures, medications can be prescribed to help maintain or build their bones. Also, besides increased intake of calcium, progressive weight resistance exercise has been proven to help build and strengthen muscle around the bone and also increase bone density. In addition, prolonged sitting at a computer can lead to problems as well; muscles begin to shrink and bone density decreases. Muscles protect bones and prevent falls. Workers of all ages, particularly older workers, should be allowed opportunities to get up and stretch and move around. This is a healthy practice and, after an individual returns to the workstation, he or she may be more productive after moving around and getting the blood circulating. Consequently, management should encourage bone density testing of older workers and increase health education programs in the workplace that stress the importance of increased calcium intake, provide weight resistance programs that increase muscle strength and build bone, and provide periods throughout the day for exercise. Employers of the future should stress healthy lifestyles for all workers.

STEREOTYPES ABOUT AGING

Misperceptions of older adults many times affect an organization's practices toward older workers.[51] (See Figures 2–5 and 2–6.) These issues are many times determined by the culture of the organization, and they can affect how older workers are treated. Ageist attitudes can lead to decreased opportunities for professional development of older workers. "An organization's human resource policies and practices will, in turn, affect its culture, and stereotypes, norms and values."[52]

As a result of stereotypes, many older workers are classified as being more dependent on others because they lack certain physical abilities. On the other hand, baby boomers are more comfortable with aging than previous generations. It is because of these attitudes that many older adults try to maintain their youthful image by masking the effects of the aging process. Men and women alike will color their hair, try to keep physically fit, and sometimes try to act and dress like younger adults.[53] Since Western culture seems preoccupied with perpetual youth, the workplace should be a safe environment

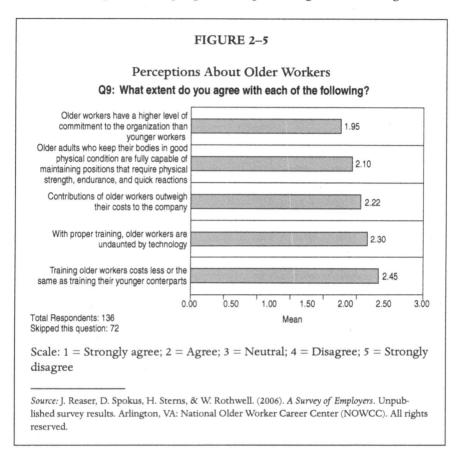

FIGURE 2–5

Perceptions About Older Workers

Q9: What extent do you agree with each of the following?

Older workers have a higher level of commitment to the organization than younger workers — 1.95

Older adults who keep their bodies in good physical condition are fully capable of maintaining positions that require physical strength, endurance, and quick reactions — 2.10

Contributions of older workers outweigh their costs to the company — 2.22

With proper training, older workers are undaunted by technology — 2.30

Training older workers costs less or the same as training their younger conterparts — 2.45

Total Respondents: 136
Skipped this question: 72

Mean

Scale: 1 = Strongly agree; 2 = Agree; 3 = Neutral; 4 = Disagree; 5 = Strongly disagree

Source: J. Reaser, D. Spokus, H. Sterns, & W. Rothwell. (2006). *A Survey of Employers.* Unpublished survey results. Arlington, VA: National Older Worker Career Center (NOWCC). All rights reserved.

where older workers feel safe from the stereotypical attitudes arising from previous generations.

THE AMERICANS WITH DISABILITIES ACT

As we grow older, from youth to middle age and older adulthood, our needs change. This is particularly true of our needs in the workplace. When acute or chronic illnesses affect older workers, employers must take steps to ensure that the value of the worker is respected. Interpersonal communication at these crucial times helps maintain organizational commitment and worker satisfaction. In the

FIGURE 2–6

What Are Your Perceptions Based on Experiences with Older Workers?

Q2: To what extent is each of the following true in your experience with your older workers?

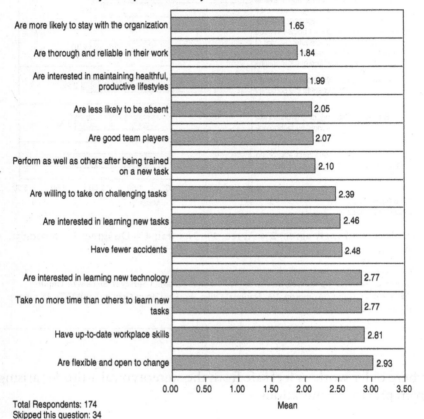

Total Respondents: 174
Skipped this question: 34

Scale: 1 = Strongly agree; 2 = Agree; 3 = Neutral; 4 = Disagree; 5 = Strongly disagree

Source: J. Reaser, D. Spokus, H. Sterns, & W. Rothwell. (2006). *A Survey of Employers.* Unpublished survey results. Arlington, VA: National Older Worker Career Center (NOWCC). All rights reserved.

workplace this can be fostered through an open-door policy where older workers feel safe to confide their needs to their supervisors.

As older adults, we are not doomed to a life of disabilities, but when accidents happen or disease develops, we may lose the ability to perform everyday activities of daily living (ADLs) or workplace functions as we did in the past. Related to this, the Global Aging Report[54] states that an "international survey of 773 corporate executives found workers reached peak performance in their 40s, then their peak performance declined in their 50s. However, it was found that white collar workers do not experience such a decline in productivity as those workers who have to do more physically demanding work."[55] In addition, like many other studies, older workers are capable of adapting to workplace demands and changes and are very reliable, are absent from work less and show more organizational commitment.[56]

The 1990 Americans with Disabilities Act (ADA)[57] is actually the first federal government legislation that addresses the rights of disabled citizens. By definition it assures that Americans "who are disabled have the same opportunities and access to transportation, government programs, access to employment and telecommunication that everyone has."[58] The act defines a disability as anything that diminishes the quality of one's physical or mental health. Examples of this disability might include vision, hearing, mobility, and communication needs.[59] Figure 2–7 summarizes ways to accommodate these age-related disabilities.

A disability could include "cosmetic disfigurement, or anatomical loss affecting one or more of the following body systems: neurological, musculosketal, special sense organs, respiratory, and cardiovascular and could include infectious and contagious disease."[60] ADA employment regulations are applied to organizations that employ more than fifteen workers.

The regulations that set guidelines must be adhered to by organizations when and how they hire workers with disabilities. The ADA guidelines require employers, regardless of the number of people they employ, to provide accommodations for those with disabilities. These accommodations could include providing a wheelchair-accessible ramp or sharing in the cost of some accommodations with the disabled worker. It should be noted that all instances of worker disability are handled on an individual basis and are evaluated according to

FIGURE 2–7

Typical Human Factors Accommodation Procedures

Purpose	Specific Aim	Examples	Accommodation Range	Critical Limits Used by the Designer
Communication fit	Ensure match of product to user and of effective use	Car restraints, helmets, wheelchairs	Complete or almost full range of the user population, such as 5th to 95th percentile	Both minimal and maximal expected values
Reach	Placement to ensure access and appropriate and effective use	Grab bar, handrail, step height	Smallest of the potential users	Minimum expected value
Clearance	Set to avoid undesirable or unintentional contact	Desk-seat gap, access hatch	Largest of the potential users	Maximum expected value
Entrapment avoidance	Prevent unintentional retention of the whole body or of a body segment	Washing machine opening, maintenance access, folding chair	Usually the largest of the potential users	Usually meet or exceed the maximum expected value
Exclusion	Achieve inaccessibility and inoperability	Barriers, railings, guards, packaging, controls	Full range of the user population	Either below the smallest expected value or above the largest expected value, or both

Source: Reproduced from K.H.E. Kroemer (2006). Designing for Older People. *Ergonomics in Design 4*, 25–31, with permission by the author and the publisher, Human Factors and Ergonomics Society.

individual differences. In addition, accommodations are made "that cost at least $250, but less than $10,250. Another tax credit of up to $15,000 per year is available if employers remove certain architectural or transportation barriers, such as steps, narrow doors, inaccessible parking spaces, and restrooms that do not meet ADA standards."[61]

When training individuals with a disability, it is necessary to avoid evaluating them on an impaired area where they are deficient. For example, in an organization where the majority of a day's work involves working at the computer, proofreading text, and a small portion of the job analysis requires an individual to walk long distances, drive, lift or bend in odd positions, the work of a person with an impaired function could be given to another individual. Therefore, it is important to understand the effects of certain health conditions on specific job-related activities.[62] "O*NET collects, organizes, describes, and disseminates data on occupation characteristics and worker attributes to define key elements of an occupation: descriptions of the worker and requirements of work of over 1,100 occupations."[63]

The website provides:

• Information about what skills are in demand.
• Information to help workers with proven skills transfer to new careers.
• National labor market information on employment levels, occupational outlook, and wages.[64]

According to research,

it is important to look at the functional capacity[65] of older adults: Consideration of the health of the population from a work life perspective with its focus on supply, demand, productivity, costs, health maintenance, necessitates a shift from the ideal view of health to the inter-individual view. Employment analysts need to be more concerned with the functional abilities than with the ideal levels of health. It matters little from an employment perspective whether worker A has arthritis and worker B does not, unless worker A feels unwell and risks health impairment through employment, performs poorly and/or costs the company more than worker B because of the arthritis.[66]

Table 2–1 gives tips on age-related changes, and Table 2–2 lists examples of human factor designs. (See Tables 2–1[67] and 2–2.[68])

TABLE 2–1

Tips on Age-Related Changes

Physically Demanding Jobs Leading to Higher Workplace Attrition Rates	Tasks That Increase Risk
TIP:	• Repetitive loading
• Design/redesign workstation/ workplace to accommodate physical changes	• Twisting of the torso
• Horizontal work-surface design	• Rapid lifting
• Seated work-surface height adjustments	
• Standing work-surface heights	
• Provide lifting aids	
• Provide rest	
• Give good foot traction to avoid tripping	

Changes in Anthropometry	Carpal tunnel syndrome:
TIP:	• Highly repetitive manual actions and use of small tools
• Managers should pay attention to seat height and width	• Performing manual tasks that involve force
• Good work postures decrease physical strain, disability, and impairment	• Awkward hand motions
• Tool redesign (e.g., longer-handled tools)	• Carrying small objects (e.g., books)
• Proper temperature control	• Using tools with low-frequency vibrations
• Systematic variations in movement during task performance	• Using short-handled tools
	• Wearing gloves that do not fit properly
	• Working in conditions of low temperature

Changes in Vision	• Use more contrast; blue-green should not be used for visual displays (computerized or written)
TIP:	
• Install soft white reader bulbs for lights	• Using larger black print on white computer screen is most effective
• Install adjustable glare-free screen monitors	• Useful field of view (UFOV): Driving research indicate that peripheral view changes as we age
• Use of computer mouse may reduce differences between old and young users	
• Install adjustable light sources	

(continued)

(continued)
Changes in Vision
- Consider where computers are placed to avoid glare
- Increase illumination (e.g., at the top and bottom landings of stairs, hallways, and elevators)
- To compensate for decreasing dark adaptation capabilities, avoid pronounced transitions in the level of illuminations
- Use consistent levels of lighting between different locations.
- Design workstations with lighting focused on select areas to enhance perceptual and selective attention capabilities

Changes in Hearing
TIP:
- Eliminate possible echoes in a room
- Enhance visual cues of communication to compensate for older adult changes
- Place seating arrangement of a group such that it is in a circle to improve visual cues of older adult
- Limit the size of the group to help integration of auditory and visual communication

Source: A. A. Sterns, H. L. Sterns, & L. A. Hollis. (1996). The productivity and functional limitations of older adult workers. In W. C. Crown (Ed.), *Handbook on Employment and the Elderly.* (pp. 276–303). Westport, CT: Greenwood Press.

MINORITIES IN THE WORKPLACE

In most of the research that has been done, men have been the target audience. However, since more women are entering the workforce, more research is needed on both women and minorities as they age in the workplace, looking at health problems, education, and work-family life issues.

TABLE 2–2

Examples of Human Factors Designs for the Elderly and for Children

	Examples	Design Aim	Useful Data
Interaction with Products	Medicine packaging	Make usable by elderly people but unattractive for, resistant to, or inoperable by children	Hand size, hand strength, color, understanding symbols, mouth size
	Medicine bottles, child pacifiers, toys	Prevent swallowing, breakage	Mouth size, hand strength
	Cooktop and oven controls	Facilitate use by elderly but prevent operation by children	Reach data, hand strength especially in twisting, understanding markers and symbols
	Bicycles, tricycles	Suitable size of handlebar, good reach to handle and pedals	Lengths of arms and legs, sitting shoulder height, hand size
Personal space	Space in bathrooms, bedrooms, kitchen	Provide ample space for dressing, washing, toileting, especially when less mobile because of age or disability; grab bars may be desirable	Body size, mobility, strength, and stamina
	Safety mesh	Prevent penetration by hand or other body part	Hand size, digit length and diameter, push strength
	Fire escapes	Allow quick access or operation when needed, but otherwise prevent unauthorized and inadvertent operation	Reach, strength, manipulation under normal and emergency conditions

Interaction with Surrounds	Examples	Design Aim	Useful Data
	Window and door handles	Facilitate use by elderly but possibly prevent operation by children	Reach data, hand and arm strength, understanding mode of operation
	Railings at balconies and stairs, playpens, stair guards	Prevent falling over or through, prevent unwanted opening of locks, prevent entrapment	Body size, height of center of body mass, head and chest width, climbing ability
	Room climate	Automatically achieve and maintain suitable surround temperature via well-located and easily understood controls	Eye height, easily read markers of existing and desired temperature, adjustment capability in terms of hand/digit motions
	Containers and drawers	Operable by elderly and disabled person but preferably not by children	Strength, mobility, motor skills

Even though more than 80 percent of both African American and Whites graduate from high school today, there is still a difference in the unemployment rates for both African Americans and Hispanic Americans. Actually, these rates are almost twice as high as for White people.[69]

Because of the high rate of immigration to the United States, there has been an increase in the number of Hispanic, African American, and Asian populations. These changes in immigration rates are increasingly higher than for Whites.[70] The Health and Retirement Longitudinal Survey report states that among men ages 51–55, Whites are more employed, and Blacks are most likely to be out of the workforce. The Survey results also indicate that Hispanic women were less likely to be employed than either Black or White women. It also reports that in older adults between the ages of 45 and 64, Blacks are 2½ times as likely as Whites to suffer from hypertension, circulatory problems, diabetes, and nervous disorders and that the decline in Black men at work reflects higher rates of disability.[71]

WORK ISSUES

Certain occupations, especially those that are physically challenging, might have hazards for individuals in the workplace. In addition, some jobs are much more dangerous physically than others.[72] However, "older adults may face more hazards due to falls, assaults, harmful exposures, or transportation incidents."[73] These are issues that organizations need to be cognizant of when providing a safe environment for workers of all ages, particularly older workers.

ACTIVE OLDER WORKERS

The baby boom generation will be a more educated and talented base whose continued employment actually benefits the nation's economy. Research has also shown that the more productive individuals are as they age, the healthier they remain both cognitively and physically. As people age, it is important for their health that they not lead a sedentary lifestyle. Keeping active can actually decrease the risk of chronic diseases and help prevent depressive symptoms, which will keep individuals living independently and leading a better quality of life for longer periods of time.

Historically, before the computer technology explosion, organizations used hard copy files in large filing cabinets. Workers used slow manual or electric typewriters. Next, they were introduced to computers and word processing. Today, as technology in the workplace becomes more important, job demands are continually increasing, requiring older workers to keep abreast of current advances in technology. Organized workplace training will be critical for certain older workers who do not have the skills to use this advanced technology. Without proper workplace training and education, older workers can face skill obsolescence.

As discussed, normative changes take place with our vision, hearing, cognition, psychomotor abilities, and perception.[74] All these factors play a significant part in how older workers perform their jobs. However, through adaptation and experience, little productivity is lost. Despite this fact, proper training is necessary when considering the importance of an older worker keeping up with rapidly changing technology because of how important that is to the economy.[75]

ADAPTING THE WORKPLACE FOR OLDER ADULTS

The International Society for Gerontechnology is an organization devoted to bridging the gap between technology and aging. This society was formed to study aging and technology in order to improve the functioning ability of older adults with regard to mobility, vision, hearing, and workplace challenges.[76] Another organization devoted to the study of ergonomic risk factors that affect individuals is the Human Factors and Ergonomics Society. Both organizations are working to enhance the continued contributions of older workers. They are also providing workplace designs that help older workers maintain a good quality of life, helping older adults maintain their independence, and helping them function with modifications in the workplace.

A computer workstation design study was conducted with 206 university employees. Fifty percent of the target audience included individuals who were over age 50, and the other 50 percent included individuals who were age 40 or younger. The study examined age and gender as they pertained to pain experienced by workers using computers at the university. The factors examined included pain in the arm/shoulder and wrist. Job class and number of hours worked were also factors that were addressed. The results indicate that there were gender differences, and both young and older workers experienced pain. Another suggestion from the study was that women may react differently to what is termed "ergonomically correct." There are many variables that have to be considered, such as whether the individual's body dimensions are the same, whether people had pre-existing conditions, and whether women who also cared for children had more symptoms.[77]

SUMMARY

In this chapter we discussed health-related issues that can be addressed through ergonomics in the workplace. Taking action to make this difference can have a positive effect on the retention, managing, and training of an older adult worker. Since many older adults spend most of their time in the workplace, this is a good place to begin with interventions that lead to increased job satisfaction and performance.

Redesigning jobs and training to fit individual needs may offer interventions that promote more positive health outcomes. Therefore, it is necessary to continue researching the health and job performance of older adults so that accommodations can be made to help retain them in the workplace. When an organization is designing environments for older workers, it must be aware of the vision, hearing, and mobility issues that older workers face. These age-related changes can affect communication and the ability to comprehend instructions. By realizing the potential benefits of ergonomic interventions and creating workstations that contribute to an older worker's comfort, age-related losses can be reduced.

3 | HOW TO TRAIN OLDER ADULTS: AGING INFLUENCES ON COGNITIVE TASKS

A popular belief is that we all go downhill as we age. While this may be true for some individuals, it is definitely not true for most people. As we discussed in Chapter 2, biological changes occur in some people. However, there is no time clock that states that cognitive changes happen to all adult and older adult workers. Many biological changes occur when individuals have an illness, abuse their bodies, do not exercise frequently, and remain sedentary. When this happens, changes are often the result of something other than just growing old.[1]

Changes in cognitive functioning may be both positive and negative, depending on how people react to their work situations. One person may feel challenged by management expectations, be stimulated by current work assignments, be involved in fitness activities, and participate in training and education opportunities. Another person may be depressed, feel that work assignments are not challenging, feel unsupported by the supervisor, have no desire to engage in physical activities, and see little reward for participating training and education activities within the workplace environment. This person may show a poorer level of cognitive performance. However, research suggests that, by offering training and education opportunities in the workplace for updating, adults and older adults can maintain or even reverse age-related changes occurring in cognition.[2]

For most older adults there may be few or no major changes in intellectual abilities and in learning abilities for people in good health. Performance in most work-related activities should not change. It may take longer to learn a new computer program, but once mastered, performance will be the same as everyone else's.

Learning and memory are closely related.[3] Learning involves acquiring new information, and memory is remembering what has been learned and then being able at a later date to recall that information.[4] It is easier to think of this process like a computer—input and output. (See Table 3–1.)

Memory may show changes as we age.[5] It may be more difficult to remember things that happened recently. The long-term memory, which holds information from the past and well-learned recent material, continues to function well.

Primary and working memory appear under short-term memory. *Primary memory* is related to remembering a telephone number that is just looked up,[6] while *working memory* is taking information and organizing it so that it can be retrieved at a later date. Research indicates that working memory may be affected by aging and, therefore, could be a reason why older workers may need more time to process new information. Memory strategies may include the use of *mnemonics,* which are devices to help us remember. They are memory tools for grouping information, remembering long lists, learning foreign languages, and remembering people's names; many of us use them without realizing it. For example, "To remember the spelling of the word mnemonic, use the following phrase: Monkey Nut Eating Means Old Nutshells In Carpet."[7]

Long-term memory includes episodic memory, semantic memory, procedural memory and prospective memory.[8]

- *Episodic memory* is concerned with remembering things associated with a particular time or place—remembering what was done on a particular day or remembering when to take a medication.
- *Semantic memory* involves memory for knowledge—that is, remembering simple facts about division or the capital city of Sweden.
- *Procedural memory* is the form of memory underlying the learning of skills and actions; it is often studied via routinized behaviors (walking, skating, driving, typing).
- *Prospective memory* involves memory for actions to be carried out in the future; for example, remembering to send a birthday card.[9]

TABLE 3–1

Three-Stage Model of Memory: Three Stages of Memory (Encoding, Storage, and Retrieval) and Three Systems (Sensory, Short-Term, Long-Term)

ENCODING		STORAGE		RETRIEVAL
External Stimulus → Sensory Image → → →		Sensory memory (small capacity, very brief storage) → →		Decay of image
		Transfer to short-term store		
Usually rather direct Representation (images, words, numbers) → → →		Short-term memory (small capacity, brief storage) 1. Primary memory 2. Working memory → → →		Recall or Disruption by other incoming material (forgetting)
		Transfer to long-term store		
Highly organized, by time and place (episodic) or by meaningful relations (semantic) → → →		Long-term memory (large capacity, long storage) 1. Episodic memory 2. Semantic memory → → →		Recall Cued recall Recognition or interference from other learned material (not able to retrieve)

Source: Based on J. W. Atkinson & R. M. Shreffrin (1968). Human memory: A proposed system and its control processes. K. W. Spence & J. T. Spence (Eds.), *The Psychology of Learning and Motivation* (Vol. 2). New York: Academic Press. Adapted from K. Warner Schaie & Sherry Willis, *Adult Development and Aging* (p. 318), Upper Saddle River, NJ: Prentice Hall.

There may be some age-related changes in each of these forms of memory. But for most people, this would not affect work-related activities. It is important to remember that individual differences are what matter.

TRANSLATING WHAT WE KNOW INTO ADULT AND OLDER WORKER TRAINING

Education and training can provide new opportunities for development across the life span. Older adults have been trained and retrained in the research laboratory and in work settings. This has led to the development of training principles and methods that recognize the unique attributes of adults and older adult workers.

The Age Discrimination in Employment Act of 1967, 1978, and 1986 defines older workers as individuals 40 years and older. Throughout this book the term adult and older adult worker has been used to describe individuals in this age group. However, many recommendations may well also apply more specifically to workers who are considerably older.

Education and training provide important opportunities to facilitate career development at all periods in the work life. The need to integrate work and learning is essential for continued adaptation in the work setting. For many individuals the workplace is an important source of continued learning either on the job or in planned training programs. It must be emphasized that the largest provider of adult education in middle and older adulthood is the work organization, not higher educational institutions. Many of today's older adult workers who are in need of training are casualties of a failure of the workplace, over many decades, to invest in future-focused training programs. A major issue today is ensuring equitable access to training opportunities for older adult workers.

Negative attitudes held by older workers may contribute to lack of access to training and retraining opportunities. Older workers may be reluctant to volunteer for, or pursue, training and retraining opportunities. This reluctance may be due to feelings of inadequacy about being able to do well in a training program, fear of failure, fear of competition with younger individuals, or the expectation that supervisors would encourage them if they felt it was appropriate. Supervisors, on the other hand, expect that older workers would volunteer, if interested, and interpret lack of volunteering as lack of interest or motivation.

Retraining, formal education, and self-directed learning are necessary so that older workers can continue to build on previous knowledge and experience. It is obsolete thinking to believe that older adults become obsolete. Rapid technological changes create skill obsolescence in all age groups. Middle-aged and older workers need updating, but today the need for retraining is shared by people of all ages.

The design of an effective training program for older workers draws on principles used to design any effective training program. In general, an effective training program for older workers is effective for all workers. The design of any training program should start with a needs analysis to determine where training is really necessary in the organization. The second step is a job analysis to identify what should be included in the training. The job analysis results in a job description that identifies the relevant tasks performed and the knowledge, skills, and abilities necessary to perform the job. The third step is a person analysis to identify who should be trained. This analysis is carried out through performance appraisal and testing appropriate for the older worker.

The adult and older adult training and retraining literature has documented a number of dimensions for successful training programs. Seven areas emerge that need to be considered when designing training programs. These include motivation, structure, familiarity, organization, time, active participation, and learning strategies. (See Table 3–2.)[10]

Motivation

Older workers are least likely to volunteer for instruction, so trainers may need to encourage them to participate more than others. Their desire to learn may be impeded by fear of failure or feelings of inadequacy as compared with younger workers. Older workers possessing little formal schooling may have particularly low self-esteem.

TABLE 3–2

Seven Practical Principles for Training the Older Worker

1. Motivation	Create circumstances conducive to initial entry. Older employees may fear of failure or inability to compete.	Build self-confidence by minimizing failure experiences. Proceed from simple to complex tasks and demonstrate mastery of each task before going on to the next one.
2. Structure	Adequately design and structure the training program.	Base training program on task analysis.
3. Familiarity	Older adults may not have been involved in learning new information on a regular basis, and they may not have been involved in education or training experiences. Thus, learning strategies are not well practiced. However, given the opportunity to engage in continuous activity in a particular area, age may be irrelevant.	In addition to encouraging active participation, it is critical to ensure the recall of prerequisites to further training. Training should build on the extensive skills of older workers.
4. Organization	Organizational interventions to change supervisors' and managers' attitudes.	Training should be built on knowledge, past skills, and abilities (KSAs) using relevant material from the perspective of the trainees. The future transferability and generalizations of the training experience should be emphasized.

5. Time	Adequate time should be allowed for mastery.	Older workers require longer to reach proficiency than younger workers so they may need slower presentation rates, longer periods to complete diagnostic tests, and longer periods for study.	Longer training times will allow for organization and strategy training.
6. Active Participation	Older employees may feel alienated from the environment inherent in many training programs. They may feel stressed, and they may lack confidence to complete the tasks often required in standard lecture training.	Active participation in the learning process has proved effective with older employees.	
7. Learning Strategies	Take into account the health of the learner but remember that the chronological age may have NO significant influence on performance.	Older employees may have developed alternative methods of organizing information. These methods may clash with requirements of the training program. Strategy training in organizational and memory processes can lead to improved performance.	Training program should ensure adequate retention and comprehension. Use appropriate tests before and after training modules. If you expect people to learn, you must show them how to learn. This is especially effective with older employees who have been removed from the tasks required in educational settings.

Source: Harvey L. Sterns & Dennis Doverspike. (1989). "Aging and the Training and Learning Process." In Irvin L. Goldstein & Associates, *Training and Development in Organizations* (pp. 299–329). San Francisco, CA: Jossey-Bass.

Motivation and self-concept can influence training involvement and success. Trainers can help alleviate feelings of fear or inadequacy by providing continuous positive feedback and reminders of training goals. Trainers should also ensure managers and co-workers give support and encouragement.

Structure

The training program should be relevant to the job, based on careful job analysis. This analysis can assist in the arrangement of training sequences. Participant anxiety can be reduced by ensuring that the trainee masters each simple component of a task before moving on. This mastery also gives trainers opportunities to provide positive feedback.

One approach that has been found effective is to arrange the training sequence according to increasing complexity. That must be based on a very careful task analysis. The task or material to be learned is then carefully introduced, presenting easier aspects first. After mastery of the basic skills, more difficult aspects are then introduced until the task or material is mastered. Past work on training interventions has led to the conclusion that older adult learning can be improved. A reliance on task analysis appears to be a strong predictor of the success of the training program, especially for complex tasks. The program structure should also allow for varying the time needed for individual trainees.

Familiarity

If possible, trainers build on the past knowledge and abilities of participants. Providing relevant or generalizable examples during training may also increase participant's attention, which improves training effectiveness.

Organization

Cognitive research has shown that older adults have difficulty organizing information effectively. As a result, trainers should organize the material being presented to help retention and comprehension by placing material into meaningful groupings. Teaching older trainees ways to organize what they learn is another effective option in training.

Time

Behavioral research consistently indicates slowing of reaction time and increases in learning time with age. Thus, slower presentation of training material and provision of longer study and test periods should aid older workers. Given sufficient time, older learners perform as well or better than younger learners. Self-paced learning for older workers is optimal. However, trainers should not just add more time without teaching the older adult efficient time use.

Active Participation

Active participation is desirable for older trainees, because lecture or rote memorization formats may cause difficulty. Active participation builds self-confidence and reduces cautiousness and hesitancy. Additionally, older workers' wealth of life and work experience should enhance group discussion and learning.

Learning Strategies

Training on the subject of learning strategies is a fairly new and rapidly developing area. The rationale behind learning strategies training is that we expect people to learn, but infrequently show them *how* to learn. Adults may need training in learning strategies—because either they never developed them or they have forgotten them through lack of use. Examples of learning strategies include simple tasks such as rehearsal strategies. A simple example is to repeat the names of things to memorize. An example of a complex strategy is outlining or creating categories. An example of a motivational strategy is overcoming computer, test, or math anxiety.

Attitudes toward career development activities and mobility relate to such factors as current employment, tenure or stage in career, need for achievement, and need for growth. In addition, fear of stagnation, marketability perceptions, job-market conditions, and chance encounters may play a role in decision making.

A career-goal decision, such as the decision to engage in training or retraining, can lead to identity growth and enhanced self-esteem. Enhanced self-esteem, in turn, may lead to greater commitment to future career development goals.

Research suggests that some learning may be affected by how well learners retain and recall information. Related to this, there are two types of intelligence to consider. The first, *crystallized intelligence,* is either maintained or shows gains throughout a lifetime.[11] An exam-

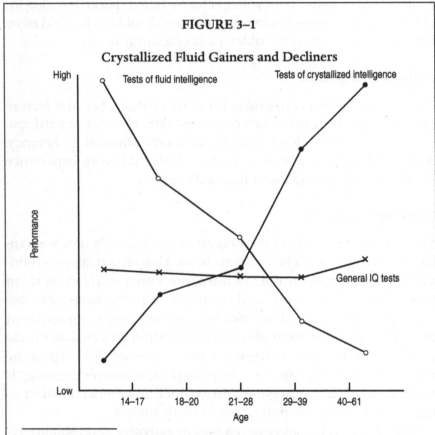

FIGURE 3–1

Crystallized Fluid Gainers and Decliners

Source: Adapted from K.W. Schaie. (1989c). "The Optimization of Cognitive Functioning in Old Age: Predictions Based on Cohort-Sequential and Longitudinal Data." In P. B. Baltes & M. M. Baltes (Eds.), *Successful Aging: Perspectives from the Behavioral Sciences.* Cambridge, UK: Cambridge University Press. In K. Warner Schaie & Sherry L. Willis (2002). *Adult Development and Aging* (5th ed., p. 373). Upper Saddle River, NJ: Prentice Hall.

ple of this would be verbal ability. It may be related to life experiences, which could include self-directed or formal education.[12] In contrast, *fluid intelligence* is not dependent on life experiences. It is related more to "on the spot reasoning."[13] Figure 3–1 shows the performance of various age groups on tests used to define fluid, crystallized, and general intelligence.[14] Crystallized intelligence may increase as a result of age, and fluid intelligence may show a decline over the lifespan; however, there are many people who show little or no change with age. Figure 3–2 shows the proportion of persons who maintain intellectual functioning over a seven-year period with

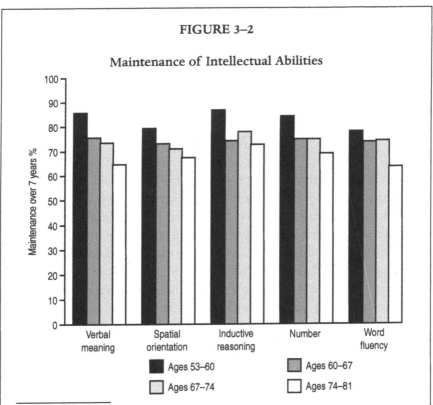

FIGURE 3–2

Maintenance of Intellectual Abilities

Source: Adapted from K.W. Schaie. (1989c). "The Optimization of Cognitive Functioning in Old Age: Predictions Based on Cohort-Sequential and Longitudinal Data." In P. B. Baltes & M. M. Baltes (Eds.), *Successful Aging: Perspectives from the Behavioral Sciences.* Cambridge, UK: Cambridge University Press. In K. Warner Schaie & Sherry L. Willis (2002). *Adult Development and Aging* (5th ed., p. 373). Upper Saddle River, NJ: Prentice Hall.

regard to verbal meaning, spatial orientation, inductive reasoning, and number and word fluency.[15]

What is important is that, even in older adulthood, some people show gains, most remain stable, and there are those who show decline. This means that there are many older workers who maintain abilities and can still perform.

Here again it is important to recognize that many people do not experience fluid decline and that most people continue to increase their crystallized abilities with age. Thus, it is important to emphasize that stereotypes about the intellectual and learning abilities of older workers can serve as a major barrier to the effective use of their talents. Even more insidious is that many older workers themselves do not know this and, as a result, accept many negative stereotypes themselves. If there are individuals who are not able to perform successfully in work settings, then it is equally important to provide opportunities for training and retraining and provide counseling.

SUMMARY

Today it is critical that managers understand what older workers are required to do in a job and then find out what knowledge, skills, and abilities individuals need to complete the job successfully. Most individuals' abilities remain stable over a lifetime. The important thing is matching individuals with jobs or work that takes advantage of what they can do. Likewise, "incorporating procedural performance in instruction where possible creates an action-based training; for example, teaching older individuals to use the internet, etc."[16]

Changes in learning may be related to many issues other than someone's age. When someone finds a particular task difficult to learn, it may not be because he or she is older. Many reasons can influence learning—such as the environment in which the learning takes place. Is the room too hot or too cold? Is the room big enough? There may be medical, psychological, or cognitive reasons for learning difficulties. Over a lifetime, however, many individuals who maintain their knowledge or skills usually maintain their ability to perform.[17]

So far, research suggests that adult and older workers may react differently to the learning process and, therefore, different approaches may need to be incorporated into training programs to accommodate older workers. Moreover, older workers may be more successful with updating when "appropriate encoding strategies are used and when a supportive retrieval context is provided."[18]

The baby boom generation represents a talented and competitive cohort that is more educated and possibly more willing to work to maintain their skills. Therefore, it is important for managers to be aware of this group of experienced workers and be sensitive to needed changes in the job task to retain older workers. In addition, it is important for managers to accommodate the needs of older workers for those workers to function at a higher level.[19,20] Thus, facilitating older adult learning can be a rewarding, challenging, and exciting experience for trainers.

II | DESIGN

4 | INSTRUCTIONAL DESIGN FOR TRAINING OLDER WORKERS

The instructional systems design (ISD) model is well known in employee training. First invented by the U.S. military to train troops, it has been adapted for civilian use to provide a most effective way to analyze training requirements, design and develop training, implement the training, and evaluate training results.[1] But what is the ISD model, and how can it be adapted to provide efficient and effective guidance for the unique challenges facing those who must analyze, design, develop, deliver, and evaluate the training of older workers? This chapter addresses this key question.

ADDIE MODEL

This chapter is organized according to the five commonly cited elements of the instructional systems design (ISD) model known as ADDIE:

- Analyze
- Design
- Develop
- Implement (deliver or facilitate instruction)
- Evaluate

In the sections that follow, each step in the ADDIE model will be described as it is typically applied. Then, each step will be described for how it should be applied when addressing the unique requirements of older workers.

Analyze

Analysis is the first step in the ISD model. Analysis focuses first on the human performance problem, ensuring that training is an appropriate solution. If training is not the appropriate solution, then management must take action to address the root cause instead. But if training is appropriate to solve the problem, then subsequent analysis must be conducted to examine who will receive training, what they should be trained to do, where they will apply what they learned from training, and what they should do upon training's completion. Without effective analysis, training cannot be successful because it will not be focused on addressing the right solution, the right people, the right setting, or the right results.

TRADITIONAL STEPS IN ANALYSIS

The traditional steps in analysis focus on analyzing the problem, analyzing the learners targeted to receive the training, analyzing the work setting in which the training will be applied, analyzing the instructional setting in which the training will be carried out, and analyzing the work to be conducted.

Performance Analysis.   *Performance analysis* distinguishes problems that can be solved by training from problems that must be solved by management action. Not all problems can be solved by training. Training should be a strategy of last, rather than first, resort because it is tough and expensive to do well. Trainers should use performance analysis when they are initially approached for help with a human performance problem by a manager, worker, or other prospective stakeholder.

Apply performance analysis by asking pointed questions. Examples of such questions may include:

- Who is affected by the problem?
- How many people are affected?
- What is the nature of the problem?
- When was the problem first noticed?
- Where is the problem most severe?

- Why does the problem exist? What causes it? How many possible causes may account for it?
- How much is the problem costing? How can its impact be measured? Is there a way to estimate the cost of the problem to the organization by assessing metrics associated with quality, quantity, cost, time, or customer service?

Learner Analysis.   *Learner analysis* examines the audience targeted to receive training. It focuses on clarifying the characteristics of those slated to receive the training at present or in the future. After all, the content of training must be adapted so that it is geared to the level of knowledge possessed by those targeted to receive it. Trainers should thus consider asking such questions as these about the learners:

- What do they already know about the topic?
- How willing are the immediate supervisors of the learners to participate in the training or reinforce, back on the job, what workers learned in training?
- What experience relevant to the topic do the targeted learners already possess, and how can their experience be assessed?
- What should the targeted learners know about the topic before they enter the training? Should workers be screened out if they lack specific knowledge, skill, or ability that they should possess in advance?
- What is the attitude of the targeted learners about the topic of the training?

In recent years, special attention has been devoted to competency identification and modeling, a process by which an organization studies the unique characteristics of its successful or outstanding performers.[2] One important goal of competency modeling is often to discover what makes some individuals so much more productive than others. The theory is that, if the reasons for that difference can be discovered, then an organization can do a better job of developing and recruiting individuals who match the profile of the most productive workers.[3]

Work Setting Analysis.   *Work setting analysis* focuses on the place in which training is to be applied. It is, after all, critical to consider the conditions under which people will apply what they learn in training. To carry out work analysis, trainers should consider such questions as these:

- Under what working conditions will workers apply what they learn in training?
- What tools, equipment, and other resources will workers have available when they apply what they have learned?
- What barriers in the workplace may prevent workers from applying what they have been trained to do, and how can those barriers be surmounted?

Instructional Setting Analysis.   *Instructional setting analysis* focuses on where the training will be conducted. Training may be conducted on the job, near the job, or off the job. Understanding the instructional setting is important in preparing for training, since training is more likely to be applied when conditions in which the training is carried out closely match actual working conditions. Training that is conducted on the job is most likely to be retained or applied,[4] but more training is increasingly being delivered by e-learning or other technology-mediated instruction.[5]

To conduct instructional setting analysis, trainers should pose questions such as these:

- Where will the training be held, and why will it be held there?
- How closely do conditions in the instructional setting match the conditions of the actual work setting?
- How can conditions in the instructional setting be made to match those in the work setting more closely?
- If training will be delivered through technology-mediated or blended learning methods, how will interactivity be encouraged and facilitated?

Work Analysis.   *Work analysis* examines the job or work people are expected to do, the results they are expected to achieve, and the procedures they should follow as they perform the work. It is an important form of analysis because many performance problems actually stem from a mismatch between what workers think they are supposed to do and what their supervisors expect of them. Consequently, work analysis alone—if it improves this match of expectations—can often be helpful in improving worker performance even without training.

Job analysis is a specialized form of work analysis. It focuses on what people do—and especially on the work responsibilities they are expected to meet, the job performance standards they are expected to achieve, the frequency with which the work is performed, and the importance (criticality) of the work duties performed. Ask the following questions to conduct simple job analysis:

- What is the purpose of the job?
- To whom does the job report?
- What kind of people does the job supervise?
- How much discretion do job incumbents exercise in carrying out their work?
- What are the primary work responsibilities or activities of the job?
- How much time is, or should be, spent on each activity?
- How critical to work success is each activity?
- What outputs are expected?
- How are outputs measured for quality? quantity?
- What qualifications are essential to learn the job?

Task analysis is that part of work analysis that focuses on how work is carried out. It goes a step beyond job analysis, focusing on the procedures to be followed rather than the mere activities to be performed. For every work responsibility or activity listed on a job description, ask questions like these:

- How is that activity carried out step by step?
- By what cues or signals does a worker know that this activity should be performed?
- By what means does a worker know that an activity has been completed successfully?

The Results of Analysis.   It is essential that analysis yield a description of the problem, the number of people affected by it, the specific learning requirements they have, and descriptions of how the instructional and work environments will affect what they learn. Job analysis is essential to clarify what people should know, do, or feel upon training completion.

Unique Issues in Analysis for Training Older Workers

The traditional steps in analysis may need to be adapted, when appropriate, to consider special issues in meeting the needs of older workers. This is not meant to imply that older workers are, in any way, less than fully productive. Indeed, most research indicates that older workers are just as capable as younger workers to learn new tasks, master training requirements, and achieve productive results.

The most important issue to consider in analyzing the training needs of older workers is to devote special attention to worker analysis.[6] Older workers may not possess the same quality of eyesight or hearing as younger workers. Hence, trainers should pose questions such as these about learners:

- What percentage of the targeted learners for the training will be older than age 55?
- How much, if at all, should training take into account reasonable accommodations for workers to reduce reliance on the sense of eyesight or sense of hearing of the training—or supplement reliance on those senses with material available in alternative formats?
- How much additional time can be devoted to training applications to help meet the special needs of older workers?

Trainers should take care to avoid generalizing that all older workers are the same or that all older workers will need reasonable accommodation. Additionally, trainers should take care to avoid making stereotypical assumptions that all older workers share certain attitudes, beliefs, or values in common. Despite much attention devoted to how generational attitudes may differ, relatively little solid research supports such assumptions.

What is known about training for older workers is best summarized as follows:[7]

> Meta-analyses have been conducted on learning success for older adults based on a mix of laboratory and applied study. Overall, the results of research in this area are encouraging in that they indicate that older adults are able to learn new skills, even ones involving new technology. Nonetheless, they are typically slower to acquire those skills than younger adults. Some of the slowing in learning new tasks may be attributable to older adults' preference for accuracy over speed, with the reverse holding true for younger adults. The literature indicates that training interventions can be successful in terms of improving performance. There have been numerous attempts over the past fifty years to find techniques that are best suited to older learners. However, very few instances of interaction between training technique and age have been observed. Generally, what is best for the young adult is also best for the older adult. In recent years, however, a few exceptions have been observed. At least two studies have shown that there are greater gains for older adults when performing procedural (action or hands on) activities compared to conceptual training. In brief, many techniques for training prove to be effective for older adults, but there is not yet an adequate research base to determine whether some training techniques are differentially beneficial for older workers on a consistent basis. The majority of older adults remain reasonably healthy and functionally able until very late in life. It is also important to recognize that conclusions regarding age-performance differences are often based on the comparison of averages and that older adults are more variable as a group than younger adults.

Design

Design is the second step in applying the ISD model. It specifies exactly the instructional solutions to be used to meet the training needs identified during analysis.

TRADITIONAL STEPS IN DESIGN

While analysis clarifies the problem and specifies its cause, design clarifies the solution and scopes out how it will be applied. Think of instructional design as akin to the process of constructing a building.

An architect prepares drawings but a building contractor then transforms the drawings into reality. In training, design is like the architect's work. But development and delivery, taken together, are akin to what a building contractor does. During the design phase, trainers formulate objectives and prepare the testing or evaluation methods.

Formulating Training Objectives.   Training objectives describe what learners should do when training is completed. While a training need describes a performance problem, a training objective describes the solution. Objectives should be stated in measurable, results-oriented terms. After the objectives for training have been formulated, they should then be placed in some order for the learners.

Preparing Testing or Evaluation Procedures.   A test assesses how much or how well participants met the training objectives. The appropriate test to select is a function of what training objectives were formulated. Some tests are administered on the computer or by paper and pencil; others are administered by demonstration, with the learner showing what he or she learned in the training.

UNIQUE ISSUES IN DESIGN WHEN APPLIED TO THE TRAINING NEEDS OF OLDER WORKERS

Design may need to be adapted, when appropriate, to consider special issues in meeting the needs of older workers. What may be needed is to plan for additional time, during the formulation of training methods, to permit older learners to apply what they have learned. That may mean planning for additional activities or exercises—and allowing more time for testing.

Develop

Development is the traditional step of the instructional systems design model in which training plans are transformed into reality. This usually means translating a training outline into instructional materials, media, and methods. This translation process may be carried out by purchasing material from other sources, preparing or writing the material from scratch, or purchasing and modifying material to meet the special requirements identified on the training outline. The way this process is carried out may differ somewhat, depending on the choice of delivery methods—such as classroom-based, on-the-job, e-learning, technology-mediated instruction, or some blend of these.

UNIQUE ISSUES IN DEVELOPING WHEN APPLIED TO THE TRAINING NEEDS OF OLDER WORKERS

To ensure that training is geared to meet the needs of older workers, run a dress rehearsal with a sample of older workers to ensure that slides are visible, training materials can be read easily, and the activities are adequate to build learners' skills. Training delivered by computer may call for extra time if older workers are unfamiliar or uncomfortable with the technology.

When training programs are developed for older workers who have vision and hearing problems, strategies can be implemented to facilitate tasks being done correctly without increasing older adult anxieties. Also, because of physical and certain psychological stages of aging, time limits can be adjusted to allow older workers more time to complete a task.

Implement

Implementation, which means the delivery or facilitation of instruction, is the fourth traditional step in the ISD model. Most trainers are quite familiar with this step. It is at this point that trainers deliver the training materials in the classroom, on the job, through technology-mediated methods, or through some blended approach.

UNIQUE ISSUES IN IMPLEMENTATION WHEN APPLIED TO THE TRAINING NEEDS OF OLDER WORKERS

If the needs of older workers have been kept in mind during the analysis, design, and development phases, then implementing the training should go smoothly. It may be useful to ask older participants how effectively the training is delivered—a wise approach with all learners—so that there is also an ample opportunity during the delivery to adapt it to any special needs of unique groups or individuals.

The authors' survey of employers revealed practices that some employers feel are appropriate in designing and delivering training for older workers. (See Figure 4–1.) Among them:

- Older workers can sometimes best be trained together.
- The pace of training may need to be adjusted.
- The format of training materials should be appropriate for those whose eyesight (or hearing) may be affected by age.
- Breaks should be frequent.
- Practice sessions are appropriate.
- Training should be designed to connect to previous work (and probably life) experience.

Other recommendations also appear in Figure 4–1. Interestingly, the small number of older workers who participated in the authors' survey expressed a preference for training sessions composed of people in their own age group. (See Figure 4–2.) For those who think that older workers do not prefer online instruction, the authors' survey results of a small number of highly educated older workers show just the opposite. That survey result simply underscores the need to ask for the preferences of the people targeted for training. (See Figure 4–3.)

Evaluate

Evaluation is the last step of the traditional ISD model. Of course, if done well, evaluation is performed before training is delivered, during training delivery, and following delivery. Analysis should provide the basis for effective evaluation by establishing measurable objectives against which to assess results.

In most cases, evaluation does not need to be adapted to the special needs of older workers if previous steps in the instructional design process have been managed effectively.

INSTRUCTIONAL DESIGN IMPLICATIONS FOR OLDER WORKERS

Researchers have addressed the issues of older worker training, and, as we have discussed earlier, older workers are trainable. Trainers should lay a good foundation that builds rapport by providing older

FIGURE 4–1

Employer Practices in Designing Training for Older Workers
Q7: When designing training for older workers, to what extent do you

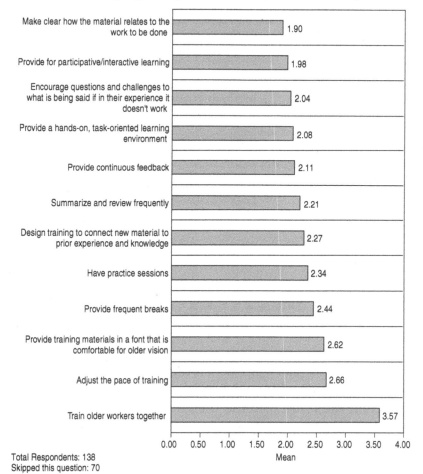

Total Respondents: 138
Skipped this question: 70

Scale: 1 = Strongly agree; 2 = Agree; 3 = Neutral; 4 = Disagree;
5 = Strongly disagree

Source: J. Reaser, D. Spokus, H. Sterns, & W. Rothwell. (2006). *A Survey of Employers.* Unpublished survey results. Arlington, VA: National Older Worker Career Center (NOWCC). All rights reserved.

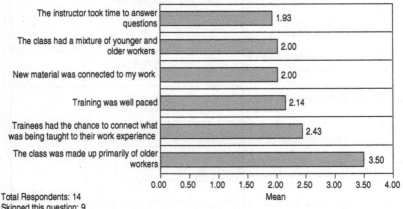

FIGURE 4–2

**What Do Older Workers Say Was Particularly Good
About the Training They Last Attended?**

**Q10: What was good about the last training program you
attended and what needed improvement?**

Total Respondents: 14
Skipped this question: 9

Scale: 1 = Strongly agree; 2 = Agree; 3 = Neutral; 4 = Disagree;
5 = Strongly disagree

Source: J. Reaser, D. Spokus, H. Sterns, & W. Rothwell. (2006). *A Survey of Employers.* Unpublished survey results. Arlington, VA: National Older Worker Career Center (NOWCC).

workers with material with which they are familiar. After older workers begin to build confidence and increase their feeling of self-esteem, the trainer should then introduce new and more in-depth concepts that require more user attention, retention, and application.

Harvey L. Sterns and Dennis D. Doverspike "emphasize that a needs analysis should be considered before any training program is initiated." In fact, they suggest that "employees of all ages need motivation to participate in skill updating. However, older workers may need additional encouragement to overcome the stereotypes and nervousness."[8] Needs analysis lays the foundation for a good training experience. The authors also suggest that, when designing training programs for older workers, it is important to encourage active

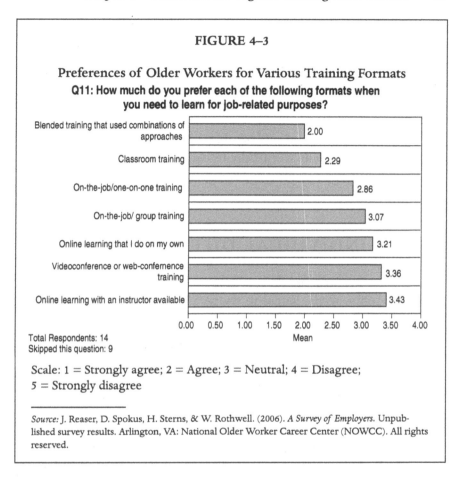

FIGURE 4–3

Preferences of Older Workers for Various Training Formats

Q11: How much do you prefer each of the following formats when you need to learn for job-related purposes?

Format	Mean
Blended training that used combinations of approaches	2.00
Classroom training	2.29
On-the-job/one-on-one training	2.86
On-the-job/ group training	3.07
Online learning that I do on my own	3.21
Videoconference or web-conference training	3.36
Online learning with an instructor available	3.43

Total Respondents: 14
Skipped this question: 9

Scale: 1 = Strongly agree; 2 = Agree; 3 = Neutral; 4 = Disagree; 5 = Strongly disagree

Source: J. Reaser, D. Spokus, H. Sterns, & W. Rothwell. (2006). *A Survey of Employers.* Unpublished survey results. Arlington, VA: National Older Worker Career Center (NOWCC). All rights reserved.

rather than passive participation and to introduce learning strategies that will help learners remember the material covered. In other words, it is important to teach the participants how they can learn the material in the best possible way. This strategy will help them to be better able to translate it back to the workplace.[9]

However, when discussing the needs of older adult learning, it is important to understand that there should be a match between what we as trainers, or facilitators, intend to teach and what the trainee actually comprehends. It is when there is a mismatch that problems in learning arise. This type of problem should be taken care of in the very beginning. "One of the hardest things teachers have to learn is that the sincerity of their intentions does not guarantee the purity of their practice."[10] As teachers of adults and older workers, it is important to do periodic "critically reflective" evaluations of the teaching and evaluate its impact on learners. Brookfield developed the Critical Incident Questionnaire as a tool to determine "what his students liked or didn't like about a class he taught."[11] This tool can be adapted to help trainers see themselves from an older worker's point of view and thereby avoid undesirable outcomes right from the start. By taking the time to do a critically reflective evaluation, a trainer can make adjustments in his or her training style that help individuals learn better.

INDIVIDUAL DIFFERENCES

Adult learners represent "diverse personalities, cultural backgrounds, genders, ability levels, learning styles, ideological orientations and previous experiences."[12] It is therefore important to recognize that learning is not universal. People learn in different ways. However, learners may not understand that. They may feel they are incapable of learning specific content because they cannot comprehend what the trainer is talking about. However, trainers are obligated to point out that everyone learns different content material in different ways. Some content can be harder to grasp than others. However, this does not mean people are incapable of learning it. It just means that trainers have to readjust their approach to the learning process. It may take more time to do this through experimentation, but it does work. The point is that several modalities may be needed to help individuals learn a specific type of content material. It is important to let the learners know that this is normal. They just have to work a little harder.

When designing programs for older adults, individual differences must be taken into account. Related to this are individual learning styles. "Learning styles refer to the individual characteristic ways for processing information, feeling, and behaving in learning situations."[13] Moreover, it is important to recognize that some training programs for older workers may need to be individually oriented.

The workplace can be thought of as a salad bowl of individuals with many characteristics. People come from all walks of life, different socioeconomic statuses, language proficiencies, and cultural backgrounds. As trainers of older adults who have special needs that need to be considered, it is recommended that a Critical Incident Questionnaire be used to examine cultural attitudes and stereotypes that could affect their interactions with older adult students.

> "Fear of, and lack of technical skills . . . can affect the speed of processes, as well as hinder the communication cycle. There was an incident that due to a lack of technical skills, communication was impacted negatively. I ensured that there was a face-to-face followup to electronic communication, and this helped the communication process."[14]

There is also an indication that, when designing learning experiences for older adults, the "designer often unknowingly incorporates degrees of complexity into devices, interfaces, and instruction that create imbalances between the demands imposed by these products and the mental and physical resources at the disposal of the user." Along these lines, the most commonly accepted process is one that is "user-centered."[15]

TRAINING

Although the baby boomer generation has been examined from a marketing and growth perspective over many years, it is surprising that more companies have not taken a highly visible role in developing and implementing strategies to retain, manage, and educate this cohort, taking into consideration the importance of individual needs. Many management behaviors greatly influence many employee characteristics, and they are determined through either a macro or micro management approach.[16] Some industries, particularly the healthcare field, because of critical shortage areas presently being felt, have been forerunners in Best Practices, addressing factors that lead to the retention of older workers. As a result of tuition reimbursements, sign-on bonuses, and more flexible work hours, healthcare institutions are strategically planning for managing, retaining, and training their experienced aging workforce. It is very possible that, in the near future, more organizations globally will compete for older workers.

Organizations that focus on the principles of adult learning theory by helping older workers overcome barriers to continued employment will be uniquely positioned to better recruit, train, retain, and manage future workers. The future will not be business as usual. There will simply not be enough young people to fill traditional entry-level positions for which they are typically hired. A crisis of this scale calls for new strategies if employers are to get the work done. They must rethink their traditional workforce strategies, devoting more thought to creating access to continuing educational opportunities that address multiple learning concepts (such as blended learning) that improve older workers' knowledge and improve their skills while providing a positive environment that enhances life-long learning experiences.

As a result, managers and employees have opportunities to work together to develop strategies to optimize human potential and avoid skill obsolescence by taking an active role in their careers through self-directed management skills. If individuals want to continue to work, they would be wise to participate in training or educational programs to maintain their skills and knowledge. In other words, the training of older adult workers should include career planning and succession planning programs that encourage workers to take charge of their careers by providing them with the tools necessary to make good decisions financially, socially, physically, and psychologically. To that end, training and education serve several purposes. They can provide comprehensive strategies that create long-term success while expanding human capital and building worker self-esteem.

Researchers have argued that training programs targeted at meeting the needs of the adult or older adult learner are most successful when there is a "shared responsibility on the part of the learner."[17]

"An older worker tried to tell me how to run the office, as she had previously done with other managers. Instead of dismissing her ideas, I spoke to her individually. We discussed respect, and I put her in charge of special projects. This older worker became a team player, and other managers could not believe the turnaround in her behavior."[18]

Workers, therefore, benefit most when they become active participants in implementing strategies for optimizing their individual
potential. As a result, managers and employees have opportunities to
work together to develop strategies to optimize human potential
and avoid obsolescence by encouraging self-directed learning and
management skills. This will be discussed more in Chapter 6.

THE VALUE OF TRAINING OLDER WORKERS

At present some employers train younger workers but older workers are not offered the same training opportunities. The thinking is
that older workers cannot be retrained, or they do not want to be
trained because they will soon retire. Also, the rationale is that, because they have an increased rate of morbidity, if they are trained,
they will not be of benefit to the organization for as long as younger
workers. In other words, there would be a reduced return on the
training investment. However, in reality, seasoned older workers, if
challenged and offered training, could be used to coach others, develop better consumer relations with customers, and implement a
wide array of tools from their years of experience that would benefit the organization.

> "Many times the approach to older workers is to treat them the same
> as some of the younger workers. Just because they are older doesn't
> mean that they are capable or maybe even more capable than the
> younger workers. Granted, there is a difference in how you interact,
> but I think sometimes people think just because they are older, they
> can't be fun to be around, which just isn't true."[19]

In addition, these experiences, coupled with additional training,
could put organizations at an advantage if they utilize these older
workers' experiences to the organization's benefit. If this is not working, examine the task analysis and how older workers are functioning
in various areas. Perhaps all that is really needed is a re-examination
of the responsibilities that have been given to older workers and,
perhaps, a re-examination of the strengths of the workers and a

rematch of tasks. Related to this, it is advantageous for organizations to help older workers manage their careers, and thereby modify their training to take advantage of strategies and approaches that capitalize on this type of investment.[20] In other words, capitalize on the strengths of older workers both through properly designed training programs and placing older workers in positions that maximize their talents and leverage their strengths.

An aging individual who does not want to maintain professional competence or update skills usually leaves the workplace and retires. This might be due to lack of motivation to update skills and knowledge, or because of poor health. In the past, we would make such recommendations to the managers, but now the situation is much more complex. Training techniques should be implemented that take into account individual differences. There is no question that these differences exist. It is a matter of bringing these differences to the forefront for workers as well as trainers.

> "Sometimes training times may take longer. Resistance to technology can occur."[21]

A new approach requires trainers to be aware of multiple approaches—a "buffet" approach that would be feasible for each individual and manager of an organization. For instance, adults and older adults may learn in different ways and may have to be offered different ways of learning—such as face-to-face or e-learning, accelerated learning, self-directed learning using modules, traditional courses, or classes offered in the evening through continuing education programs. The main issue is to rethink attitudes or stereotypes about aging and work and rethink one-size-fits-all approaches to training. Moreover, it should be noted that the work environment also contributes to whether an older adult continues to work, and whether he or she remains motivated to maintain the skills that optimize performance. Managing the work environment so that older workers feel welcome is essential to retention.

Related to this, Expectancy Theory[22] is an important concept whereby adults and older workers know that their efforts will be rewarded and that their training can be translated back into the field. Today, strategies for managers and employees include helping adult and older workers be responsible for self-management while address-ing the issue of active versus passive worker learning. In other words, in order to prevent obsolescence, creative and challenging learning environments should incorporate training techniques that target the special needs of individual older workers. Belbin and Belbin[23] used methods of discovery, activity learning, and programmed instruc-tion. These authors were early pioneers in older worker training, and many of their conclusions are still used by researchers today, benefiting both lower- and upper-level training programs.

Older adult learners, in order to update their skills, may require special learning situations, which are favorable environments for building the needed competencies to remain abreast of workplace developments. Kolb indicated that, when adult learners make the choice to participate in a new learning activity, they take "risks."[24] Perhaps because of intergenerational differences, they might not be as open to communicating their needs as a younger generation. In a classroom setting with younger adults, they might fear losing face and, therefore, might not be as honest in communicating how they learn best.

Another key issue about age differences is that training can exercise mental ability and possibly reverse some decrements that result from sheer misuse. Changes transpire in intelligence throughout the life-span. Many older workers do not participate in learning and training opportunities that would help them maintain or increase their abili-ties through mental and physical stimulation. It is also possible that age differences among colleagues intimidate older workers' ability to learn. They may fear failure, which leads to a self-fulfilling prophecy. Therefore, when an instructor is delivering training programs, it would be wise to understand various learning philosophies to accom-modate adult learners.[25] As people age, there are apparent age differ-ences in how the information is processed in our brains. It is related to short-term memory—what happened in the last two weeks—and long-term memory—remembering information from years past. And, although learning differences occur between young and older adult workers, effective training programs can be implemented that in-crease the use of implicit and external aids that improve learning, which will improve performance and possibly motivate older adults to learn through work experiences that have meaning to them.

As previously stated, older workers are as productive as younger workers in skilled labor and in the speed of processing new skills. However, other studies show that older and younger adults have age-related differences in their speed of processing and retaining newly acquired skills. One study suggests that "younger adults experienced a 26 percent decline in performance from single- to dual-task processing. Older adults experienced a 55 percent decline in their performance but adapted strategies during dual-task performance. However, increased practice by both older and young adults actually improved dual-task performance."[26] It is important to note that age is a factor that accounts for only a small amount of individual variability in performance, and experience is actually a better indicator of job performance than increased age.[27] Moreover, the ability to adapt and be flexible in a changing environment is a factor that determines whether adult and older workers maintain their performance in everyday activities.[28] These are examples of how employers can provide workplace training that can be successful in retraining, retaining, and managing older workers.

Another study[29] examined the performance of computer data entry tasks and how well experience dictated the extent to which age differences were maintained. Older people completed significantly less work than the middle-aged and younger people across all three days of a specific task. However, when there was a control factor for differences in the quantity of work produced, there were no age differences in errors. The findings also suggest that "visuomotor skills and memory were significant predictors of quantity and quality of work which are factors to be taken into consideration when planning older adult training programs. These predictors can be addressed readily through new technological advances that help older workers adapt to decreased vision, memory and motor skills."[30]

HOW OLDER ADULTS LEARN BEST

Identifying one's philosophical orientation whereby learners reflect and share in writing with their trainer how they learn best is a tool developed to be self-administered and self-scored. Before a training program is implemented, it would be a good idea to do an anonymous survey of the individuals participating. Some adults may learn better with experiential learning than with didactic learning, or perhaps they learn different content material using different modalities. There are many "variables involved such as education, experience, socioeconomic background, cultural background, personality, physical condition, roles, and relationships."[33] It is also important for older adults "to know how to learn."[34]

GUIDELINES FOR TRAINING OLDER ADULTS

In Chapters 2 and 3 we discussed the various sensory changes such as vision, hearing, and motor coordination as well as the changes that take place with memory and other cognitive abilities in older adults. These changes affect the way older adults learn, and the way they react to training.[35]

The information processing model is sometimes referred to as a good way to explain how individuals process new information. It is similar to the way a computer works with inputs and outputs.

TRANSFERRING TRAINING RESULTS

Having a challenge keeps an individual motivated. Considerable research exists describing deterrents and motivational factors that affect participation in training, professional development, and continuing professional education credit opportunities for healthcare positions, especially for nurses. This issue is of particular interest because of the present and predicted increase in nursing shortages and because of the high attrition rate among healthcare workers who are overworked, experience burnout, and feel underpaid. Therefore, the work is not only difficult and the level of responsibilities increasing, but there is an increasing need for more specialized knowledge and skill-based training and education for older adult healthcare workers. A major barrier for successful educational and training programs is the inability to transfer the results of individualized training, education, or professional development to the workplace. Thus, unless an employee can apply the training in his or her own real-world situation, participation in programs has little significance or reward. In addition, this frustration on the part of the employee decreases motivation for attendance at future programs. This concept can be applied across all occupations.

Further research[36] suggests that training transfer strategies have to be created to aid trainers. However, an employee's perceptions of how these types of barriers affecting the workplace climate has received little research attention. Consequently, because of the workforce shortages, organizations need to address the barriers that prevent professionals from applying what they have learned when they return to their work settings from retirement. In other words, for the training to be successful, trainers must enjoy the support of many stakeholders, and the employees must be able to translate what they have learned to the workplace.

TRAINING MODALITIES

Corporate universities, training departments, and institutions of higher learning in the United States provide training opportunities through online courses rather than using face-to-face interaction because it is impossible for many individuals to attend onsite training because of travel cost and conflict with work schedules. Since online registration is growing, more research indicates that online learning can be a successful, fulfilling experience for learners. This mode of learning can compensate for the inability to travel distances. It also enables individuals who might have physical limitations to learn when they want to and without leaving the comfort of their own homes or offices. However, for older adult learners this might present a challenge if they are not computer literate, if they are not comfortable with online learning, if they do not have access to high-speed Internet services or if they lack knowledge of necessary software applications.

For instance, a study[37] showed that people enrolled in a Web-based class because they were curious. They felt they needed to learn how to use this new technology. They also enrolled for the convenience it afforded. Moreover, this study examined gender differences and revealed that there were no differences in anxiety between men and women or between ethnic groups.

Students enrolling in online courses tend to be self-directed learners trying to make a difference in their lives or gain control of them. They act as agents eager to bring about change that can be due to personal, financial, social, or career change choices. In fact, many organizations now pilot self-directed learning techniques to reach busy people who might not otherwise attend a workshop. It can be argued that this self-directed approach to learning may be a cohort factor. Schaie and Willis[38] found that there is supporting evidence that older adult learners may score higher than younger people on specific types of intelligence and not as good on other measures of intelligence. Fluid intelligence is knowledge an individual possesses when trying to solve a difficult problem or when doing abstract reasoning. Crystallized intelligence refers mainly to an individual's acquired knowledge over a long period of time. Older adults are often superior in their crystallized intelligence.

In addition, online learning provides flexibility when adults have to juggle work, family, and educational responsibilities. As a result, older workers should be offered choices to learn. These may include a smorgasbord of approaches such as self-study techniques, on-the-job learning, group training around desks, peer training, videoconference experiences, face-to-face, e-learning, accelerated learning, and blended learning.

OLDER ADULTS AS LEARNERS

Educational approaches for adults and older learners were researched by H. R. Moody (1976).[39] Moody's landmark model suggests a four-stage approach to educating and training adults. For instance:

> *Stage 1* is a reflection of negative attitudes about older adult learning. These attitudes include aging stereotypes such as envisioning older workers as too frail to work, too poor, too poorly educated, or in poor health.[40]

Baby boomers are probably more educated than past generations.[41] In addition, 47 percent of older adults classify themselves in
excellent to very good health, and 53 percent classify themselves in
good-fair-poor health.[42] There are also stereotypes that older workers are not as productive as younger workers and that training older
workers costs more than training younger workers.[43] In addition,
stereotypes suggest that older workers might not be as creative as
they age. However, even President Jimmy Carter, who was unexpect-
edly unseated at an early age for his second-term presidential bid,
has continued to be innovative in his humanitarian activities for the
Habitat for Humanity. Now in his eighties, he still travels the world
to promote world peace as an elder statesman.

Cultural aspects also play a role in many stereotypes. Racial differences, whereby less educated ethnic individuals are required to take
physical jobs and work at them all their lives, continue to force older
workers out of the workplace. They find that a strenuous workload
decreases the quality of their lives.

Previously, providing learning opportunities for older adults was
looked upon as wasted time because older adults feel they may not
have much time left due to increased risk of mortality. In addition, in
this stage there are pervasive attitudes that suggest cognitive decline
occurs in all abilities for everyone. However, this view does not take
into account that there is great variability among individuals with
age. Moreover, recent data suggest that little research has been done
on older adult workers who seek training on their own outside the
organization.[44]

Stage 2, according to Moody (1976), describes the social services
model where adult and older workers are seen as nonactive participants. These older workers are retained on important projects only
because of their experience, while younger workers are offered the
updated training programs. In this stage, older learners are also negatively viewed as needing all the help they can get. Consequently,
older workers might be unjustly excluded from career-ladder decisions and may not get to participate in new technology training. To
management, training older workers may be seen as a waste of time.
In contrast, this contingent work could have a win-win solution to
both employer and older worker where the older adult worker could
more easily be transitioned into partial or phased retirement and still
contribute in valuable ways to the needs of the company by working
on special projects.[45]

Stage 3, according to Moody (1976), is a more positive stage. Individuals are encouraged to take responsibility for participating in self-directed education and training programs that would support their individual career development and promotion. Rather than completely changing the workplace, this stage encourages a change in workplace strategies and policies that challenge aging stereotypes and promote active learning for older workers. This discourages older workers from disengaging themselves from others in the workplace. In this stage there is acknowledgement of the biological changes associated with aging. However, it does suggest that older workers can compensate or adapt in ways to improve and maintain their functions. This stage is positive because it suggests changing the environment to accommodate cognitive and biological processes of aging while allowing room for older workers to adapt, thereby continuing to work. Intrinsic benefits go far beyond good health and increased incomes. Older workers may want to work because they see it as a meaningful activity that gives them not only a sense of identity but also preserves self-worth.[46]

Stage 4, according to Moody (1976), allows for the uniqueness of each individual and acknowledges variability in age differences. However, most importantly, this stage stresses the importance of achieving self-actualization, similar to Maslow's Hierarchy of Needs,[47] and the potential for growth that the older workers can develop and use to their benefit. In addition, the organization also benefits through the new role responsibilities of older workers that optimize their talents and full potential. It is having experiences that are very meaningful and relevant that keeps many talented workers in the workplace.[48]

DIVERSITY TRAINING

The racial and ethnic composition of the future workforce will be different than it is today due to shifts in population distribution and immigration patterns. Historically, concerns centered on gender, ethnicity, and racial issues. However, there is now a concern over age diversity. Early work histories affect later life-work patterns. When all age categories are taken into account, Black and Hispanic men, and also some women, are out of work for longer periods of time than other workers. In many cases, it is a matter of discrimination. It begins with schools being underfunded, which leads to more underskilled and undereducated older workers in the job market.

An organization's corporate culture can greatly influence the work climate of older workers. The culture can either make or break an intergenerational relationship that could produce positive effects on the individual as well as the company.[49] It is also important to engage in intergenerational communication, with two important key factors to be considered—that is, aggressive communication and what they term *difference deployment*. In other words, instead of treating older workers negatively, an organization's leaders can reduce conflicts by increasing diversity training to include not only racial and ethnic diversity but also age diversity.[50]

Today's younger generation is highly educated with more individuals postponing marriage to pursue advanced degrees. And baby boomers in the workforce in the year 2020 will be more educated than past generations of older adults. Therefore, if an organization values the wisdom, skills, knowledge, and experience of an aging workforce, instructional design techniques must accommodate the diversity in the learning needs of this projected population.

SUMMARY

This chapter summarized the traditional steps in the instructional systems design (ISD) process based on the so-called ADDIE model. It thus examined analysis, design, development, implementation, and evaluation. The ISD model is rigorous, yielding effective training. Each step of the model may be adapted to meet special needs of older workers, but the research generally indicates that older workers are generally just as capable of learning as younger workers. The old adage about teaching old dogs is just patently false.

As research has shown, older adults can learn new skills. They are capable of change. They are capable of learning both consciously or subconsciously. This can be accomplished through formal or informal learning. It is only a matter of empowering them with the necessary tools to take the risks to learn.[51] Many times, it is with some frustration that individuals make significant strides in learning a new task or gaining new knowledge. It is also important for trainers to be critically reflective teachers of older adults and help them recognize learning styles that will work best for them if they are to remain in the workplace.

Two of the most important things to provide to attract older workers to training programs are respect and a safe, low-stress environment where they feel comfortable to express themselves.[52] It is also important to explain to older workers that they are not being "singled out for training because the company is dissatisfied with their performance, but rather because they are valued employees who deserve to be kept up-to-speed professionally."[53]

At this time, many of the baby boom generation are reaching old age. In fact, today's challenge is in providing opportunities that motivate older learners to take charge of their careers even after traditional retirement age and to play a more active role in remaining current in the workplace. Many corporations are looking for resources and are rethinking how they invest in their older workers.[54] It is no longer acceptable to disengage older workers from training opportunities due to the wrongheaded assumption that they would not use the updated training for long. The baby boom generation is more educated and less likely to be unemployed than other generations. Therefore, not only are technological advances challenging employers and workers, but there is also a need to provide workers with a smorgasbord approach to learning opportunities that allows for individual differences.

Futurist Alvin Toffler wrote that twenty-first-century illiterates would be those who could not learn and not, as in previous centuries, those who cannot read or write.[1] Management gurus Michael Lombardo and Robert Eichinger pointed out that *high potentials,* meaning those who are exceptional performers capable of higher level responsibility, differ from average workers in that they possess superior learning ability.[2] Despite much attention in recent years to the competencies considered essential to successful trainers,[3] little research has been directed to building the competencies of learners.[4] And while much attention has been devoted to the differences between learning as oriented to children and learning as oriented to adults, less attention has been devoted to the learning characteristics unique to older workers.[5]

But what is workplace learning competence, and why is it important? What research has been carried out on workplace learning competence and workplace learning climate? What characteristics distinguish the learner characteristics of older adults from those of younger people? What are the implications of those differences for training older workers? This chapter addresses these questions.

WORKPLACE LEARNING COMPETENCE AND ITS IMPORTANCE

Competencies have revolutionized current thinking about human resource management.[6] One reason is that individual differences, best described by job competencies, help to explain why some individuals are so much more productive than others.[7] These differences amount to differences in individual characteristics. In fact, any characteristic that leads to successful or superior work results is a *job competency*. And any characteristic that leads to successful or superior learning results is a *learning competency*. A key difference is that a job competency focuses on what is necessary for individuals to achieve successful work results, but a learning competency focuses on how individuals learn.

While competence is essential to produce effective work results, learning competency is essential to keep pace with the changes of a dynamic world. Many people continue to act as though the world is static and knowledge remains static. But this is not true. Today knowledge constantly changes due to the speed of information available on the World Wide Web and in other media. "The total quantity of data on computers worldwide doubles every five years. With the widespread use of client/server technologies, including the Internet, expectations are that this doubling factor may soon occur yearly," writes John Stanard in "Information explosion yields data nightmare."[8] (See www.govtech.net/publications/gt/1998/June/story2/story2.htm)

One result of the information explosion is that individuals must continuously learn to avoid the risk of skill obsolescence. Improving how people learn how to learn is essential to helping them keep their skills current and remain employable. It is thus only through learning that knowledge is rendered useful.

WORKPLACE LEARNING COMPETENCE AND WORKPLACE LEARNING CLIMATE

William J. Rothwell examined workplace learner roles, competencies and work outputs, and the conditions of the workplace learning climate that encourage or discourage individuals to learn in real time. The full results of his study were reported in a different book.[9] Individuals can build their learning competence by focusing attention on improving how well they learn how to learn. Organizational leaders can improve their learning climate by measuring it and then setting priorities to improve it. The workplace learning competencies are listed in Figure 5–1; the conditions associated with the workplace learning climate are listed in Figure 5–2. Workers young or old can improve their learning competencies and thereby improve their ability to learn how to learn. And employers can improve learning climate, encouraging the conditions that lead workers of any age to learn how to learn.

FIGURE 5–1

Workplace Learning Competencies

1. Reading Skill
2. Writing Skill
3. Computation Skill
4. Listening Skill
5. Questioning Skill
6. Speaking Skill
7. Cognitive Skills
8. Individual Skills
9. Resource Skills
10. Interpersonal Skill
11. Informational and Technological Skill
12. Systems Thinking
13. Personal Mastery
14. Mental Modeling
15. Shared Visioning
16. Team Learning Skill
17. Self-Knowledge
18. Short-Term Memory Skill
19. Long-Term Memory Skill
20. Subject Matter Knowledge
21. Enjoyment of Learning and Work
22. Flexibility
23. Persistence and Confidence
24. Sense of Urgency
25. Giving Respect to Others
26. Work Environment Analytical Skills
27. Sensory Awareness
28. Open-Mindedness
29. Humility
30. Analytical Skill (synthesis)
31. Intuition
32. Information-Sourcing Skill
33. Information-Gathering Skill
34. Information-Organizing Skill
35. Feedback Solicitation Skill
36. Willingness to Experiment and Gain Experience
37. Internalization Skill
38. Application of New Knowledge Skill
39. Ability to Adapt Knowledge to New Situations or Events
40. Critical Examination of Information Skill
41. Learning How to Learn Skill
42. Self-Directedness Skill

FIGURE 5–2

Conditions That Encourage Workplace Learning

Workplace learning is encouraged to the extent that each of the following conditions is perceived to be met:

- Sufficient financial resources exist to support workplace learning.
- Realistic goals and expectations for learning have been established.
- There is commitment by the organization to the learning process.
- Sufficient trust exists in the organization.
- Management shares a common understanding of vision and goals.
- Sufficient time is provided to permit learning.
- Good communication exists in the organization.
- The organization fosters a means by which to collect and use feedback from customers.
- Workplace learning is made a priority and is tied to performance expectations.
- The leadership of the organization is perceived to support workplace learning.
- Clear milestones have been established for the workplace learning process.
- Managers, union leaders, and learners exhibit buy-in and commitment to learning.
- Individuals are matched to learning experiences for which they have the appropriate education and background.
- The learning effort is closely tied to business needs.
- Work standards are consistently applied within the organization.
- The organization possesses clear methods by which to examine and measure work performance.
- Learners are open-minded and possess an attitude that favors learning.
- Measurement and accountability have been established and linked to the workplace learning process.
- The workplace learning process is guided by a plan.
- A clear sense exists about "next steps" following the workplace learning process.
- The organization's union, if the organization is unionized, supports the workplace learning process/effort.
- External environmental factors support the workplace learning process.
- Fear has been reduced within the organization so that individuals are not afraid to take risks and learn.
- Learners feel empowered.
- Learners feel they have incentives and rewards sufficient to encourage them to pursue workplace learning and see "what's in it for them."
- Responsibilities for who should do what in the workplace learning process have been clarified.

Source: W. J. Rothwell. (2000). *Models for the Workplace Learner.* Unpublished research report.

LEARNER CHARACTERISTICS OF OLDER VERSUS YOUNGER ADULTS

While much has been written about adult learning and adult learning theory,[10] it seems clear that most of it can be summarized in ten key foundational principles.

1. Adults are often problem-centered in how they regard learning experiences. They approach learning experiences with an expectation that they can solve their immediate problems and thereby meet their immediate needs. They often want to move directly to grapple with key issues and skip preliminary discussions of background or theory.

2. Adults are motivated by considerations of personal growth or gain. They wish to know "what's in it for them." Unlike young people, adults are self-confident and are thus impatient with trainers who do not make it clear why learners should care about what they are learning. Some adult learners tune out if appeals to self-interest are not made manifest quickly and compellingly.

3. Trainers can plan ways to increase learners' motivation to learn. By demonstrating to learners how a program can help them, trainers can build interest and motivation. Of course, it is important to remember that not all learners want the same things or learn effectively in exactly the same ways.

4. Gauging expectations before a learning event is critical. What do learners believe about a topic before they participate in a learning event? Trainers must find ways to gauge the answer to that question.

5. Trainers should plan to provide feedback and recognition to learners. Indeed, learners should be given ample feedback. And, when learning events are delivered through electronically mediated instruction, interactivity is essential to preserve learners' interest, attention, and involvement.

6. Individual differences in learning style should be considered when learning activities are planned. People do not all learn in the same ways, and one size does not fit all. Care must be taken to encourage learning to appeal to each learning style.

7. Planned learning experiences should take into account adult lifespan development, needs, and values. Individuals will not learn

effectively when learning events are inconsistent with their needs and beliefs. And what is important to them can change over time.

8. Learning experiences should take into account ways to encourage on-the-job transfer. How can participants be encouraged to apply on the job what they learned? How can their supervisors and co-workers hold them accountable for doing so?

9. Mature workers need a psychologically supportive climate in which to learn. If they feel that failure will lead to the loss of their job or of employment opportunities, then their fear may have unintended negative side effects. Hence, adults should be given freedom to learn without fear of punishment for the natural mistakes made while in training.

10. Hands-on activity promotes learning. Lectures lasting hours are not effective with mature workers. It is thus best to challenge these learners with problems to be solved. If done right, the problems solved will in turn encourage the learning process.

IMPLICATIONS OF LEARNING PRINCIPLES FOR TRAINING OLDER ADULTS

Generally speaking, older adult workers are about the same as younger adult workers in their learning abilities. But it is also true that research results presented in *Adult Education Participation in 2004–2005* reveal that there is a dropoff in participation by adults over age 54 in formal adult education activities.[11] (See Figure 5–3.) That same difference also holds true for adults enrolled in formal work-related courses or trainers who reported specific numbers of classroom instructional hours (see Figure 5–4), and adults reporting participation in distance education (see Figure 5–5). However, many older adults continue to participate in informal learning events rather than in formal, planned events (see Figure 5–6).

Both individuals and employers must take steps to change the mistaken stereotype that older adults cannot learn. This idea is very damaging at a time when the future U.S. and global workforce may consist of many retirees who must work, or retirement-age persons who have not retired. Both individuals and employers alike must foster the new assumption that no one stops learning—unless they

FIGURE 5–3

Percentage of Adults Who Participated in Adult Education by Type of Educational Activity and Selected Adult Characteristics: 2004–2005

Characteristics	Number of adults (thousands)	Any formal adult education	ESL classes	Basic skills GED classes	Part-time college degree program[1]	Part-time vocational degree/ diploma program[2]	Apprentice-ship	Work-related courses	Personal-interest course
Total	211,607	44	1	1	4	1	1	27	21
Age									
16 to 24 years	25,104	53	2	6	9	2	3	21	27
25 to 34 years	38,784	52	2	2	7	2	3	32	22
35 to 44 years	42,890	49	1	1	4	1	1	34	22
45 to 54 years	41,840	48	#	#	3	1	1	37	20
55 to 64 years	29,068	40	#	#	1	1	#	27	21
65 years or older	33,922	23	#	#	#	#	#	5	19

Source: K. O'Donnell, & C. Chapman, (2006). Adult Education Participation in 2004–2005 (p. 7). Washington, DC: U.S. Dept. of Education.

FIGURE 5-4

Percentage of Adults Enrolled in Formal Work-Related Courses or Training Who Reported Specific Numbers of Classroom Instructional Hours in the Past 12 Months, by Selected Adult Characteristics: 2004–05

Characteristic	Number of adults (thousands)	Total instructional hours across courses or training			
		10 hours or fewer	11–25 hours	26–50 hours	51 hours or more
Total	57,004	33	24	20	22
Age					
16 to 24 years	5,332	43	19	16	22
25 to 34 years	12,283	32	25	23	21
35 to 44 years	14,472	32	25	18	25
45 to 54 years	15,289	34	24	20	22
55 to 64 years	7,851	29	28	22	21
64 years or older	1,778	35	24	20	21

Source: K. O'Donnell & C. Chapman (2006). *Adult Education Participation in 2004–2005.* Washington: U.S. Dept. of Education, p. 26.

FIGURE 5-5

Number and Percentage of Adults Participating in Adult Education Activities Who Reported Using Any Type of Distance Education Method in the Past 12 Months, by Selected Adult Characteristics: 2004–2005

Characteristic	Number of adults (thousands)	Percentage of adults
Total	93,939	32
16 to 24 years	13,286	28
25 to 34 years	20,229	28
35 to 44 years	20,896	35
45 to 54 years	20,032	36
55 to 64 years	11,715	33
65 years or older	7,781	25

Source: K. O'Donnell & C. Chapman (2006). *Adult Education Participation in 2004–2005.* Washington: U.S. Dept. of Education, p. 34.

FIGURE 5-6

Number and Percentage of Adults Who Reported Participating in Informal Learning Activities for Personal Interest, by Type of Educational Activity and Selected Adult Characteristics: 2004–2005

Characteristic	Number of adults (thousands)	Any informal learning activities	Type of informal learning activities for personal interest				
			Computers, CD-ROM and Internet	Books, manuals, audio tapes, videos, or TV	Magazines or other publications	Clubs or groups	Conventions or conferences
Total	211,607	70	28	47	53	20	23
Age							
16 to 24 years	25,104	69	29	42	45	18	25
25 to 34 years	38,784	70	33	49	50	20	25
35 to 44 years	42,890	73	32	51	56	21	23
45 to 54 years	41,840	73	31	51	59	23	27
55 to 64 years	29,068	70	27	47	56	21	23
65 years or older	33,922	64	15	38	49	17	17

Source: K. O'Donnell & C. Chapman (2006). Adult Education Participation in 2004–2005 (p. 38). Washington, DC: U.S. Dept. of Education.

FIGURE 5–7

**A Worksheet to Guide Instructional Design Consistent
with Principles of Effective Adult Learning**

Directions: For each principle of adult learning listed in the left column below, write notes in the right column to indicate how you plan to ensure that the principle is met in your planned learning experience. There are no "right" or "wrong" answers in any absolute sense, but some answers may be better than others.

Principle of Adult Learning	How Do You Plan to Ensure That the Principle Is Met in Your Planned Learning Experience?
1 Adults are often problem-centered in how they regard learning experiences.	
2 Adults are motivated by considerations of personal growth or gain.	
3 Trainers can plan ways to increase learners' motivation to learn.	
4 Gauging expectations before a learning event is critical.	
5 Trainers should plan to provide feedback and recognition to learners.	
6 Individual differences in learning style should be considered when learning events are planned.	
7 Planned learning experiences should take into account adult life span development, needs, and values.	
8 Learning experiences should take into account ways to encourage on-the-job transfer.	
9 Mature workers need a psychologically supportive climate in which to learn.	
10 Hands-on activity promotes learning.	

FIGURE 5–8

A Worksheet to Guide Individuals in Taking Initiative
for Their Own Informal Learning Experiences

Directions: Use this worksheet to help individuals guide their own informal learning experiences. For each question posed in the left column below, encourage individuals to do some planning in the right column.

What Can You Do to Guide Your On-the-Job, Informal Learning?	What Steps Should You Take in a Specific Situation?
1 What questions can you pose to help you discover more about what you wish to learn?	
2 Who can you watch, and what can you learn from what you watch, to see someone who is very good at what you wish to learn? What can you imitate from what you see?	
3 How can you establish a situation in which you can practice carrying out something and have someone who is more experienced watch you?	
4 How can you ask for feedback from those who are good based on your effort to practice applying what you have learned in number 3 above?	

FIGURE 5–9

Training and Older Workers

A training policy that sets out individuals' right to training is a key factor influencing access. Without a policy to guide organizational thinking, decisions about access can be haphazard and impede efforts to implement equality of access. Companies that exhibit good practice view training as a strategic issue closely linked to business performance—the question for them is less about whether to provide training and more about the business impact of not training staff. However, even where formal policies exist, there may still be a passive attitude toward the training of older workers. If this is the case, what else needs to be done?

- *Make sure all managers understand and implement the policy.* Line managers are key intermediaries in facilitating access to training and there may be tension between policy, led by those in human resources, and practice, led by line managers and supervisors. It is essential to address any negative perceptions line managers might hold, since they are often gatekeepers of training and development.

- *Monitor training take-up.* It is essential to monitor the take-up of both mandatory and optional training. Most businesses keep a close eye on essential training such as health and safety or training associated with the introduction of new technology. However, training that contributes to wider staff development may not be so carefully observed. Take-up of such training may be suggestive of the career aspirations of different workers. More importantly, monitoring training is likely to indicate employees with skill sets that fit the requirements of new roles, thereby potentially avoiding the need to recruit from outside.

- *Relate training to career pathways.* Linked to the monitoring of training take-up, emerging good practice is to relate both mandatory and optional training to career pathways through the company. This allows employees to make informed decisions about the training they might take and promote their engagement with the company through making visible the routes to career development. This is particularly important for older workers whose career aspirations may be different from those of younger workers. For instance, some older employees may prefer a sideways move into a new project rather than progression up the management scales.

Source: Becci Newton. (2006). "Training an Age Diverse Workforce." *Industrial and Commercial Training,* 38:(2), 93. Used by permission of Emerald Group Publishing Limited.

(continued)

FIGURE 5–9 *(continued)*

Training and Older Workers

- *Discuss training as part of staff appraisal.* Good management and appraisal systems are a driver of employee engagement. An emphasis on training and career development here is key. Discussing training needs and career aspirations during staff appraisal helps to promote the company training policy as well as emphasize the importance of continuous development. Such discussions also allow managers to identify whether confidence barriers exist—and to address these to ensure all staff engage in their own development.

- *Training delivery and learning preferences.* There is evidence to suggest that older workers may prefer training that allows for group learning opportunities, is work-based, delivered in bite-size chunks, draws on their knowledge and experience; and offers opportunities to apply newly gained knowledge and skills. In fact, these preferences may not be so different from those of other employees. The rise of blended learning—for instance, e-learning mixed with face-to-face group sessions—offers opportunities to deliver learning in multiple ways—and the chance to revisit content once the training module is completed. It may also be a cost-effective way to deliver nonessential training geared toward staff future career aspirations.

choose to do so. The reality is that older adults will not learn if they do not want to, or if employers or organizations discourage them from doing so.

What is known about adult learning can be readily applied to older workers.[12] Use the worksheet in Figure 5–7 to structure your thinking whenever you or your organization begins the instructional design process to plan formal instruction for adults. Use the worksheet in Figure 5–8 to structure your thinking about ways to encourage older workers to learn on or off the job. Employers may also encourage team learning—that is, action learning[13]—to foster interaction between younger and older workers so that they may learn from each other and thereby foster knowledge transfer from those with more experience to those with less.[14] By taking these steps—and others (see Figures 5–9 and 5–10)—employers and individuals may encourage learning among older workers.

FIGURE 5–10

A Worksheet for Improving Training for Older Workers

Directions: For each desirable practice in the left column below, indicate in the right column possible action strategies that your organization might take to ensure that those practices are applied.

Desirable Practice for Training Older Workers	What Action Strategies Might Your Organization Take to Ensure That the Practices Are Applied?
1 Make sure that the organization has a training policy that sets out individuals' right to training	
2 Make sure all managers understand and implement the policy	
3 Monitor training take-up	
4 Relate training to career pathways	
5 Discuss training as part of staff appraisal	
6 Make sure training delivery matches learning preferences	

Source: This list is taken from Becci Newton. (2006). "Training an Age Diverse Workforce," *Industrial and Commercial Training, 38(2)*, 93. Used by permission of Emerald Group Publishing Limited 2006.

SUMMARY

This chapter defined workplace learning competency and reviewed why it is important. The chapter also reviewed research that has been conducted on workplace learning competence and workplace learning climate as well as the characteristics distinguishing older from younger learners. Finally, the chapter offered some conclusions on what implications can be drawn from the research for training older workers.

6 | CAREER DEVELOPMENT FOR ADULTS AND OLDER WORKERS

Middle-aged and older adult workers represent a talented group of people who will be able to continue working for many years, perform at high levels, and be competitive with younger workers. A select group of today's retirement-age older workers are excellent models for the emerging middle-aged workforce. Many of this group will continue to be productive, characterized by its continual updating of skills, excellent work habits, and sophistication in working with other people. These people will be strong contributors as long as they choose to work. They are the survivors with expertise.[1, 2, 3] Others in this age group are facing early buyouts, downsizing, layoffs, and the challenge of reemployment. Self-management is essential for the career success of workers in a highly volatile, ever-changing world of work. There is much that we know and more yet that we need to better understand in order to facilitate and provide support for individuals in the future.

SELF-MANAGEMENT: CAREER AND RETIREMENT

Conceptualizations of work and retirement continue to evolve, and in the mid-1990s, Hall and associates published three very important publications in this regard.[4, 5, 6] *The Career Is Dead: Long Live the Career* by Hall and associates in 1996 presents the strongest statements about the protean career referred to throughout this book. Their emphasis was on self-management of career in a dramatically changing work environment.

Sterns and Gray[7] emphasize the challenge faced by midlife and older workers in terms of self-management. As organizations transition from pyramid to flatter, more streamlined configurations through downsizing and restructuring, employees may experience job loss, job plateauing, and skills obsolescence.[8, 9] These changes suggest that older workers may need to have increased involvement and responsibility in terms of career management.

Organizational changes are also altering the nature of the relationships between organizations and employees. Employers' commitment to employees may last only as long as there is a need for their skills and performance. Similarly, employees' commitment to the employer may last only as long as their expectations are being met. Hall and Mirvis[10] conceptualize this as a change from a relational to a transactional relationship. These changes place greater emphasis on employees' adaptability and abilities in learning to learn.

Career self-management is included by Hall and Mirvis in their careful discussion of the protean career.[11] A protean career means one that is directed by the individual rather than by the employing organization. Greater responsibility for learning, skill mastery, and updating is placed on the individual. The individual is in control and able to change the shape of his or her career at will—similar to a free agent in sports. This perspective and the goals of this type of career (e.g., psychological success, identity expansion, and learning) also recognize the artificiality of the distinction between work and non-work life. Personal roles and career roles are highly interrelated, and the boundaries between these roles tend to be fuzzy rather than clear cut. This fits well with Super's definition of career as the combination and sequence of roles across the life-span.[12]

It has been suggested that taking the responsibility of career self-management may hold special benefits for older workers. Greater tenure in a protean-type career may lead to increased value of older workers. However, it may be rather costly to replace such knowledgeable, adaptable, and continuously learning employees with younger workers with less protean-type career experience. Protean careers may increase the organization's options for deploying older workers, however. Similarly, the options older workers may pursue in changing their careers are also increased. Potential alternatives include moving to a new field (i.e., second or third careers), building new skills in their present field, changing organizations, phasing into retirement, or joining the contingent workforce.

Older workers may also be at a disadvantage, however, in terms of moving toward greater career self-management. Transitioning from a typical, organizational-driven career to a protean career may be a rather daunting task, particularly if an individual initially entered the workforce with a one career–one employer ideal. Problems of self-definition may arise from one's personal identity's no longer being connected to a formal organizational work role. This is likely a problem especially for earlier cohorts who have worked through the period of the changing relationship between employers and employees. Additionally, stereotypic beliefs about older workers may lead to the underutilization of this group within organizations.

Evidence is mounting that the intrinsic rewards of work—satisfaction, relationships with co-workers, and a sense of participating in meaningful activity—become more important as an individual ages, although this is not necessarily true in all instances.[13] The abolishment of the mandatory retirement age allows working older adults to continue to participate in these benefits until they feel that they have the financial resources and personal network outside the workplace to retire.[14] Job satisfaction research shows consistently that work-related attitudes are more positive with increasing age in surveys of employed adults.[15] Older adults may have a different perspective on work than younger adults. For older workers with high tenure, survival needs may be less urgent as they will probably have reached a maximum income for their jobs. Desire for personal control is still strong.[16, 17] However, older workers have seen less evidence that hard work leads to promotions, salary increases, or other rewards. Goals may not change with age but expectations of achieving these outcomes can diminish.

Sterns,[18] in his model of career development and training, sees the option of full or part-time retirement as part of the decision to no longer be actively involved in career development and work activities. Decisions regarding career and updating are based on many factors. However, individuals can move in and out of the work role.

A multidimensional model initially proposed for self-management of retirement also elucidates the variety of factors influencing career decisions for middle-aged and older workers.

One of the major goals of career self-management is to identify key influences on the decision-making process. Much of the emphasis is on consciousness raising, values clarification, getting in touch with personal feelings, and awareness of viewpoints held by significant others. A primary step in self-management involves reflection on the self as a knowledge structure providing a basis for retrieval of past information and developing a context for evaluating and responding to present circumstances

The first component of Sterns's model deals with the individual's self-concept, how it is influenced, and how it influences career decisions. A person's self-concept is influenced by many factors in consideration of career issues (see Figure 6–1). First, there is the understanding of our past selves and what values, preferences, and desires are based on our past. This is countered and complemented

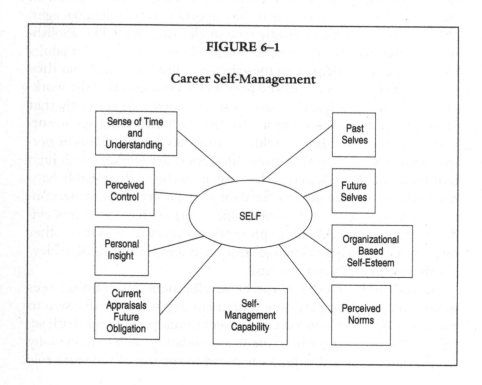

FIGURE 6–1

Career Self-Management

- Sense of Time and Understanding
- Perceived Control
- Personal Insight
- Current Appraisals Future Obligation
- Self-Management Capability
- SELF
- Past Selves
- Future Selves
- Organizational Based Self-Esteem
- Perceived Norms

by our future selves. Three factors are important here. One is the understanding of change and an awareness of the passage of time. How we view change in others and ourselves over time and how we see and understand the implications of future time are major aspects of personal integration, leading to self-understanding.

The second factor influencing self-concept is the perceived control that we have about our lives at the personal level, in relation to significant others and in our work, career, business situations, etc. We may feel in control based on financial resources, position held, or seniority, or we may feel extremely vulnerable based on the current financial situations and/or business climate. For example, in one year we have gone from the highest level of employment to a sense of great vulnerability. The summer of 2002 forced many midlife and older workers to come to terms with the fact that they may have to work longer based on the decline of their investments. More middle-aged adults' current and future goals are in the work domain more than any other. Work success seems to be closely tied to perception of control at midlife, such that each builds upon the other.[19] The third factor is personal insight—how well we understand ourselves, our motivations, our personal desires, our work approaches, our relations to family, friends, and organizations. Self-study, education, and counseling may aid this process.

Organizational-based self-esteem (OBSE) is the bridge to the world of work. How valued one feels, how one feels in relation to one's fellow workers, the feeling of contribution that one gets from one's work are all part of OBSE. One's OBSE may undermine the stance required for effective self-management, i.e., that one's self-development should be independent of a specific organization. If the relationship between the employer and employee is more transactional, and the typical psychological contract with the employer can no longer be depended upon, OBSE may become a liability to employees if it impedes them from focusing on their own needs (which may conflict with those of their employing organization). Another important area is how one perceives the work and retirement norms around them. One's personal social clock and one's understanding of social norms will influence self-perceptions and actions to be taken.

The orchestration of all of these influences on self and the needed interpretation, planning, sophistication, and wisdom are all part of self-management capability. Staudinger[20] and Smith[21] have both presented important work regarding the development of planning capability, wisdom regarding life events, and the development of an approach to the art of living. An important continuing area of research will focus on how well people are able to self-manage the planning and execution of their careers.

Figure 6–2 focuses on the work influences. Briefly, one is concerned here with one's self-evaluation of the employment situation. Part of this relates to one's appraisal of the current situation: how one believes he or she is viewed by supervisors, outcomes of performance appraisals, perceived growth opportunities within the organization, and observations of treatment received by other, later career employees. Another part is an understanding of personal

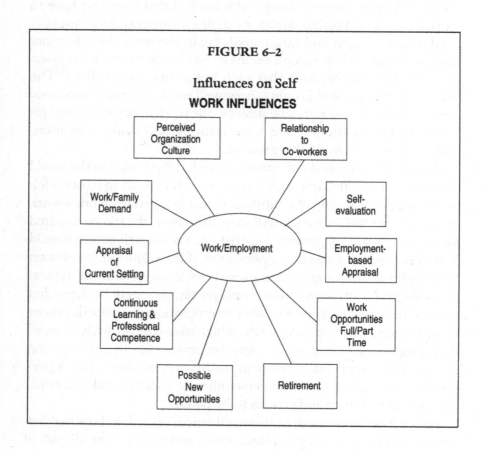

FIGURE 6–2

Influences on Self
WORK INFLUENCES

strengths and weaknesses that one knows about oneself and one's approach to work related tasks.

Within this portion of the model, employment-based appraisal refers to the formal and informal feedback that one receives from supervisors—outcomes of performance appraisals, salary increases, involvement in organization planning and policy. Work opportunities refer to future plans within the work context and potential opportunities over time. New work opportunities may be an important incentive for job or career change. A major dimension is one's activities in continuous learning and maintaining professional competence. Remaining competitive with up-to-date skills may make one valuable to the organization, or make it possible to move to other employment.

Relationships with co-workers may be extremely important in decision making. How a person feels about his or her work situation is highly influenced by co-worker interactions in many cases. Middle-age and older workers value relationships on the job. A negative relationship with co-workers may lead a valuable employee to seek alternatives. Perceived organizational culture is another dimension that provides important messages to current employees. Choices made by current organization leadership and how these are transmitted to current employees provide important general information. Middle-aged and older employees are usually very aware of changing climate and how long-service employees are being treated.

Employers in the authors' survey felt that some management practices are particularly important to managing older workers and creating a work environment friendly to them. Such management practices included permitting extended lunch breaks and flexible workdays. Sponsoring health fairs was also named as a desirable practice. Numerous other practices were rated but did not stand out as particularly desirable. (See Figure 6–3.)

The few older workers who participated in the authors' survey indicated that the single greatest reason that they might consider leaving an employer had to do with the way they are treated. (See Figure 6–4.) But most feel challenged in their jobs. (See Figure 6–5.) They prefer managers who create a sense of teamwork, provide guidance on what they could improve, and provide promotion and

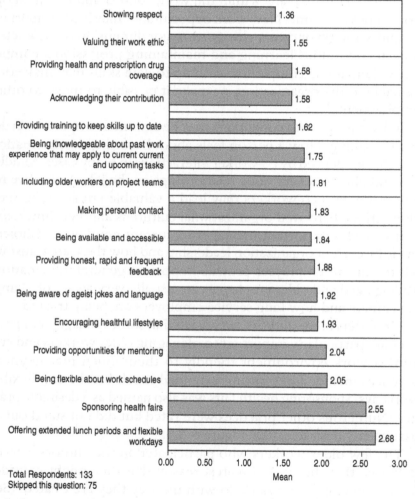

FIGURE 6–3

Perceptions About the Importance of Different Actions in Managing Older Workers

Q11: How important do you think each of the following is when it comes to managing older workers?

Action	Mean
Showing respect	1.36
Valuing their work ethic	1.55
Providing health and prescription drug coverage	1.58
Acknowledging their contribution	1.58
Providing training to keep skills up to date	1.62
Being knowledgeable about past work experience that may apply to current current and upcoming tasks	1.75
Including older workers on project teams	1.81
Making personal contact	1.83
Being available and accessible	1.84
Providing honest, rapid and frequent feedback	1.88
Being aware of ageist jokes and language	1.92
Encouraging healthful lifestyles	1.93
Providing opportunities for mentoring	2.04
Being flexible about work schedules	2.05
Sponsoring health fairs	2.55
Offering extended lunch periods and flexible workdays	2.68

Mean

Total Respondents: 133
Skipped this question: 75

Scale: 1 = Strongly agree; 2 = Agree; 3 = Neutral; 4 = Disagree; 5 = Strongly disagree

Source: J. Reaser, D. Spokus, H. Sterns, & W. Rothwell. (2006). *A Survey of Employers.* Unpublished survey results. Arlington, VA: National Older Worker Career Center (NOWCC).

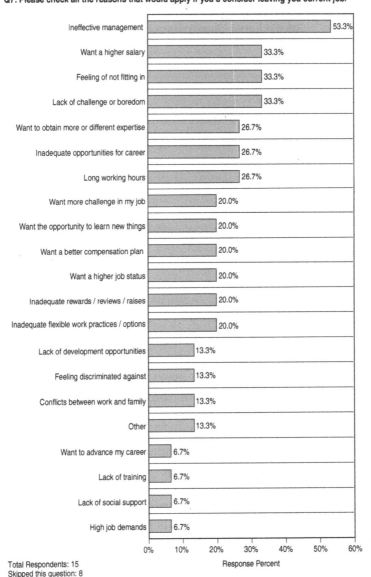

FIGURE 6–4

What Are Some Reasons You Would Consider Leaving Your Job?

Q7: Please check all the reasons that would apply if you'd consider leaving you current job.

Reason	Response Percent
Ineffective management	53.3%
Want a higher salary	33.3%
Feeling of not fitting in	33.3%
Lack of challenge or boredom	33.3%
Want to obtain more or different expertise	26.7%
Inadequate opportunities for career	26.7%
Long working hours	26.7%
Want more challenge in my job	20.0%
Want the opportunity to learn new things	20.0%
Want a better compensation plan	20.0%
Want a higher job status	20.0%
Inadequate rewards / reviews / raises	20.0%
Inadequate flexible work practices / options	20.0%
Lack of development opportunities	13.3%
Feeling discriminated against	13.3%
Conflicts between work and family	13.3%
Other	13.3%
Want to advance my career	6.7%
Lack of training	6.7%
Lack of social support	6.7%
High job demands	6.7%

Total Respondents: 15
Skipped this question: 8

Response Percent

Source: J. Reaser, D. Spokus, H. Sterns, & W. Rothwell. (2006). *A Survey of Employers.* Unpublished survey results. Arlington, VA: National Older Worker Career Center (NOWCC).

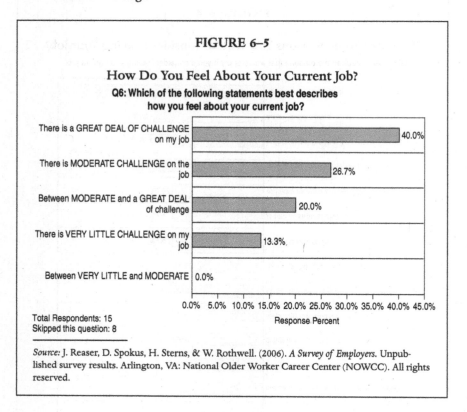

FIGURE 6–5

How Do You Feel About Your Current Job?

**Q6: Which of the following statements best describes
how you feel about your current job?**

- There is a GREAT DEAL OF CHALLENGE on my job — 40.0%
- There is MODERATE CHALLENGE on the job — 26.7%
- Between MODERATE and a GREAT DEAL of challenge — 20.0%
- There is VERY LITTLE CHALLENGE on my job — 13.3%
- Between VERY LITTLE and MODERATE — 0.0%

0.0% 5.0% 10.0% 15.0% 20.0% 25.0% 30.0% 35.0% 40.0% 45.0%

Response Percent

Total Respondents: 15
Skipped this question: 8

training opportunities open to everyone. (See Figure 6–6.) They would consider standing most of the day and commuting half an hour or more to work. (See Figure 6–7.)

Employers in the authors' survey felt that offering employees incentives for referrals and using newspaper advertisements were particularly good practices in recruiting older workers. Of lesser value were other common recruiting options, such as online ads on the web that have grown popular with the advent of so-called e-recruiting. (See Figure 6–8.) In contrast, individuals participating in the authors' small-scale survey of older workers indicated that they were attracted to employers most by positive referrals coming from friends or colleagues. (See Figure 6–9.) Challenging work is the thing that older workers want most. (See Figure 6–10.)

Another dimension is possible in new opportunities. This refers to looking for new employment opportunities within or outside of

FIGURE 6–6

Preferred Management Practices for Older Workers, According to Survey Respondents

Q13: What aspects of his/her management style was he/she good at and not good at?

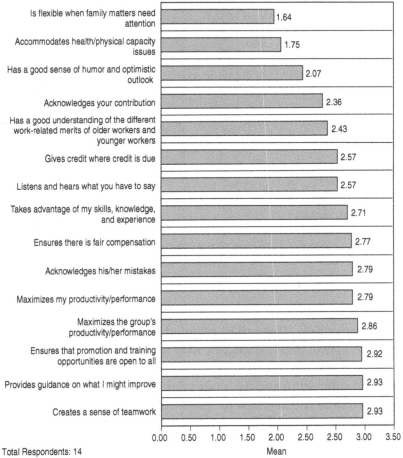

Total Respondents: 14
Skipped this question: 9

Mean

Scale: 1 = Strongly agree; 2 = Agree; 3 = Neutral; 4 = Disagree;
5 = Strongly disagree

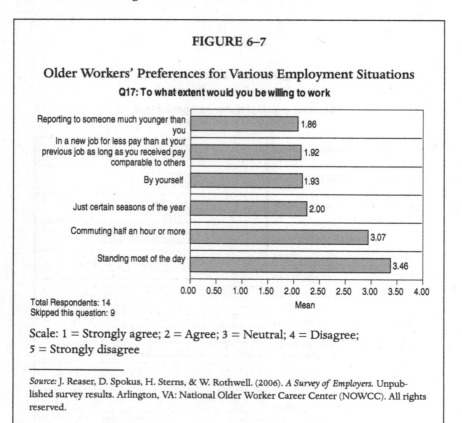

FIGURE 6–7

Older Workers' Preferences for Various Employment Situations

Q17: To what extent would you be willing to work

	Mean
Reporting to someone much younger than you	1.86
In a new job for less pay than at your previous job as long as you received pay comparable to others	1.92
By yourself	1.93
Just certain seasons of the year	2.00
Commuting half an hour or more	3.07
Standing most of the day	3.46

Total Respondents: 14
Skipped this question: 9

Scale: 1 = Strongly agree; 2 = Agree; 3 = Neutral; 4 = Disagree;
5 = Strongly disagree

one's organization. This can be planned in terms of second- or third-career education and training, or may be related to chance encounters or in response to a corporate recruiter. In these cases, where one is self-managing and no longer desires to continue in one's employment, then the decision to retire may be the decision of choice. Often middle-aged and older employees may not be in a position to choose to retire.

Self-concept is influenced in many of the previously described ways. What is critical is our ability to bridge from the individual level to the broader work and societal context.

Early models of career development were linear models, which assumed that individuals moved through predictable career stages and then retirement. For older adults, maintaining skills for a period of time and then declining was the predicted pattern. This notion that

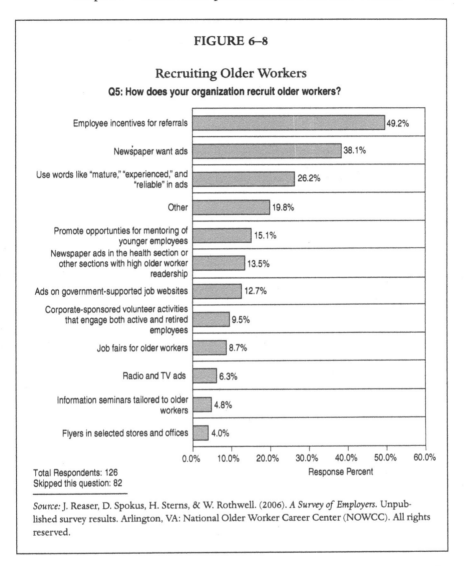

FIGURE 6–8

Recruiting Older Workers

Q5: How does your organization recruit older workers?

Category	Response Percent
Employee incentives for referrals	49.2%
Newspaper want ads	38.1%
Use words like "mature," "experienced," and "reliable" in ads	26.2%
Other	19.8%
Promote opportunties for mentoring of younger employees	15.1%
Newspaper ads in the health section or other sections with high older worker readership	13.5%
Ads on government-supported job websites	12.7%
Corporate-sponsored volunteer activities that engage both active and retired employees	9.5%
Job fairs for older workers	8.7%
Radio and TV ads	6.3%
Information seminars tailored to older workers	4.8%
Flyers in selected stores and offices	4.0%

Total Respondents: 126
Skipped this question: 82

Source: J. Reaser, D. Spokus, H. Sterns, & W. Rothwell. (2006). *A Survey of Employers.* Unpublished survey results. Arlington, VA: National Older Worker Career Center (NOWCC). All rights reserved.

career stages are linked to age will lead practitioners to incorrectly develop career development opportunities that are congruent with the age and life-stage of various cohorts. These models ignore individual differences and the contributions that older workers make.

As evidenced in the background just given, the social sciences have informed us about the importance of understanding individual differences in career self-management and decision making. Demographic changes are increasing the need to better understand older

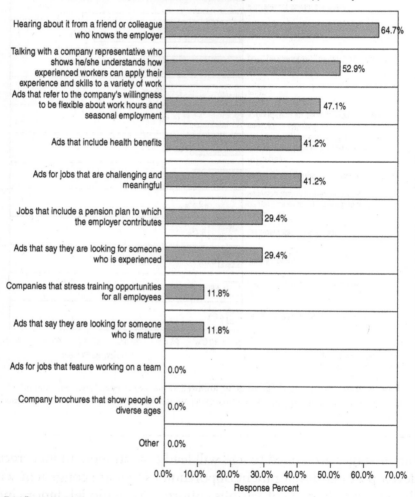

FIGURE 6–9

What Do Older Workers Say Attracts Their Attention When Seeking Employment?

Q2: What attracts your attention when looking for a new job opportunity?

Response	Percent
Hearing about it from a friend or colleague who knows the employer	64.7%
Talking with a company representative who shows he/she understands how experienced workers can apply their experience and skills to a variety of work	52.9%
Ads that refer to the company's willingness to be flexible about work hours and seasonal employment	47.1%
Ads that include health benefits	41.2%
Ads for jobs that are challenging and meaningful	41.2%
Jobs that include a pension plan to which the employer contributes	29.4%
Ads that say they are looking for someone who is experienced	29.4%
Companies that stress training opportunities for all employees	11.8%
Ads that say they are looking for someone who is mature	11.8%
Ads for jobs that feature working on a team	0.0%
Company brochures that show people of diverse ages	0.0%
Other	0.0%

Response Percent

Total Respondents: 17
Skipped this question: 8

Source: J. Reaser, D. Spokus, H. Sterns, & W. Rothwell. (2006). *A Survey of Employers.* Unpublished survey results. Arlington, VA: National Older Worker Career Center (NOWCC). All rights reserved.

FIGURE 6–10

What Makes a Difference to Older Workers When Deciding Whether to Take a Job?

Q4: What makes a difference to you when deciding whether to take a job?

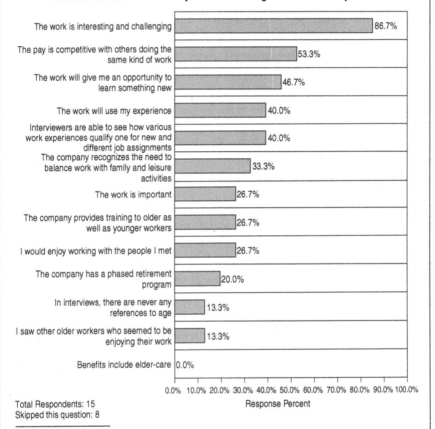

Total Respondents: 15
Skipped this question: 8

Response Percent

workers and how to attract, select, guide, and assess this part of the population. Change in the employer/employee dynamic has led to a need for increased personal responsibility among all workers for their own development and skill maintenance.

Gerontology has provided a great deal of information on both the capabilities and the limitations of older workers. We have been aware of the existence and effects of negative aging stereotypes for decades and the effects on employment decisions about older workers, as well as on the behavior of older workers themselves. What is needed is a comprehensive, interdisciplinary review of what we know about factors contributing to or detracting from successful career self-management. The remainder of this chapter briefly outlines some of these factors, providing a basis for examining what we do not know in order to inform further research.

Individual Factors in Success

There is much available to the individual in terms of resources in the career self-management process. Hall and Mirvis[22] suggest that in order to be successful, the individual needs to develop enhanced adaptability and growth and flexibility in identity. Career adaptability, according to Savickas,[23] involves developing planful attitudes, engaging in ongoing exploration of self and career, and developing adaptive decisional skills for coping with a dynamic environment. This is also referred to as adaptive competence.[24]

Part of this planful approach to employment in later life[25] is discussed in four approaches related to the Selective Optimization with Compensation theory developed by Baltes and Baltes. The first involves developing strategies for *psychological* accommodation of potential loss of ability and/or status. The second is planning in order to prevent or defer declines in functioning. Third is the identification and utilization of interventions for recovering lost capacities. Finally, there is the need to develop meaningful ways to compensate for inevitable age-related declines.

Important to career self-management from the cognitive psychology perspective are the individual's level of self-knowledge and broader occupational knowledge, such as familiarity with career alternatives and knowledge of recent changes within the current employment field. What the individual is capable of doing with this knowledge is affected by his or her decision-making skills as well as higher order cognitive processes called metacognition or executive processing skills. Executive processing involves the ability of the individual to regulate and integrate information and how the individual makes use of that information. Staudinger[26] would refer to this as a part of the "art of life," or development of wisdom in self-management. The work of Maurer and Tarulli[27] supported the importance of career insight, perceived need for skill enhancement, job involvement, and self-efficacy to individual development.

As previously discussed, perception of control is also important to career self-management.[28] Individuals must see potential benefits to the process in order to fully engage themselves. If control is seen as in the hands of others, such as the organization, career self-management efforts will seem futile. Encouraging individuals to take a proactive approach and to see the benefits of a protean career and the variety of opportunities for learning and development as well as skill maintenance available to them are steps in developing self-management skills. It requires helping individuals to appreciate the control over their growth and development that they already possess, if they will only recognize and take advantage of it.

Career commitment, increased education, work as a source of identity, and the existence of social networks at work are additional variables that contribute to career development and the likelihood of remaining in the workforce. Occupational self-efficacy, the individual's belief in his or her ability to do the job, to learn, and in his or her own social competence within the organization are also relevant to career self-management decisions.[29]

Environmental Factors

The perception of supportive policies, rules, and guidelines contribute to higher participation. Also important for older workers is access to a career counselor. A positive work environment, relatively free of grumbling and complaining, in which the individual feels supported to the extent that he or she feels safe to experiment and to make mistakes from which learning comes, can also facilitate an attitude consistent with growth and development.

OBSTACLES TO SELF-MANAGEMENT

Growth, need, strength, and the intrinsic importance of engaging in developmental activities may be negatively related to increasing age and may be potential obstacles to continued development in late career. Perceived age-inappropriateness of changes, concerns about age discrimination, and a perception of occupational obsolescence detract from the individual's desire and perceived ability to change job or career.[30] Negative aging stereotypes affect older workers' behaviors as well as their self-image. Older workers may have decreased training self-efficacy and negative attitudes based on prior experience. In addition, individuals may not have the necessary cognitive or psychological resources for career self-management.[31] Individuals may also be wary of the financial costs of training and updating.

Organizational factors also create obstacles to the development of older workers. The stereotypes that affect the individual worker also affect employment decisions made by the organization, such as hiring, job assignments, and training opportunities.[32] While supervisor support has been identified as important to the development of older workers, evidence indicates that most supervisors pay little attention to the functioning of older workers. Opportunities for expanding the employee's career view are nonexistent, as any career discussion that does take place only examines short-term goals. Generally, the literature cites fewer development opportunities for older workers, decreased likelihood to volunteer for development, decreased prevalence of on-the-job training or supervisor career counseling, and fewer opportunities for challenging work.

Feldman[33] documented a continuum of late career issues in his discussion of managing careers in organizations. He argues that more attention to the late career is important for three reasons. First, it represents a significant portion of one's career, potentially fifteen to twenty years of an individual's working life. Second, it is likely that as older adults become a larger segment of the workforce, a larger percentage of the workforce will be in the later stages of their work life. Third, changes to the Age Discrimination in Employment Act ended mandatory retirement for many individuals and solidified protections that would allow individuals to work beyond the then-standard retirement age of 65 years. Feldman also raised several issues with regard to career planning, including careful planning to ensure that one's late career was professionally satisfying, active, and provided financial security.

Besides the aging of the workforce, other trends are occurring as well: the shift to an information / services economy, the influx of communications technology, and increased globalization—all will continue to impact the workplace. With lifetime employment no longer valued or pursued and the pace of change only increasing, organizations have not remained static either, and their processes for developing staff to be managers and managers to be executives have continued to advance. To remain on the creative cusp of market changes, organizations have instituted new structures and personnel development programs that facilitate remarkable adaptability to changes in the external environment. These learning organizations practice continuous renewal of their structures and processes.[34] Larger organizations are also seeking to identify areas for improvement at the personnel and at the organizational levels through feedback systems. These organizations have formal processes for getting feedback from subordinates, peers, supervisors, and customers. Information from these processes can drive the agenda for the types of training and career development processes embraced by an organization.

Clearly, there is a need for current and flexible models of career development that reflect this new reality. A lifespan developmental perspective on career development holds a promising future as it places a changing individual in a changing environment. This perspective has proven very robust in the work environment. The decision to pursue promotions, change jobs or careers, find new employment, or engage in career development activities may come about as a result of changes within the individual, the environment, or both in combination. The professional role of the older worker is being redefined in the rapidly changing environment of work in the twenty-first century. Industrial gerontologists have also redefined how they model career development from its beginnings in the 1940s to the present.[35, 36] This chapter will review the major influences on career development theory of the past fifty years and propose some considerations and challenges for career development models as we move deeper into the century.

MODELS OF CAREER DEVELOPMENT

Feldman[37] defines "career" as the progression of events of a person's work experience from the formation of career interests through retirement. "Career development" refers to those activities that pertain to managing the progression of a career. These activities may be initiated by employers (e.g., hiring and promotion policies), professional organizations (e.g., certifications), supervisors (e.g., performance appraisals), or the individual involved (e.g., self-directed study). Career development models attempt to summarize the progression of career events and decisions to two ends. First, these models are useful to predict the behavior of individuals. Second, and of more personal interest to each of us, these models can be used to better understand our own career behavior and provide recommendations that can aid each of us to maximize our personal growth and development during our working life. The ultimate goal of a career development model should be to contribute to maximizing the potential of all individuals as they navigate their careers.[38]

In the 1970s

The 1970s saw age and life stage as an important determinant of behavior, and these elements were incorporated into career development theories. Numerous models suggest that the mobility rates of younger persons (up to around age 30) are much higher than those of older persons as the younger generations move about seeking their niche in life while the older ones maintain theirs as they plan for retirement.

Schein[39] describes three stages in a career: socialization, performance, and obsolescence versus the development of new skills. In the third stage, the obsolete person may be retained as "deadwood," with no options for mobility, or he or she may be retrained, transferred into a lateral position, or forced into early retirement. Although career development could be helpful to the employee in all three stages, it seems likely that the person who would most strongly desire such help would be in a third stage of Schein's model. In terms of actual research, mobility in an early career has a relationship with one's later career. Thus, the person who is mobile early on is most likely to be mobile in his or her later career.

Hall's model of career growth[40] conceptualizes career planning from a goal-setting perspective. Once a career-goal decision—such as the decision to engage in training or retraining—is made, then goal attainment should lead to identity growth and enhanced self-esteem. Such enhanced self-esteem may then lead to greater commitment to future career-developmental goals. Goal attainment enhances self-esteem, which may increase perceptions of self-efficacy and future commitment to career-development activities.

In the late 1970s, theories of career progression began to be criticized for following a "linear life plan," the pattern in which education is a task for the young, work is for the middle-aged, and leisure is for the elderly. The criticism of using the linear life plan as a basis for theory is that it perpetuates the notion that these are the appropriate tasks for each life stage, discouraging intermixing of all three tasks across the life span.

The work of Levinson[41] added new dimensions to life-stage theories by incorporating biological, psychological, and social development constructs. Levinson and Sheehy[42] have contributed by popularizing the idea of midlife transition issues and raising the possibility of different career development patterns for males and females.

In the 1980s

The life-span orientation combines the above approaches with a recognition that behavioral change can occur over the entire life cycle. This approach emphasizes substantial individual differences in aging.[43] Individuals are influenced by normative, age-graded biological and environmental influences (physical and cognitive changes as one ages), normative, history-graded factors (generational events), and non-normative influences unique to every individual. The influences interact to determine an individual's career path. Over the course of a career, a person will be presented with increasingly complex work roles, which play a crucial role in stimulating the development of mental models of how people interact, how projects are successfully completed, and how to gain recognition from the organizations. Individuals begin with different potentials and will improve at differing rates.

Katz[44] moved the focus of career development into the organizational setting. In a model of job longevity, Katz describes three successive stages: socialization, innovation, and adaptation. Stage I, socialization, occurs during the first few months on the job. During this stage, one tries to establish a situational identity, decipher situational norms, learn role expectations, build social relationships, and prove oneself as an important contributing member of the organization. Stage II, innovation, is characterized by a transition in employee job concerns. Occurring approximately between the sixth month and the third year of job longevity, the major concern is on achievement and accomplishment. Attempts are made to improve special skills, enlarge the scope of one's contributions, enhance visibility and promotional potential, and influence the organizational surroundings. Gradually, however, if promotion or movement does not occur, tasks become less challenging and more routine, and the person enters into Stage III, adaptation. In this stage, the individual adapts to remaining in that job or leaves the organization. If the organization is left, then the socialization phase (Stage I) is reentered in the new job. Thus, the socialization stage can occur throughout the span of the career.

Similarly, in 1984, Super[45] updated his theory to include "minicycles" that revisit the career stages across the life span. Career growth, exploration, maintenance, and decline may occur at any or at many points in the life span. An individual can continue to grow, explore new interests and career directions, establish new competencies, maintain those new skills, and then disengage and take on a further set of new interests. The continued relevance of Super's theory hinges on the notion of career adaptability—a construct that encompasses a willingness to plan a career, participate in ongoing exploration, and develop adaptive decisional skills. Although research validating Super's theory has been sparse, numerous studies support the utility of his approach.

The early 1980s also brought research attention to personality variables. "Need for achievement" and "locus of control" were variables hypothesized to affect mobility and career development attitudes.[46]

Neopolitan[47] investigated occupational changes in mid-career and found that people who made changes regardless of great obstacles tended to reflect an internal locus of control. A comparison group of people dissatisfied with their careers who did not make changes tended to perceive great risk beyond their control, which would doom any such efforts. Thus, we might expect internals to engage in greater career planning activity than externals. Research by Gould[48] and by Beehr, Taber, and Walsh[49] lends support to this hypothesis. We may conclude that persons with an external locus of control are less likely to view a career development program as beneficial to them and, hence, are less likely to participate in one.

In the early 1980s, Veiga[50] discussed "individual barriers to moving" in the context of seniority and age. Veiga suggested that perceptions of one's own marketability might strongly influence one's efforts to explore alternative career opportunities, both within one's own organization and in an outside firm. Since holding a particular position within the same organization for an extended period of time may only reinforce feelings of specialization and/or obsolescence, older workers are at higher risk of perceiving low marketability. Moreover, the longer people remain with a company and the older they get, the more likely they will be to think twice about risking any benefits accrued through the years in order to move to a new organization. The same may be true for the person who strongly values job security, regardless of age. In sum, if the perceived risks associated with career moves are too high, people are unlikely to participate in career development programs.

Veiga also identified five motives that significantly influenced propensity to leave a job: fear of stagnation, career impatience, and dissatisfaction with one's salary, recognition, and/or advancement. Again we assume that people with a desire to move will react positively to the initiation of a career development program that could conceivably help them on their way.

In the 1980s, life-cycle and life-stage theories were criticized for using male workers as the basis for the development. It is becoming increasingly evident that career progressions of women may be quite different from those of men, as the former juggle the roles of student, housewife, paid worker, mother, etc. Life-cycle and life-stage approaches have also been criticized for failure to test propositions adequately. Particularly lacking is longitudinal research using subjects over age 50. A criticism of stage theories is that they tend to ignore the interaction of work and nonwork aspects of life.[51] Sterns and Patchett[52] and Patchett and Sterns[53] have attempted to develop and refine a model of adult and older adult career development that is not age-specific.[54] The model assumes that transition in work life may occur many times throughout a career. It shows that the decision to change jobs or careers or to exit the system is directly influenced by attitudes toward mobility and success or failure in previous career development activities. Numerous factors are hypothesized to affect mobility attitudes, such as employment, career stage or tenure, growth need, fear of stagnation, marketability perceptions, job market conditions, and chance encounters. The decision to change jobs or careers may also affect one's attitudes toward entering or reentering the workforce. The effects of various personality variables could also mediate any of these variables. The model incorporates Hall's model of career growth.[55]

In the 1990s

Hall[56] revisited his goal-setting career model in 1996 with a popular book entitled *The Career Is Dead: Long Live the Career.* Based on his 1970s' goal-setting perspective, he emphasized the importance for people to now manage their own careers. This represents a clear turning point, as previously it had been the organization that directed increases in responsibility and growth through training. Career growth and development were no longer confined to the context of the employing organization. To represent this shift in responsibility to individual workers, we now use the term "self-management" of careers.

Two schools of thought characterize this new approach to career development. In the context of Hall and Mirvis' protean career model, Hall now looks at advancing one's career by moving between as well as within organizations. Loyalty is to oneself, and the opportunities are provided by the industry as a whole, not just by a single employer.

The other school of thought, represented by Sterns' self-management model,[57] emphasizes training and the acquisition of new skills through formal education, short-term training, and self-directed study. While early career theory assumed that key career decisions were made early in life, and models from the 1970s called attention to additional career decisions taken in midlife, Sterns's model recognizes that these decisions are taken throughout the lifespan. People are not bound to any particular track, as they can change employers, re-enter school, learn new skills, or change careers at any point in their working lives. These decisions are influenced by a variety of factors, including technological change, evolving interests, or unexpected opportunities.

In the self-management model, people engage in career planning and goal-setting, leading to the necessary training and updating to not only maintain currency but also to set the stage for new employment opportunities. If employers do not provide those opportunities, then outside training must be sought. This could be formal (e.g., through colleges, universities, or computer training centers) or informal (e.g., subscriptions to journals or technical publications). Training offered by organizations tends to focus only on skills that benefit the company, while outside training tends to focus on developing the individual in a broader sense. According to the self-management model, people are likely to be ready to change careers or retire when their interest in updating skills declines.

LOOKING TO THE FUTURE

Early in the twenty-first century, we find career development still in a state of flux, while the gap between theoretical models, empirical research, and practical application remains wide. We have made great progress in recognizing the cyclical nature of career development and have begun to understand the implications of a dynamic model of career development. However, much remains to be done. There is a great need for career development theories that are valid, have utility in practice, and take into account the recent changes that have occurred in the workplace. It is our belief that the concept of self-management has great potential for this purpose. To further refine this concept, the relationship between individual career decisions and their effects on the individual, on groups within the organization, and on organizations as a whole must be better understood. The environment in which career decisions are made (external factors) and the intrinsic elements that contribute to the individual's awareness and motivation (internal factors) must be better conceptualized, measured empirically, and tested to determine the utility and validity of emerging career development theory. Before presenting recommendations for future research and practice, we present a synthesis of career development research: What have we learned?

External Factors

As Sterns and Sterns have emphasized,[58] the organization that employs the older adult contributes in important ways to the desire of that worker to engage in career development activities such as training.[59, 60] Because organizational factors are outside the individual, they are referred to as external factors.

1. *Opportunities for training.* Training opportunities are very different in the twenty-first century, with many new training modalities available through dramatic advances in networking and multimedia technologies. However, at least in the near term, older workers may be given fewer opportunities to train because they are likely to have greater responsibilities than younger workers and may not be given time or encouragement to continue to update skills. When given the opportunity to participate in self-paced modes of instruction, they have excellent mastery of material.
2. *Flexibility.* Employees must feel free to approach their managers with new ideas and be encouraged to discuss, pursue, and apply them. This does not suggest a radical and global change every time an employee has an idea, but creating an environment that is flexible enough to discuss new ideas and to invest resources in learning about and trying new ideas. A flexible managerial style will encourage older and younger workers alike to learn about, develop, and implement conceptual and mechanical tools to improve performance, productivity, and profitability.[61]

3. *Reward systems.* A reward system is necessary to encourage training behavior. An organization must provide release time for updating skills.[62] This is especially important for middle- and higher-level managers, as their large staffs and time-consuming responsibilities often leave them little time to train and update skills. Training periods often allow additional benefits by giving managers time to associate with peers and to exchange ideas and get expert feedback outside of a formal office setting.
4. *Challenging work.* This is another key external factor.[63] A work situation of this nature provides intrinsic motivation for employees to seek out new strategies and tools to accomplish assignments. This in turn leads them to embrace their work and enjoy the endeavor and the success.
5. *Differences in organizational level.* Personnel at different levels of the organization will have different training needs.[64, 65] This applies not only to the skills they will be trained in, but also the techniques used for the training. Older workers who have been out of school for long periods of time (and tend to be at higher levels in organizations) tend to respond better to training that involves case studies and discussion and active learning.

In sum, opportunities for training, the nature of the work, flexibility, reward systems, and organization level all have an impact on career development behavior. While organizations and jobs vary widely along each of these parameters, individual workers must navigate these opportunities and manage their career growth. Not surprisingly, then, internal factors (those intrinsic to the individual) also have a significant impact on career development behavior.

Internal Factors

In previous sections, several personality traits have already been presented, such as locus of control and need for achievement. Besides traits, attitudes also contribute to the desire to continue to work and to maintain the skills required to excel. These attitudes have been researched under the topic of organizational commitment.

Organizational commitment is a process of identification with the goals of an organization's multiple constituencies.[66] Randall[67] speculated that commitment is an inverted-U function with the apex at a moderate commitment level. A healthy level of organizational commitment allows the balancing of work-related and personal responsibilities. Low levels of commitment generally are detrimental to both individual and organization. High levels are good for the organization, but hurt the individual's other responsibilities.

Meyer and Allen[68] distinguish between two dimensions of organizational commitment: continuance commitment and affective commitment. Continuance commitment is the perceived cost of leaving, exacerbated by a perceived lack of alternatives to replace or make up foregone investments. The longer one remains with an organization, the more "side bets"[69] one is likely to have. Examples of such side bets are social networks, organizations, clubs, and participation in family-related activities. Vacation time, investing in retirement plans, and seniority-related perks are other examples. Clearly, side bets are important to older workers and their families and represent a major determinant for their continuance commitment.

Affective commitment is the emotional orientation to the organization and can be seen in two ways. One focuses on the attributions that are made to maintain consistency between one's behavior and attitudes. Simply becoming a member of an organization creates an affective commitment. The longer the tenure with that organization, the more likely it is for the worker's identity to become tied to that membership. While less common today than in the past, individuals can still work for many years for the same company. In the case of small business, it is also likely that commitment will be even stronger since the business is likely to dominate a person's time and attention.

The other version of affective commitment defines it as the congruence between individual and organizational goals. Commitment is strongest when workers identify with and extend efforts toward organizational goals and values. As workers increase their tenure with an organization, they may feel increasing continuance commitment because they have established a home and friendships in the area; they have become specialized in a skill that they feel cannot be transferred, or they feel they could not get the same benefits if they moved to a new organization. On the other hand, affective commitment gives the employee an emotional tie to the organization that motivates him or her to remain, not because he or she cannot afford to leave, but because he or she feels a sense of contribution and growth from and with the organization.

Organizational commitment has proven useful in predicting job performance, and its role should be expanded in future career development models.[70] Organizational commitment is driven to some extent by organizational characteristics (external factors). Organizations that encourage maintaining and improving the skills required to excel and provide challenging work and the opportunity to inject new ideas will have employees with higher affective commitment, leading to reduced turnover and increased productivity. An organization can measure the success of its efforts by examining organizational-based self-esteem (OBSE).

OBSE has been operationalized as the degree to which organizational members believe they could satisfy their needs through their participation within the organizational context. Matheson[71] explored age-related differences between OBSE and other work satisfaction and commitment measures and found that age was significantly and positively related to organizational satisfaction, continuance commitment, and self-esteem. However, after controlling for job and organizational tenure, two variables that have been found to co-vary with age, only self-esteem was significantly associated with age. Employees over age 50 had significantly higher self-esteem than did younger age groups. Employees who perceived that they are valuable as organizational members were more satisfied with their jobs and organizations, more committed to the organization (in terms of both affective and continuance commitment), and less likely to leave. These finding show the importance of understanding employees' perceptions and interpretations of organizational policies, procedures, and culture.

RECOMMENDATIONS

Again drawing on the earlier discussion of Sterns and Sterns,[72] regardless of whether the organization is large or small, the message of self-management must be emphasized from the earliest career interest programs and continuously throughout the career. This task is likely to become easier with increasing resources available online in both free and subscriber forms. Accelerating technologies and increasingly portable, flexible, and multifunctional electronic tools available to individuals make this job easier and more challenging at the same time.

Self-management does not absolve employers from their responsibility for career development. The following recommendations for human resources practitioners and career development practitioners may help them take that responsibility:

- Spread the message of career self-management. Educate employees on the new workplace and its consequences for career development activities.
- Concurrently, support employees in their self-management efforts by collecting and disseminating information about training opportunities and resources inside and outside of the organization.
- Examine training policies, procedures, and practices that could be discriminatory in their impact on specific populations, particularly aging workers. Since all employees age 40 and up are protected by the Age Discrimination in Employment Act, there is a real business imperative to do this.
- Train both managers and employees on training: Ageist stereotypes are so pervasive that older workers themselves may have internalized that stereotype, which would prevent them from participating in training. Management needs to take responsibility for educating older workers on their own ability to learn, and in the process, they need to become sensitized to how these stereotypes manifest themselves. Such sensitivity trainings could easily be expanded to include race, gender, and ethnicity.
- Adjust reward systems to reflect a commitment to career development. Hold employees accountable for managing their own development efforts (for example, through individual development plans, which can be seen as an official agreement between employer and employee) while holding managers accountable for their employees' training utilization rates. Policies that do not reward older workers for acquiring new skills may actually encourage retirement by not using these productive workers.
- Maintain an appropriate balance between routine tasks and challenges in all jobs at all levels. Consider drawing on mentoring programs, cross-training, temporary assignments elsewhere, sab-

baticals, or any other program that might stimulate learning and development.

FUTURE DIRECTIONS

Much work is needed to better understand the position of older workers, their perceptions of their careers, and how these perceptions affect their self-management behaviors. Many factors involved in the career self-management process have been identified, but we need to better understand the processes affecting when and how these factors act and interact to affect the career self-management behaviors of the individual.

Recent statistics suggest that far more midlife and older workers are participating in development activities than has been previously believed. This may be due to either actual increased involvement or changes in the nature of the measurement of these activities.[73] There is evidence that workers aged 50+ are over *two times* more likely to be involved in credentialing programs and more job or career-focused courses than younger workers. We need to better understand who is updating and why. We need to identify what are cohort effects and what changes are due to perceptions of change in the nature of employment.

In order to be able to recommend approaches for encouraging and supporting career self-management, we need to better understand underlying processes, and employers and trainers alike need to better understand how existing programs work, such as phased retirement and proposed changes to Social Security. Information available to us from a wide variety of disciplines needs to be better integrated within and across research to gain a broader and more complete picture of the knowledge currently available about career change and development among older workers.

This knowledge needs to be condensed to suggest useful interventions in career self-management and development activities. Field studies of interventions and suggestions for improving older workers' self-efficacy for learning and development are necessary to examine their viability in the organizational environment, as well as unexpected factors at play in our ability to successfully implement them.

We have reviewed the factors that contribute to the need for continuous skill development and self-management of careers across the lifespan. No matter what age, updating is valuable to the organization and the individual employee. Changes in organizations and the nature of work make it necessary for individuals to take responsibility to ensure that their own skills stay up to date and that they are ready when those changes directly affect their employment situation. While we have information on many factors involved in updating, training, and career management, much of the research is disjointed and requires integration. We need to take what we know about individual and organizational factors and develop and test interventions to increase the value of midlife and older workers.

SUMMARY

The first career development theories, hailing back to the 1950s but still influential today, were characterized by an assumption of a linear career progression through time, culminating in stages of maintenance and decline when retirement age approached. The 1970s and 1980s yielded increased recognition that career behavior is essentially cyclical in nature, regardless of age. The layoffs, mergers, takeovers, and downsizing efforts all underscored the realization that lifetime employment was no longer feasible and that older workers are as much in need of career development as younger ones are. The 1990s embraced the new workplace reality, placing the responsibility for career development primarily with the individual employee. This was called the protean career or career self-management.

It is imperative that more research be conducted to more fully understand career self-management behavior, particularly for older workers. Future career development models must incorporate and quantify external and internal factors that predict career development behavior. The ultimate goal of career development should be to contribute to maximizing the potential of all workers—regardless of age, gender, race, or ethnicity—as they negotiate their careers.

And employers have much that they can do to recruit, retain, and manage older workers. Employers would be well advised to plan carefully for doing that. Use the tools and information appearing in Figures 6–11, 6–12, 6–13 and 6–14 to plan for taking action.

FIGURE 6–11

A Worksheet for Overcoming Barriers to the Recruitment of Older Workers

Directions: For each possible barrier to recruiting older workers listed in the left column below, indicate in the right column possible action strategies that your organization might use to overcome them.

Barriers to Recruiting Older Workers	What Action Strategies Could Your Organization Take to Overcome the Barriers?
1. Attitudes about age prevailing in the organization are unfavorable to older workers	
2. *Nonlinear career paths:* Older workers may not have career paths that conform to management expectations	
3. *Surplus experience:* Older workers may have experience that justifies a higher position than they are applying for, and this creates skepticism about the willingness of the candidate to stay with the job if offered	
4. *Giving older workers little "benefit of the doubt":* Hiring managers make snap judgments about people during selection interviews based on appearance	
5. *Short-term hiring strategies:* The organization selects for immediate needs, ignoring an individual's long-term potential to develop	

Source: This list is taken from Katherine L. Y. Green, Ph.D., and Andrea Hodson, SPHR, "The recruiting challenge: What do *you* know about older workers?" Downloaded from www.shrm.org/diversity/library_published/nonIC/CMS_012885.asp on 11 March 2007.

FIGURE 6–12

A Worksheet for Improving Employment Practices
for Older Workers

Directions: For each desirable practice in the left column below, indicate in the right column possible action strategies that your organization might use to ensure that those practices are used.

Desirable Practice	What Action Strategies Might Your Organization Take to Improve on Current Practices?
The organization sets out to:	
1. Recruit older workers	
2. Tap and draw on the retiree base when needed for short-term and long-term employment or consulting services	
3. Train workers on job interviewing techniques or other selection practices that do not discriminate overly or covertly against older workers	
4. Provide onboarding and orientation experiences geared to the unique needs of older workers	
5. Demonstrate sensitivity to older workers when delivering training without appearing to underscore how sight, hearing, or other senses may change with age	
6. Leverage the work or life experiences of older workers by positioning them in ways that they can mentor others	
7. Train managers to treat workers fairly regardless of age	

(continued)

FIGURE 6–12 (CONTINUED)

Desirable Practice	What Action Strategies Might Your Organization Take to Improve on Current Practices?
The organization sets out to:	
8. Apply innovative policies that show sensitivity to the needs of older workers in dealing with matters of leave	
9. Monitor turnover of older workers, looking for any unfortunate trends that may need to be addressed by the organization	
10. Other (*list and describe it*)	

FIGURE 6–13

AARP Honor Roll: Diverse Group of Employers Use Flexible Work Options to Retain 50-Plus Workers
By Lydell C. Bridgeford

Martha Cyr had never heard of AARP's list of best employers for older workers until the day an employee told the vice president of human resources at L.L. Bean, Inc. about the list.

"Gee . . . you do great things," when it comes older workers, Cyr recalls the worker saying.

So in 2005, the 94-year-old company decided to submit an application to AARP, an advocacy group for older Americans, for its 2006 Best Employers for Workers over 50 competition. Not only did the mail-order and retail outfit make the 2006 list on its first try (it's ranked No. 42 on a list of 50), but it's also the first time a Maine-based business has won such an honor, Cyr points out.

The New England operation employs about 4,000 year-round workers with 36% over the age of 50. Its main store, located in Freeport, Maine, is open 24 hours a day, seven days a week, as well as its call center.

"As an organization, we have lots of programs that support all ages of workers, including senior workers. Our part-time schedules with flexible hours fit very well with senior workers, who don't want to work full-time," Cyr explains. Seasonal workers, many of whom are older workers, can also enroll into the company's 401(k) plan and receive deep discounts on clothes and outdoor equipment.

During the Christmas season, the retailer sees its fair share of older workers. But Cyr also points out that an influx of retirees come to Maine for the summer. The company's flexible work schedules are attractive to retirees who want to earn some extra money over the summer.

Making the List
To capture and retain older workers, employers will have to offer flexible work options and benefits. As AARP's CEO Bill Novelli points out about the companies on the list, "These dynamic employers recognize the importance of creating a mutually beneficial work environment. Flexible arrangements can be a big part of that positive environment, enabling workers to balance both work and family obligations."

Now in its sixth year, AARP's Best Employers for Workers over 50 includes 50 organizations from a cross-section of industries, but hospitals and health-care facilities make up nearly half of the winners.

Source: Lydell C. Bridgeford (2006, November 1). "AARP Honor Roll: Diverse group of employers use flexible work options to retain 50-plus workers." *Employee Benefit News*, 1. Copyright by Thomson Media. All rights reserved. Used by permission.

(continued)

Companies vying for a spot on the list must complete and submit a questionnaire that is then reviewed and scored by a panel of judges. Both outside experts and AARP representatives examine each employer's answers and conduct a background investigation into the company, focusing on recruitment practices, age discrimination record, flexible work options, and benefits offerings to current and retired workers.

Topping the list as the nation's best employer for older workers is Mercy Health System of Janesville, WI. The healthcare provider, which was ranked No. 11 last year, runs three hospitals and over 50 outpatient clinics and other healthcare facilities.

The not-for-profit organization employs 3,500 people in southern Wisconsin and northern Illinois with about 28% of them 50 or older. AARP praised Mercy because it offers many flexible work options, such as weekend-only schedules, telecommuting, sabbaticals with benefits, and on-call assignments.

Cornell University, which has a workforce of 9,000 to 11,000, was chosen because of its recruitment strategies, flexible work options, and educational and learning opportunities, which include employees taking courses at a discounted rate or for free, says Lynette Chappell-Williams, director of workforce diversity, equity and life quality at Cornell University in Ithaca, New York.

At the Ivy Leaguer, 18% of the nonacademic staff is 55 and over, while 44% of faculty and 30% of the staff have 15 years of experience.

"Since 2000, we have been aggressively working to identify programs and services that address the diversity of our workforce, including our older workers," Chappell-Williams explains. "There have been a number of targeted efforts, whether it's in terms of providing long-term care or workshops on preparing employees for retirement" that the university utilizes to retain and attract older workers.

In 2005, the university was ranked No. 5, but fell this year to No. 32. "We attribute it to the fact that more organizations are becoming aware of this valuable segment of the population. It's a reminder that we need to stay on the ball," says Chappell-Williams.

"We are definitely seeing more companies applying to get on the list, which changes the competitiveness of it," says Deborah Russell, director of workforce issues at AARP.

Still, the healthcare industry dominates the list because of its current labor shortage, especially with nursing, which means the industry has to actively and creatively look for ways to retain and lengthen the amount of time its current workforce might consider staying in the workplace. Moreover, industry is always creating new measures to recruit retired workers back into the workforce.

Prescription Drugs Matter

Meanwhile, more organizations are reevaluating their policies and practices to meet the needs of workers 50 and older.

"We are seeing evidence of employers making retiree medical benefits more affordable, even though Medicare has made some improvement—particularly with the prescription drug provision—it still does not cover a lot and prescription drugs are expensive," says AARP's Russell. Retirees and employees, especially those on prescriptions, see it as a tremendous benefit to have an employer who can offset the cost through an insurance company.

"Some employers are looking for ways that they can try to help offset those costs without it still being a big financial liability for the employers," observers Russell, citing California-based Scripps Health (No. 13) as an example of an employer who addresses retiree medical health costs.

"We offer a retiree medical benefit that includes prescription drugs," says Cyr at L.L. Bean. "In fact, our people have not even gone to the Medicare Part D because our drug plan is so good."

Recently, AARP teamed up with HR consulting firm Towers Perrin to look into building a business case for employers as to why they should consider 50-plus workers. Russell points out employers continue to perceive the cost of older workers as not affordable.

"We look at the areas of healthcare, benefits, and paid time off, focusing on labor costs and the older worker. Clearly with healthcare, older workers are slightly more expensive," Russell notes. "However, if you look at the cost holistically, turnover and engagement, there are some off-setting costs there.

"It may be a better deal to look at a strategy that includes older workers rather than dismissing the opportunity that you might have there, especially given the future demographics of few younger workers," she says.

FIGURE 6–14

A Worksheet to Foster Experience Sharing

Directions: Older workers have much life and work experience. On occasion it is worthwhile to tap that experience, if relevant, to mentor younger workers or those with less experience. One powerful way to do that is through the critical incident method. Ask older workers to complete the questions below and then share them over a brown bag lunch or in other venues as appropriate to foster experience sharing.

1. Tell me a story about a time when you experienced the single most difficult situation in your work life. Describe as completely as you can what happened.
   Write your notes here:

2. When did this happen? How recent was it?
   Write your notes here:

3. What did you do in the situation, and what happened as a result of what you did?
   Write your notes here:

4. What made the situation so difficult?
   Write your notes here:

5. If you faced this situation again, what would you do? Would you handle it exactly the way you did, or would you use another approach? Explain why. Then try to summarize the key points about what you learned from experience in the situation.
   Write your notes here:

III | MANAGING ORGANIZATIONAL KNOWLEDGE

7 | WHAT EMPLOYERS CAN DO TO PLAN FOR AN AGING WORKFORCE

In Chapter 1 we asserted that it is important for U.S. businesses to address the issues of the aging of our nation's workforce. This chapter is a roadmap for successfully working with an aging workforce. It is addressed to human resources professionals and human capital planners. It is important because employers—both public and private sector, profit and nonprofit—who are not successful with their aging workforce will likely struggle to maintain a qualified, competitive workforce. We have made this discussion as practical as possible in light of the fact that although many organizations are becoming aware of the issues, few have developed an approach for dealing with them.[1]

First, we will define the workforce of the future that employers are likely to have to deal with. Then we will lay out actions that employers can take at various stages of an employee's career. A range of actions is suggested, taking into account the size of the organization and the level of resources available to the employer to address the issue.

THE EVOLVING WORKPLACE

A number of the trends in the workplace are evident. The challenge for managers and trainers is to know what to do about them given the uniqueness of their business situation and the direction of the trends.

There is a wide range of predictions regarding the impact of the aging of the U.S. population on the aging of the workforce. As mentioned in Chapter 1, U.S. Comptroller and Director of the Government Accountability Office (GAO) David Walker summarized the long-range implications for the nation's economy at the 2005 White Conference on Aging and argued that the economy needs older workers.

As shown in Figure 7–1, growth in the U.S. workforce has been declining since the mid-1970s and is predicted to steadily decline over the next several decades. This fact, together with the fact that twice as many of those in the workforce will be age 55 or over compared to those in the core workforce age group of 25 to 54, will redefine the way employers look at older workers in the near future.

Concomitantly, the costs of entitlement programs are increasing and are one significant component of government costs projected to far exceed revenues. (See Figure 7–2.)

Walker declared that current fiscal policy is "unsustainable," pointing out that "real annual economic growth in the double digit range every year for the next 75 years"[2] would be required.

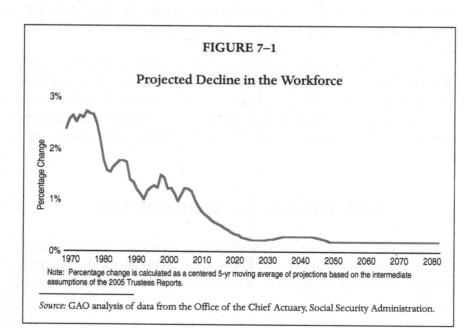

FIGURE 7–1

Projected Decline in the Workforce

Note: Percentage change is calculated as a centered 5-yr moving average of projections based on the intermediate assumptions of the 2005 Trustees Reports.

Source: GAO analysis of data from the Office of the Chief Actuary, Social Security Administration.

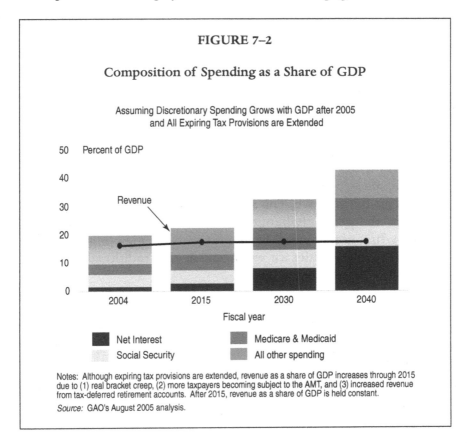

FIGURE 7–2

Composition of Spending as a Share of GDP

Assuming Discretionary Spending Grows with GDP after 2005
and All Expiring Tax Provisions are Extended

Notes: Although expiring tax provisions are extended, revenue as a share of GDP increases through 2015 due to (1) real bracket creep, (2) more taxpayers becoming subject to the AMT, and (3) increased revenue from tax-deferred retirement accounts. After 2015, revenue as a share of GDP is held constant.

Source: GAO's August 2005 analysis.

One question Walker posed at the White House in 2005 was this: How can existing policies and programs be reformed to encourage older workers to work longer? Their working longer would impact the economy (size of the workforce and thereby economic growth), the federal budget (tax revenues and ameliorated entitlement expenditures), and the workers themselves (enhanced financial security and quality of life). Clearly, organizations will be required to become adept at attracting, retaining, developing, and sustaining older workers.

Economist Martin Sicker[3] commented as follows about the present and future workforce:

- Job tenure of middle-aged men declined sharply from 15.3 years to 10.5 years for workers 55 to 63 over the thirteen-year period between 1983 and 1996.

- Because of the decoupling of labor from productivity due to factors like globalization, technology may well result in significantly diminished high-wage employment opportunities.
- The nonstandard workforce will grow substantially. During the period 1980 through 1996 this group grew between 9.9 and 22 percent faster than general employment figures.
- As Robert Reich has noted, "The most important part of the [employment] contract is that if the worker is diligent and reliable, and if the company is making money, that worker keeps his or her job. The second principle is enjoying rising wages and benefits as a company's profits improve. This social contract is not longer with us."
- One of the great challenges that will confront society in the twenty-first century will be the creation of meaningful and rewarding opportunities for work outside the traditional economic framework of employment.
- We are moving from a production-based industrial economy to an information-based network economy. And, as a result, the principles that have governed both business and society for the past two hundred years are becoming obsolete.
- Thirty years ago, new entrants to the labor force typically had higher levels of education than the older workers who were retiring. That is no longer true. . . . Improvements in skills sought by employers will have to come primarily through investment in the human capital of existing workers (p. 18).
- Small businesses provide the jobs—56.6 percent in businesses of fewer than 100 employees, and 82.2 percent in businesses of fewer than 500.

GETTING AHEAD OF THE TRENDS

Individual industries and even individual companies must determine their own workable responses to these issues. For our purposes here, we have simply categorized some of the initiatives along the lines of those provided in Figure 7–3. The difference between columns (business size) is the time and money that might be needed to implement the initiatives. The activities in the small business plan are those that almost all organizations can implement. They take a minimum of

FIGURE 7–3

Employer's Guide for Workforce Planning

Retire the worker and retain the knowledge	Small employers	Mid-size employers	Large employers
Assess your organization's situation			
Attract and recruit older workers			
Retain and sustain older workers			

time and funding but will increase management attention to the issues that may be facing the organization.

The large business initiatives are appropriate for organizations with large workforces and the need, and the resources, to invest in more extensive assessments of their workforces and in the development of human capital, skill, and knowledge management. In the following section, we describe how to carry out the initiatives according to the business size.

Small Business Initiatives

ASSESS YOUR ORGANIZATION'S SITUATION

One of the most basic steps an employer can take is to assess the "older worker friendliness" of the organization. There are two sources to help you do this. You will find the "Older Worker Friendly Employer Assessment Tool" on the Wisconsin State website: www.wisconsin.gov/olderworker/pdf/OW_Assess_Tool2.pdf. AARP offers an employer's checklist on its website: www.aarp.org/ money/ careers/findingajob/readytosearch/a2004-04-08-careers-clues.html.

These simple assessment tools can stimulate some thinking about what the issues are for your organization and help its leaders begin to look at older workers and the importance of their continued contribution to business success.

ATTRACT AND RECRUIT OLDER WORKERS

One of the most basic issues is the attitude of recruiting staff and hiring managers toward older workers. There are a number of deeply ingrained myths about older workers that can be addressed head-on. Neil Charness of Florida State University provided an overview of this issue at the conference "Maximizing Your Workforce" in November 2004, sponsored by the Wharton School and AARP, and offered the following background:

- Productivity: A meta-analysis of 100 studies of worker productivity showed that "there is no significant relationship between job productivity and the age of the worker."
- Absenteeism: In a similar study it was found that "younger workers have more avoidable and involuntary absenteeism than older workers."

- Turnover: "Job change rates are generally much lower for older than younger workers."
- Job-related injury: "The trend is for fewer injuries with age, though more costly ones that keep older workers off the job longer."
- Speed: "There is a general slowing with age . . . [however] despite slowing in reaction time, older typists type at the same rate as younger ones." (They train themselves to look farther ahead in the text as they type.) Also, the Days Inn study showed that "older sales reps handled calls more slowly, [but] they had higher booking rates for rooms."[4]

Technology is often cited as an area in which older workers lag behind, but according to the Houston-based "Media Audit data, [the percentage of] the 55 to 64 age classification . . . who access the Internet regularly increased from 45.8 percent in 2000 to 56.7 percent in 2003. . . . 65 to 74 year olds who access the Internet regularly increased from 26.2 percent to 35.9 percent."[5]

"Contrary to the popular belief that older Internet users were taught how to use the Net by their children or grandchildren, SeniorNet finds that 76 percent [of older persons] say they taught themselves. Another 37 percent say they took a class to learn and just 30 percent say they got help from a relative."[6]

RETAIN AND SUSTAIN OLDER WORKERS

There are also some very basic steps that can be taken to improve retention. Consider Barbara McIntosh's *An Employer's Guide to Older Workers: How to Win Them Back and Convince Them to Stay* available on this website: www.doleta.gov/Seniors/other_docs/EmplGuide.doc. McIntosh especially addresses the need to attract retiring members of the baby boom generation back to work and to retain them.

In its report "Staying Ahead of the Curve 2004," AARP identified some relatively straightforward benefits practices used to support retention efforts. These include:

- Providing 401(k) "catch-up" contributions [AARP's Fall 2006 survey].
- Ensuring that employees are aware of their options for caring for family members under the Family Medical Leave Act (FMLA).

- Establish leave banks to allow employees to donate some of their leave to others who need it.
- Providing personal telephone accounts to permit calls for long-distance elder-care.
- Following the lead of Volkswagen of America, which provides Flexible Spending Accounts that include Elder Care expenses.[7]

There are also some basic management issues to keep in mind. As pointed out by The Conference Board's Dr. Linda Barrington at the Wharton conference on Maximizing Your Workforce: Employees Over 50 in Today's Global Economy in November 2004, "employers will find it more difficult than expected to manage a three- or four-generation workforce that is increasingly diverse and progressively more global."[8] Supervisors and managers will need to be reminded to:

- Communicate.
- Show respect.
- Ask for feedback.
- Acknowledge contributions.
- Promote continuous learning/training.
- Be flexible.
- Recognize the inclination to want to be a team player (more than younger workers).
- Handle conflicts openly.
- Look for negotiated Win-Wins.
- Be culturally, chronologically, sexually, professionally, intergenerationally, and politically sensitive and aware.

A very simple and direct approach to carry out these guidelines is to simply ensure that older workers are given an equal opportunity for training. A Hay Group study showed that "the opportunity to learn new skills is directly linked to how long employees plan to stay with their companies."[9]

There are some powerful messages in the cartoon in Figure 7–4: the impact of technology on the workplace and on the actual work we do each day, the need for continuous training, the need to be aware of the concerns our employees have about the changes in the

FIGURE 7–4

The Impact of Technology on the Workplace

By permission of John L. Hart FLP and Creators Syndicate, Inc.

workplace, and the need for employers and employees to anticipate those changes.

Additionally, when training older workers, keep in mind the training issues for older learners, using these training techniques and principles:

- Do not rush.
- Connect new material to existing knowledge.
- Solicit connections between new material and past experience; provide the rationale for how the material relates to making a difference on the job.
- Use contrasting colors on PowerPoint figures (avoid red lettering).
- Remember that "age alone does not account for obsolescence of knowledge, skills, or abilities"; rather, obsolescence can be frequently attributed to the failure of companies to provide continuing education to mature workers.[10]
- Remember that, while older adults may take longer to learn, they are more accurate once they have learned the skill.
- Also, ensure that diversity training activities include the issue of age diversity.

RETIRE THE WORKER AND RETAIN THE KNOWLEDGE

William J. Rothwell at The Pennsylvania State University points out that: "Succession planning to most . . . means executive replacement planning. But succession planning actually means far more than that. It is not just about finding replacements. It is also about developing talent and building sufficient bench strength and preserving the organization's institutional memory as embodied in the heads of veteran performers *at all levels*. . . . This has to do with technical succession planning." In the first reference in the matrix sheet, Rothwell provides a "Checklist for Assessing Agency Technical Succession Planning."[11]

As examples given by Rothwell:[12]

> The Pennsylvania Department of Transportation employs 12,000 people. It uses a Position Analysis Workbook (PAW) process to help capture tacit knowledge from "best-in-class" performers and transmit it to others through a formal training course, on-the-job training, and cross-training activities. (p. 412)

The U.S. Postal Service has introduced an innovation in its succession planning procedures. The Postal Service is unveiling a new corporate succession planning process. The innovation is that it invites employees to nominate themselves for higher level positions. Part of the rationale for the program is that we often eliminate very competent and dedicated employees simply because they have become a part of the fabric of a specific department and, on paper, lack some key element (like a college degree) that has made it difficult for them to be considered for more responsibility. The self-nomination process is open to all and lays out the process for them to make a case for their being considered for a position at higher levels of responsibility.

Mid-Size Business Initiatives

ASSESS YOUR ORGANIZATION'S SITUATION

In the last section, we mentioned doing a basic assessment of your situation using the Wisconsin assessment. However, a number of other questions need to be answered to get a better understanding of the potential knowledge loss you face with older workers retiring, and the attitudes of your managers and employees regarding this issue. For example:

- What production/product quality issues in the organization are you experiencing?
- Do managers already have a feel for who might be retiring and what special knowledge might be lost when they go?
- How does the human resources staff approach interviews with older applicants?
- Is there evidence in your organization that there is age bias at work in hiring, training, or promotions?
- How does your training department approach the training of older learners?
- What is the opinion of the organization held by your older employees?
- Why are your older workers opting for retirement—to pursue a personal dream, to volunteer or contribute to society, because they do not feel respected by their employer, or because their financial goals have been met?
- What interests does each knowledge-rich older worker have that can be used as an incentive to stay involved with the organization?

Some of this assessment involves conducting in-depth surveys. When carrying out employee studies of this kind, there are several factors to consider. Any survey of employees must be done with care. This is especially true when dealing with retirement and older worker issues. In *Lost Knowledge: Confronting the Threat of an Aging Workforce,* David DeLong recounts the experience of the Tennessee Valley Authority with surveys. When it began surveying its staff in 1999, only about 50 percent participated. But "TVA employees have increasingly recognized that their personal responses about retirement plans were only being used to drive workforce planning and not to make individual personnel decisions. As a result, response to the annual e-mail survey has increased to 80 percent."[13]

Conducting surveys or at least holding focus groups can be important tools for assessing the workforce. But they must be done with great care because both the intent and the appearance of the

intent must be for the good of the employee as well as for the employer.

ATTRACT AND RECRUIT OLDER WORKERS

We spoke earlier about biases toward older workers. One of the places in which biases get translated into practice is in the recruiting process. So it is important to review recruiting and advertising materials to ensure that the images and language that are used in your materials are not biased against older applicants.

Do your materials make the applicant think the employer wants a younger person—lively, ambitious, bright, upbeat, energetic? When an employment ad uses words like mature, dependable, responsible, reliable, experienced, is the employer looking for an older person?

Consider these ads that were recently placed on an online jobs website.

Position advertisement 1

Energetic take-charge person with excellent communication skills

Post all month-end journal entries and closing

Produce month-end management reports

Cash flow analysis

Preparation of financial statements

Payroll management

Proficiency in Excel a must

Bachelor's degree in accounting or finance

Minimum of 5 years experience

Ability to demonstrate good judgment and exercise discretion and confidentiality pertaining to the work environment a must.

Position advertisement 2

One of the city's best public companies to work for needs an experienced, dependable Payroll Clerk. Excellent working conditions, great benefits, and convenient location. Will produce paychecks for about 1000 people, update computer files, and perform other payroll functions. Super opportunity to take your payroll experience to the next level and have future career opportunities based on your hard work.

In its September 3, 2003, testimony before the U.S. Senate Special Committee on Aging, the Society for Human Resource Management reported that the most commonly used strategies for recruiting older workers was through employee referrals and networking. This being the case, employers might save some recruiting funds by reallocating advertising expenses to incentives for referrals from employees.[14]

RETAIN AND SUSTAIN OLDER WORKERS

Most organizations would be well advised to review their policies and practices to ensure that there is no implicit or explicit age bias. On March 30, 2005, the Supreme Court rendered a major decision on age bias. The long-term effect of the decision, *Smith v. City of Jackson, Miss.*, will be to elevate age discrimination legally to nearer the level of race or gender bias.

If claimants can tell a story with statistics, they no longer need to have a "smoking gun," such as a memo showing hostility toward older workers, to persuade a judge to move their case to the evidence-gathering phase. There was one such front-page story in the May 2005 issue of *AARP Bulletin*.[15]

A policy review should identify both biases and disincentives that need to be eliminated as well as policies and practices that will serve as incentives for retaining the talent needed to be remain competitive.

In the Committee for Economic Opportunity's 1999 landmark study, "New Opportunities for Older Workers," they discuss physical and financial barriers. Pension plans can strongly discourage continued working. Even Social Security may be an issue in this regard. "One of the goals of the program at its inception was to draw older workers out of the work force in order to make jobs available to younger workers." Further regarding private sector plans, "For workers participating in defined benefits plans, the disincentive to work after the age of earliest eligibility—typically age 60, but as young as age 55—can be great. A survey of 1,000 pension plans showed that continued work after early retirement eligibility typically reduced the lifetime value of the pension by the equivalent of a 30 percent pay cut."[16]

Incentives to remain in the workforce include:

- Flexibility in benefits, working arrangements, work schedules, compensation (deferred salary).
- Benefits—health, dental, family coverage, vacations.

Some of these benefits cost money, and their flexible administration can cost money. However, it is important to do the homework. For example, there is evidence that "for every $1 companies spend helping employees care for aging family members, they save $3 to $5 in productivity."[17]

The Wharton study[18] suggests:

- Continue to offer defined benefit plans.
- Pare early retirement subsidies.
- Adjust health benefits.
- Introduce work-life programs.
- Institute eldercare: "employer provided eldercare assistance programs increase the average retirement age of men by eight months."
- Phased retirement programs increase the average retirement age among women by 21 months.
- A combination of strategies can extend the retirement age by nearly two years.

You may remember hearing the public service message from the National Institute on Aging featuring the comedian George Burns. When Dr. Gene Cohen of the NIA was interviewing Mr. Burns, he asked, "What does your doctor say about your smoking and drinking?" Burns paused a second and in his inimitable style replied, "My doctor is dead."

We think that Burns didn't have the right answer—he WAS the right answer. He spent his career making people laugh. Dr. Michael Miller's study at the University of Maryland's School of Medicine showed volunteers comedic and dramatic films to gauge the effect of emotions on heart health. In their March 2005 study, the researchers found a medical basis behind the adage that laughter is the best medicine. They linked laughter, for the first time, to the healthy function of blood vessels and emphasized the importance of laughter at all life stages.

We have not learned of a employer program to ensure that employees are getting enough laughs in everyday, but aside from benefits, there are other ways by which employers can enhance their employees' quality of life and retain their workforce. One such innovation is the Happy Returns Program™ that was initiated by the Principal Financial Group (PFG). Through a special arrangement through Manpower Principal Financial, PFG offers retirees the opportunity to come back to work without interruption to their benefits. The program allows them to work on a full-time, part-time, or temporary basis without any adverse impact to their retiree benefits. In many cases this lets the retiree get back to enjoying the trade or profession he or she originally went into without the administration and organizational politics that are a large part of the stress in a job. The program also has benefits for the employer since it can bring back the talent it needs with extensive interviewing and have confidence in having immediate productivity.

The John Deere Company has undergone a dramatic restructuring of its healthcare benefits to refocus on "healthcare" rather than on "sick care." That is, they provide a high deductible health insurance program that has allowed them to redirect savings to cash incentives through having and regularly using health club memberships, smoking cessation, weight loss, cholesterol reduction, and other employee-initiated activities to improve health and reduce health problems. Other possibilities in this health-oriented insurance program include:

- Health risk assessments.
- Prescription coverage.
- Weight-loss/weight-management programs.
- Nutrition counseling.
- Fitness classes.
- Massage.
- Quiet rooms.
- Approaches that recognize that those ages 65 to 74 are more similar in health status to those ages 45 to 64 than to those over 75.

RETIRE THE WORKER AND RETAIN THE KNOWLEDGE

At a conference on workforce trends and issues for environmental organizations and industries, the issue of brain drain in the environmental area was addressed. In a Q&A session dealing with the potential loss of organizational knowledge, a representative of a government agency related the results of an internal study on the effects of their mentoring program. The results were dramatic. They looked at the rate of those leaving who had participated and not participated in the mentoring program. Among their middle managers who did not participate, there was a 20 percent attrition rate. Among those who did participate, the attrition rate was between 1 and 2 percent. This is just one example of how much these programs can have a measurable impact on the bottom line.

Large Business Initiatives

ASSESS YOUR ORGANIZATION'S SITUATION

We introduced the need to do a basic assessment using surveys to get a more in-depth picture of an organization's situation. Some organizations have gone to great lengths to determine exactly what exposure they have regarding potential retirements in their workforce. To share more of the Tennessee Valley Authority approach: The TVA gathered data on retirement projections by skill/knowledge category and managers' estimates of "indispensability" of the people in that category and developed a "knowledge risk factor" to identify the business activities that were at greatest risk. This required a survey of employees followed by individual interviews with employees in critical categories. The interviews were conducted to get a better understanding of a job's specific knowledge content.

There is another aspect to assessing the issue of older workers. It is also necessary that the business community be actively engaged in the national policy discussion in regard to the aging workforce issue. Let's take a look at the projections from the GAO.

We hear a lot of talk about Social Security, debt, and implications for tax policy for the future. Figure 7–2 shows that government spending exceeds revenues and that in twenty-five years interest on the debt will about equal the other large expenditure areas—Social Security, Medicare/Medicaid, and all other government entitlement programs.

Social Security is an issue, but only one issue. We need a national response to the aging of the workforce issue that is comprehensive and complementary. Reforms in Social Security need to be part of changes to:

- Employer-provided pension systems.
- Related social insurance programs (e.g., disability insurance).
- Labor market policies (e.g., retirement age).
- Health and long-term care programs (including shifting the focus to prevention and healthy lifestyles).
- Immigration and off-shoring policy and practice.

Employers and labor representatives need to have a significant voice in the national debate.

ATTRACT AND RECRUIT OLDER WORKERS

The goal of recruiting is to find the person with the right skills, knowledge, and work ethic to make the needed contribution. The recruiting decision should always be made within a context of understanding both the short-term and long-term needs of the organization.

There has been a major effort in recent years to recruit young people to the federal workforce while continuing reductions in force (RIF). However, as pointed out in a Federal Deposit Insurance study,[19]

> But for federal agencies a RIF is a roll of the dice where the final outcomes with regard to skills and experience cannot be accurately predicted. Quite frequently, the employees who are separated are the ones that the agency needs to retain, while the bumping and retreating of employees across the organizational units can result in chaos and disruption that takes years to erase.

RETAIN AND SUSTAIN OLDER WORKERS

Another initiative that can be undertaken is to redesign the work and the work arrangement. For example, employers can provide:

- Extended lunch periods.
- Liberalized use of vacation time.
- Short leaves of absence with benefits.

- Flextime.
- Job sharing.
- Part-time work.
- Consulting (issues of taxes, comfort level of retirees with the mechanism).
- Seasonal work.
- Compressed scheduling.
- Short-term assignments/special projects.
- Reduced hours.
- Job rotation.
- Telecommuting.
- Membership in emergency response teams (with stipends).

All of these are possibilities to enhance older worker retention. The best options for an individual employer and its workforce depend on benefits, types of work, and other factors specific to the situation.

Helping older workers to deal with physical changes can be another way to retain and sustain older workers. Losing vision due to aging does not mean the older worker is in failing health or is losing faculties generally. An older person with diminishing eyesight can be as mentally sharp and fit as ever. Losing eyesight due to aging does not mean a worker must retire either. It just means he or she needs to learn new ways to do things for which sight was previously used. Below are some examples of how companies have helped these workers.[20]

> The Principal Financial Group purchased a magnicam for an employee with vision problems. Pitney Bowes retrained an employee who developed a chronic heart condition. DantaQuest Ventures provided a new computer mouse and armrests for an employee who developed carpal tunnel syndrome. Adecco Employment Services provided an enlarged workstation for an employee to accommodate a guide dog.

Microsoft has Microsoft Accessibility Resources Centers[21] throughout the country that provide a wide range of resources to ensure that users can make use of technology in spite of physical limitations of all kinds.

Several federal agencies have longstanding programs to extend work life. These include the Environmental Protection Agency's Senior Environmental Employment (SEE) Program, the Agriculture Conservationist Enrollee / Seniors (ACES) project of the Natural Resources Conservation Service (NRCS) in the U.S. Department of Agriculture, and the When Actually Employed (WAE) program for foreign service officers of the State Department. The first two of these are grant-funded programs administered by the National Older Worker Career Center (NOWCC) and other organizations. The WAE program is administered directly by offices within the State Department.

Watson Wyatt reported these findings in the 2004 study *Phased Retirement: Aligning Employer Programs with Worker Preferences:*[22]

- Phased retirement programs can encourage older workers to delay retirement (a third would take the option).
- A sizable gap exists between what workers want and what employers currently allow in terms of phased retirement opportunities (e.g., reduced hours).
- Workers currently in phased retirement arrangements are motivated to "work in retirement" for a variety of reasons.
- Even informal phased retirement arrangements can create an incentive for workers to extend their working careers.
- Phasers who work primarily for enjoyment are more likely to experience higher job satisfaction, enjoy good health, and receive higher pay raises that their peers.

Many older workers, when they finally do retire, still "work" as volunteers in their communities. We mentioned earlier that 28 percent of those planning to retire cite volunteering or contributing to society as a reason for retiring. The 3M Corporation's CARES (Community Action Retired Employee Services) Program[23] is one of the premier examples in the country. In 1984, the CARES Program was created to bring together retiree volunteers under the 3M banner and match them to specific community needs.

In 2004, as a result of this program,

- 1,625 volunteers had their time matched by 3M with $325,000 awarded to 823 organizations in 45 states.

- 25 employees and retirees received the Community Volunteer Award; $25,000 donated to their charities.
- Community participation is especially encouraged at management levels. In turn, management should support volunteer service by employees.

The stated purposes of the CARES program are

To encourage volunteerism to enhance the quality of life in our communities.

To support their efforts by sharing information about community needs and volunteer opportunities.

To recognize the sharing of their time and talents to make a difference in our communities.

Programs like CARES keep retirees connected to their former employers and help keep them healthy and active.

Another retiree volunteer program, TAP-IN, is designed to boost Free Clinic volunteerism among six groups of retired healthcare professionals: physicians, dentists, nurses, pharmacists, psychologists, and social workers. The program uses focused marketing and Web-based communications and dialogue to link retired healthcare professionals with Free Clinics throughout Virginia and North Carolina. It will be field tested and implemented initially with retired physicians in the nearly 100 Free Clinics in these two states. The program will then be expanded to include other retired health professionals and Free Clinics in other states.

The program is designed to assist Free Clinics nationally in recruiting volunteers to help serve the more than 45 million Americans under age 65 who are currently without health insurance. At present these uninsured turn to a complex safety net that includes physician offices, hospital emergency rooms, Federally Qualified Community Health Centers, and Free Clinics. Some 1,700 Free Clinics operating in 47 states are an increasingly important part of that safety net, accounting for more than 8.9 million patient visits annually. Free Clinics, staffed primarily by actively practicing and retired volunteers, now turn away thousands of patients each week due to a lack of volunteers. This program will focus on tapping into the hundreds of thousands of retired healthcare professionals to help Free Clinics meet their growing need for volunteers.

Phased retirement programs are a part of the solution. However, there are impediments. As Sara Rix of AARP points out, "Employers face numerous impediments —many of them legal—to formalizing phased retirement. . . . These include pension plans that require termination upon receipt of pension benefits and possible violation of [ERISA] regulations." . . . This is also the issue of "how, under formal phased retirement programs, employers can retain only the workers they want without violating the Age Discrimination in Employment Act (ADEA)."[24]

Regardless, employers need to find creative, effective solutions for providing phased retirement to extend work life. One of AARP's fifty best employers allows mature workers to cut down on hours without risking reduction in retirement benefits in the final years of mandatory employment.

RETIRE THE WORKER AND RETAIN THE KNOWLEDGE

Create a retiree / employee knowledge network to retain knowledge in the organization and share it among its employees. Figure 7–5 shows how knowledge networks work, using AskMe's[25] knowledge management program at Eli Lilly.

"Knowledge Management caters to the critical issues of organizational *adaptation, survival,* and *competence* in face of increasingly discontinuous environmental change. . . . Essentially, it embodies organizational processes that seek synergistic combination of data and *information processing* capacity of information technologies, and the creative and innovative capacity of *human beings.*"[26]

Pharmaceutical industry leader Eli Lilly and Company is an innovation-driven corporation, and it has always known that at the root of every innovation is its people. From the company's founding 126 years ago to the present, with annual sales topping $11 billion, Lilly has relied on the varied perspectives, knowledge, and experience of its global community of employees to fuel the creativity and the energy that pioneered medical breakthroughs such as Prozac®, Sarafem®, and Forteo®, to name a few.

Lilly has R&D facilities all over the world and conducts clinical research in more than sixty countries. It's impossible for members of

FIGURE 7-5

How Knowledge Networks Work

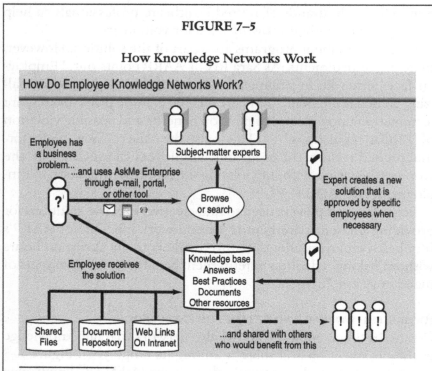

Source: Employee Knowledge Networks: A Broader Perspective. (2003, February 11). Downloaded November 11, 2007, from www.hss.energy.gov/csa/analysis/ll/proceedings/proceedings0403/askme.pdf Reprinted by permission of AskMe Corporation.

such a large and diverse community to all know about each other's work and expertise. To alleviate this problem, Lilly has undertaken several well-publicized knowledge management initiatives. For example, it created data-management tools for doctors to better record the results of drug tests so that information could be more easily analyzed. It also implemented a portal that enables employees to access various enterprise applications and data about the company's products and research. Specifically, in the areas of communities of practice in the new drug development process, Lilly has deployed AskMe's software.

Lilly is using AskMe to enable research scientists to share experiential knowledge and provide feedback on each other's ideas. After the first six months, results have exceeded expectations, and Lilly has begun to look for opportunities to broaden its use of the solution. "One of our most significant research cost-savings suggestions came from several users not formally identified as subject matter experts for the project, and the rest of the group strongly supported them," said Alph Bingham, Ph.D., Vice President, R&D, Eli Lilly. "It's one thing to believe you'll get that kind of result from an informal network of employees, and another to have it in hand."[27]

Here is a basic approach to knowledge and skill retention we call Knowledge Retention 101.

Step 1. Have a human capital plan that defines short- and long-term workforce needs. This is a difficult task even for experienced managers and HR professionals. I remember sitting on a task force for my former employer trying to develop a strategic training plan for the newly created learning center. I suggested that in order to accomplish that, we need to know what skill mix to which we needed to train and what skill set we currently had. The HR director sat there with a blank look on her face like I had just suggested jumping off the roof with chicken wings taped to my arms.

Step 2. Define what portion of the existing and future desired skill mix exists in the minds and hearts of those soon to retire. David De Long tells the story in *Lost Knowledge* of the Tennessee Valley Authority initiative to answer this question. Supervisors were asked to identify the "go-to" people in the organization. They identified what skills were critical to the organization. They identified who was considering retirement. They developed a rating process to help prioritize the areas of vulnerability for the organization.

Step 3. Decide on which employees you need to keep. Once the employer knows what it needs, and how much of what it needs may be walking out the door (sometimes aided by early out programs), then it knows who it needs to keep and how important it is to keep them—or at a minimum, retain access to their skills and knowledge.

Step 4. Develop a strategy to keep whom you need. Once the employer knows who the employees are with the essential skills, then the challenge is to find out how to either (1) extend their work life, (2) retain access to their skill and knowledge, or (3) recruit other workers (including older workers) with the right skills. There are a number of specific initiatives the employer can take to accomplish each of these. Some of those initiatives serve more than one purpose so they appear in more than one of the sequences below.

Step 5. Extend work life. What can an employer do to keep an older worker working? There is not one answer to this. At this point we are dealing with individual motivation. Individual supervisors and managers of the older workers in question need to know their direct reports well enough to know what is important to each one and what to offer as an incentive to continue to work. A number of writers offer ideas about programs that might work:

- **Create an advisory team** of older employees and human capital planners to be active participants in planning and overseeing older worker retention programs.
- **Create civic engagement activities** that keep older workers involved in the local community, serve the needs of the community, provide an opportunity for younger and older workers to "connect" on other dimensions other than work; provide one important component of phased retirement (providing a mix of meaningful volunteer experiences with reduced work time), and keep older workers healthfully active.
- **Design and provide continuous training** for older workers to ensure that technological, administrative, management, and cultural skills and knowledge are up to date.
- **Train managers** at all levels in managing a diverse (multicultural, multigenerational, multilingual) workforce.
- **Embrace flexibility**—in benefits, work schedules, work assignments, compensation, and employer-employee relationships (contracting, using third party agencies specializing in older workers like NOWCC, part-time employment, temporary employment, job-sharing, telecommuting, and compressed work schedules). This is at the core of *"phased retirement."*
- **Modify benefits to incent older workers to continue to work.** Ensure that programs are provided: for retirement/financial planning, to keep older workers informed of retirement options, to provide health fairs and healthy lifestyle information, to allow workers to contribute leave time to a leave pool,

to celebrate long-term contributions of older workers, to regularly survey older workers, to fairly evaluate performance, and to provide health benefits that cover family, family care leave, and employee assistance programs.

Step 6. Retain access to skill and knowledge. Once an employee retires, either full-time or part-time, the employer will likely need the skill and knowledge of the employee from time to time. How does the employer keep an active connection with retirees so that when needed the retiree is available? Again, there is no single answer. Some strategies include:

- **Develop a knowledge management strategy** that includes retirees. The AskMe Corporation (*www.askme.com*) has a sophisticated strategy for tapping into the knowledge of active and retired workers. The strategy focuses on the human knowledge supported by access to databases and data warehouses that can be referred to in developing a response to a question that is asked. The questions can be posed by an active employee or manager who is seeking advice on an issue. The person asking the question reviews and rates the responses. For some AskMe clients, respondents are compensated for their participation in the system based on the ratings they receive from those asking the questions.
- **Create civic engagement activities** that keep older workers connected to current employees and, to the extent possible, help keep skills and knowledge up to date.

Step 7. Design effective older worker recruiting strategies. The data is clear that older workers will need to be a significant part of employers' workforce strategy. Keeping the ones you have is a part of the solution. Finding new ones will also be necessary. Somewhat different approaches to advertising, recruiting, interviewing, and selection are appropriate for older workers. Recruiters and hiring managers need to:

- Be aware of their own preconceptions and prejudices regard-ing older applicants. Be able to identify skill and knowledge that was gathered in one work situation and make it transferable to the needs identified for the position for which they are hiring.
- Understand that very qualified people who have worked for one employer for many years may not be the best at "selling themselves" in the interview situation.

- Know what qualities are truly the most important for the position for which they are hiring and what qualities an older applicant is likely to bring to the job.
- Design recruiting programs that include mature workers with the images of the workforce, use appropriate language, emphasize experience, reliability, and importance of the work or mission.

Step 8. Manage older workers appropriately. In many ways older workers are no different from other workers. They like acknowledgment for their contributions; they like being shown respect; they like to have the camaraderie of co-workers; they like to be fairly compensated; they like opportunities for learning new things; and they like being kept in the loop on what is going on and why what they are doing is important. There are ways in which they may differ slightly from their younger colleagues. They

- Tend to value, and be better at, working in a team environment.
- Work more slowly, but more reliably.
- Tend to be more dependable and less accident prone.
- Tend to take longer to train, but are more accurate and just as productive once back on the job.

Other initiatives to take with older workers include:

- Actively encouraging participation in training.
- Providing opportunities for new assignments and challenges.
- Ensure that grievances are heard and handled.
- When necessary, make workplace accommodations to ensure accessibility to physical locations and accessibility to information resources.

If there is a message for employers to be gleaned from this book, it is that

- The workforce is aging.
- There will likely be a shortage of workers, especially skilled knowledge workers.
- Employers can meet this challenge by leveraging the experience of older workers.
- Employers can learn how to expand and extend the contribution of older workers, including investment in training.

A summary covering part of the business initiatives for planning for an aging workforce is found in Figure 7–6.

FIGURE 7–6

A Roadmap to Ensure That Your Organization Is Getting the Maximum Contribution from Older Workers

Small	Medium	Large
1. Assessment	**6. In addition:**	**11. In addition:**
1. Conduct a "older worker friendly" assessment [27, 34]	1. Conduct a more thorough assessment including surveys of managers and staff [35]	1. Conduct a policy and practices review
2. Determine retirement eligibility of workforce	2. Identify operations that may benefit from a more experienced team (e.g., customer service)	2. Conduct a knowledge audit
3. Establish needed business goals and develop a plan		3. Implement a talent management strategy [31]
2. Recruitment	**7. In addition:**	**12. In addition:**
1. Inform recruiters and hiring managers about	1. Review recruiting advertising for ageist language	1. Train recruiters to ensure that age bias is not influencing recommendations and selections
a. myths and stereotypes [28]	2. Provide incentives to employees for referring older workers	2. Revise human capital plan to ensure appropriate recruiting strategies that support talent management goals
b. the demographic trends in the workforce	3. Emphasize value of the work and the social aspects of the work environment in advertising and interviewing	
2. Create an advisory group made up of older employees [29, 30]	**8. In addition:**	**13. In addition:**
3. When interviewing, explore transferability of skills, and volunteer and life experiences [28]	1. Review pension programs and policies, including early out policies [28, 29, 34]	1. Redesign workflow and restructure jobs to address fatigue, attention, and stress components [34, 36, 37]
		2. Implement a cafeteria benefit plan
		3. Pro-rate benefits [29]

(continued)

Small

3. Worker Retention

1. Provide for 401(K) catch-up contributions[34]
2. Review early out policies within the context of talent management goals[28]
3. Make sure that managers are aware of life circumstances (e.g., family care responsibilities)
4. Ensure that diversity training includes age diversity issues[34]

4. Work-Life Extension

1. Provide training opportunities for all ages
2. Implement services to match retirees to part-time and contract opportunities within the company

5. Knowledge Retention

1. Develop executive and technical succession planning[26] as a part of talent management strategies
2. Keep retiree contact information up-to-date

Medium

2. Implement retirement transition options including part-time, flex-time, selective assignments, job-sharing, telecommuting, temporary assignments, and other options
3. Address workplace ergonomic issues
4. Train managers on cross-generational workforce management[32]

9. In addition:

1. Provide health club privileges
2. Provide wellness seminars and health fairs
3. Implement work-life benefits like eldercare and phased retirement[28] including dependent care spending accounts and group long-term care insurance
4. Review training materials to accommodate learning styles of older learners

10. In addition:

1 Institute mentoring programs
2. Provide access to market sector services[34]
3. Adopt knowledge transfer strategies

Large

4. Learn the incentives to work that are important to each person and negotiate flexible "work contracts."

14. In addition:

1. Create and support civic engagement activities that keep retirees networked with current employees, and keep them active in the community.

15. In addition:

1. Create a retiree/employee knowledge network
2. Provide access to retiree health benefits[34]
3. Set up a knowledge network team to develop a knowledge management strategy

ACTION STEPS FOR PREPARING FOR THE WORKFORCE OF THE FUTURE

Finally, we offer suggestions for preparing for the aging workforce of the future for small, mid-size, and large organizations.

Small Organizations

- Have the HR director complete the "Older Worker Friendly Employer Assessment Tool."
- Have all managers and supervisors complete the "Older Worker Friendly Employer Assessment Tool" for compilation and analysis by NOWCC.
- Conduct age-diversity training for all managers to include myths vs. research on older worker productivity, absenteeism, turnover, job-related injury, working speed, management of intergenerational workforces, and technology adoption.
- Conduct training for all staff involved in recruiting regarding recruiting of older workers, e.g., communication, respect, "it's OK to be overqualified."
- Include in all staff training on diversity in the workplace a module on aging diversity.
- Provide 401(k) "catch-up" contributions.
- Train all employees on aspects of the FMLA that deal with elder care and spousal care.
- Establish leave banks to allow employees to donate their leave days to co-workers.
- Include elder-care expenses as authorized expenses against flexible spending accounts.
- Revise HR policies to provide:
  - Flexible work hours.
  - Flexible length of the lunch hour.
  - Flexible seasonal schedules.
  - Seasonal geographic reassignment (e.g., for "snow-birds").
- Revise HR policies to provide age-neutral opportunities for training.
- Design training with older learners in mind when possible, that is,
  - Don't rush, connect new material to existing knowledge.

- Solicit connections between new material and past experience.
- Relate the material to current job performance.
- Use contrasting colors on graphs and charts.
- Institute succession planning at all job levels and mentoring programs at all levels.
- Conduct a position analysis of all essential job positions and determine who has the knowledge and skill that is essential to organizational performance/competitive advantage.

Mid-Size Organizations

- Conduct surveys on broader workplace issues and analyze the results by age group. Address older worker issues.
- Establish an older worker advisory group.
- Conduct a human capital analysis to develop a picture of the staff's plans to retire and the skill/knowledge base that may be affected.
- Conduct a survey of older workers to determine the reasons for retirement.
- Develop incentives to respond to older workers reasons for wanting to retire.
- Evaluate the language used in recruiting advertisements.
- Train managers and HR staff on the implications of the Supreme Court's ruling in *Smith vs. City of Jackson, Miss.*, that elevated age discrimination to a level approximating that of race or gender bias.
- Review pension plans to eliminate disincentives for phased retirement.
- Structure benefits packages to allow for employee options (e.g., natal benefits for child-bearing women and long-term care for older workers, prescription drug coverage, FSA/HSA plans).
- Encourage managers, older workers, and HR staff to negotiate working arrangements that will accommodate the needs of older workers as well as the needs of the employer.
- Base benefits policy decisions on sound human capital planning research (e.g., there is evidence that for every $1 an employer spends assisting employees with elder-care issues, $3 to $5 is saved in productivity.)[28]
- Use early retirement subsidies only after a skill/knowledge assessment that identifies who holds the essential skill/knowledge in customer relations, operations, and management.

- Encourage healthy lifestyles and provide:
  - Workout facilities and classes or discounted health club memberships.
  - Opportunities to encourage laughter.
  - More healthful snacks in vending machines and employee cafeterias.
  - Quiet rooms.
  - Work life assistance programs.
  - Health fairs/health risk assessments.
  - Nutritional counseling.
  - Financial incentives for weight loss and smoking cessation.
- Establish contractual relationships with organizations like the National Older Worker Career Center to provide return-to-work programs for retirees.
- Retain the knowledge.
- Institute formal mentoring programs to pass on knowledge and reduce turnover.

Large Organizations

- Conduct a thorough skill/knowledge loss risk assessment.
- Identify critical skills and knowledge.
- Identify the workers who possess them.
- Determine the retirement projections for those workers.
- Determine what the Tennessee Valley Authority refers to as the "indispensability" factor for each employee.
- Negotiate retention programs for employees at risk.
- Implement a knowledge management system like the AskMe Inc. approach used by Eli Lilly and Company.
- Videotape critical processes.
- Develop an inquiry network.
- Engage in the public policy debate by working with Congressional representatives and through professional organizations to address changing federal and state laws and regulations to favor extending work life for those who wish to continue working past traditional retirement age while retaining the essence of ERISA and ADEA requirements.
- Develop a civic engagement program to engage retirees and active employees in community-related activities like the 3M CARES

program that keep retirees connected, active, and a continuing part of the community (and available to work part-time or periodically as needed.)

- Conduct a research study to establish the true cost of older workers relative to other age cohorts.
- Invest in ergonomic studies and workplace design changes needed to maximize the productivity of older workers.

SUMMARY

Our nation's workforce is aging—quickly. This will affect our economy. The degree to which this will be true will be largely dependent on how successful individual employers will be in retaining and sustaining productive older workers in the workforce. Maintaining skill levels through training is an essential component. However, as reviewed in this final chapter, there are a number of initiatives that any organization can take.

The answers for a particular organization lie in management's asking the right questions: What skill and knowledge sets will we need in the future? Who has them? Are those who have them near retirement? Would they consider staying? Would they consider consulting, part-time employment, mentoring younger employers, remaining available for short-term project assignments, documenting critical information, being interviewed on videotape describing lessons learned and best practices, or being active in an online expert panel to whom less experienced employees can pose questions? What retirement policies are creating intended or unintended motivations to leave the organization? What aspects of the organization's culture are "ageist"? What aspects of formal policies and procedures are "ageist" (e.g., training, recruiting, interviewing, testing, evaluation, work scheduling, benefits administration)?

We have endeavored in this book to articulate the issue, describe the aspects of the issue and provide some practical, actionable guidance about what to do about it so any organization can age successfully. It is part of an overall workforce plan needed by many organizations to address talent needs of the future.

APPENDIX: RESOURCES LIST

Administration on Aging, *Workforce and Aging,* **Downloaded February 18, 2007 from:**
www.aoa.gov/prof/notes/Docs/Workforce.doc#_Articles_on_Education

CONSUMER INFORMATION

Myths About Older Workers [AARP]
(WISCONSIN DEPARTMENT OF WORKFORCE DEVELOPMENT)
www.dwd.state.wi.us/dws/programs/populations/olderworker/
MythsaboutOlderWorkers.pdf

How to Attract and Retain Older Workers [AARP]
(WISCONSIN DEPARTMENT OF WORKFORCE DEVELOPMENT)
www.dwd.state.wi.us/dws/programs/populations/olderworker/
TipsforEmpcolor.pdf

Careers
AARP
www.aarp.org/working_options/home.html

Best Companies for Workers Over 50
(AARP)
www.aarp.org/bestcompanies

AGE AND DISABILITY DISCRIMINATION IN EMPLOYMENT

Age Discrimination in Employment Act
(U.S. Equal Employment Opportunity Commission)
www.eeoc.gov/laws/adea.html

U.S. Equal Employment Opportunity Commission
www.eeoc.gov
Filing a Complaint: www.eeoc.gov/facts/howtofil.html
Local Office Directory: www.eeoc.gov/contact.html

Disability Employment Rights: Who Has Them and Who Enforces Them
(Office of Disability Employment Policy, U.S. Department of Labor)
www.dol.gov/odep/pubs/fact/rights.htm

How Does the Federal Government Define "Disability"
(Office of Disability Employment Policy, U.S. Department of Labor)
www.dol.gov/odep/faqs/federal.htm

Age Discrimination in the Workplace: A 2001 Survey of Utah Residents Age 40+
(Public Policy Institute, AARP)
http://research.aarp.org/econ/ut_discrimination.html

FEDERAL OLDER WORKER PROGRAMS

**Senior Community Service Employment Program
[Title V, Older Americans Act]**
(U.S. Department of Labor)
http://wdsc.doleta.gov/seniors

**Nine Effective Practices of Highly Effective Seniors
Community Services Employment Program Projects**
(National Council on the Aging)
http://wdsc.doleta.gov/seniors/other_docs/BestPractices.pdf

Older Workers: Employment Assistance Focuses on Subsidized Jobs and Job Search, But Revised Performance Measures Could Improve Access to Other Services. GAO-03-350, January 24.
www.gao.gov/cgi-bin/getrpt?GAO-03-350
www.gao.gov/highlights/d03350high.pdf

Veteran's Employment and Training Service
(U.S. Department of Labor)
www.dol.gov/vets/welcome.html

Work Force Investment Act of 1998 (Plain English Version)
(U.S. Department of Labor)
www.doleta.gov/usworkforce/Runningtext2.htm

NATIONAL TITLE V PROGRAM CONTRACTORS

AARP Senior Community Service Employment Program
www.aarp.org/scsep/

Asociación Nacional Pro Personas Mayores [no website for program]
www.buscapique.com/latinusa/buscafile/oeste/anppm.htm

U.S. Forestry Service
www.fs.fed.us/people/volunteer/scsep.htm

Easter Seals
http://az.easter-seals.org/site/PageServer?pagename=AZDR_SCSEP&
AddInterest=1062

Experience Works [Formerly Green Thumb]
www.experienceworks.org/index.html

National Asian-Pacific Center on Aging
www.napca.org/prod01.htm

National Center on Black Aged, Inc.
www.ncba-aged.org/sep/index.htm

National Council on the Aging
www.ncoa.org/content.cfm?sectionID=17

National Older Worker Career Center
www.nowcc.org

National Indian Council on Aging
www.nicoa.org/scsep.html

National Senior Citizens Education and Research Center
www.seniorserviceamerica.org

National Urban League, Inc.
http://cgi.nul.org/directory/seniors.html

STATE AND LOCAL PROGRAMS

Alabama—Senior Employment Program
www.adss.state.al.us/senioremployment.htm

Alaska—Senior Community Service Employment Program
www.alaskaaging.org/masst.html

Arizona—Senior Community Service Employment Program
www.de.state.az.us/senior/employment.asp

California—Senior Worker Advocate Office
www.edd.ca.gov/swaorep/swaoind.htm

Colorado—Older Worker Network
www.scan.org/own

Connecticut—Senior Community Service Employment Program
www.ctelderlyservices.state.ct.us/OWP.htm

Delaware—Senior Community Service Employment Program
www.dsaapd.com/employment.htm

District of Columbia—Employment/Volunteer
http://dcoa.dc.gov/employment/index.shtm

Florida—Senior Community Service Employment Program
http://elderaffairs.state.fl.us/doea/english/senior_emp.html

Idaho—Older Worker Programs
www.idahoaging.com/programs/ps_olderworker.htm

Illinois—Senior Community Service Employment Program
www.state.il.us/aging/1athome/employ.htm

Illinois Older Worker Taskforce
www.olderworker.org

Kansas—Senior Community Service Employment Program
www.kansasjobs.org/OlderWorker.htm

Kentucky—Senior Community Services Employment Program
http://chs.state.ky.us/aging/programs/
SeniorCommunityServiceEmploymentProgram.htm

Pikesville Local Office—Older Workers
www.pikeville.desky.org/olderworker/olderworker.htm

Louisiana—Senior Employment Program
www.sremploy.org/index.html

Maine—Senior Community Service Employment Program
www.state.me.us/dhs/beas/resource/employ.htm

Maryland—Senior Employment
www.state.me.us/dhs/beas/resource/employ.htm

Michigan—Older Worker Training Programs
www.miseniors.net/weassist/jobseekers.asp?CatID=4&SubCatID=13

Minnesota—Project 2030 Report—Workforce and Economic Vitality
www.dhs.state.mn.us/Agingint/proj2030/report/workfrce.htm

Older Worker Program—Minnesota Work Force Center
www.mnwfc.org/oldwkr

Older Worker Programs (Chart)
www.iseek.org/sv/44430.jsp?textOnly=Y

Missouri—Senior Community Service Employment Program
www.dhss.state.mo.us/Senior_Services/guide00/fa/csep.htm

Montana—Employment Opportunities
www.dphhs.state.mt.us/sltc/financial/12.02.emp.opports.htm

Nebraska—Eastern Nebraska—Senior Employment Program
www.connectfremont.org/COMSER/enoasep.htm

New Jersey—Senior Community Service Employment Program
www.state.nj.us/health/senior/federalbenefits/employment.htm

New Mexico—Jobs for Seniors
www.nmaging.state.nm.us/njob.html

New York—Employment and Training Opportunities
http://aging.state.ny.us/findhelp/employment/index.htm

North Carolina—Senior Community Service Employment Program
www.dhhs.state.nc.us/aging/scsep.htm

North Dakota—Senior Community Service Employment Program
http://crisnd.com/cris/program.html?program=1164

Ohio—Senior Community Service Employment Program
www.state.oh.us/age/websites_workers.html

Mature Services
www.swap.org/docs/matureservices/about/mission.htm

Oklahoma—Senior Community Service Employment Program
www.oesc.state.ok.us/Emp-Trng/programs.htm
-SeniorCommunityServiceEmploymentProg

Oregon—Employment Opportunities for Older Adults and Persons with Disabilities
www.sdsd.hr.state.or.us/programs/employment.htm

Pennsylvania—Employment Services for Older Pennsylvanians
www.aging.state.pa.us/aging/cwp/view.asp?a=3&Q=228777

South Carolina—Older Worker Employment
www.dhhs.state.sc.us/InsideDHHS/Bureaus/
BureauofSeniorServices/other1352432003.htm

Utah—Salt Lake County Senior Employment Program
www.slcoagingservices.org/html/employme.html

Virginia—Fairfax County Area Agency on Aging—Employment Services
www.fairfaxcounty.gov/service/aaa/Employ_Services.htm

Senior Connections—Senior Employment Services (Richmond Area)
www.seniorconnections-va.org/services_for_independent_living/
services_senior_employment.htm

Washington—Older Workers and Elderly Workers
www.wa.gov/esd/lmea/sprepts/newsp/oew.htm

West Virginia—Senior Employment Program
www.state.wv.us/seniorservices/wvboss_article.cfm?atl=
ACE1FD13-D1FE-11D5-8DA00002A52CB920

Wisconsin—Senior Community Service Employment Program
www.dhfs.state.wi.us/Aging/Genage/sencsep.htm

Wyoming—Senior Community Service Employment Program
http://dwsweb.state.wy.us/community/scsep.asp

JOB PLACEMENT SERVICES FOR OLDER WORKERS

Agelight.com
www.agelight.com

Experience Works!
www.experienceworks.org/staffing.htm

Fiftysomething jobs.com
http://fiftysomethingjobs.com

Forties People—Recruitment Provider of Mature Office Personnel
www.fortiespeople.net/marketing.htm

Forty Plus
www.fortyplus.org

Hire Potential
www.hirepotential.com

National Older Worker Career Center
www.nowcc.org

Overqualified Professionals Network
www.adusa.com/invest.htm

Seniors for Hire
www.seniors4hire.org

Senior Jobs
www.seniorsjobs.com

Senior Employment Services
http://seniorjobs.org

Senior Job Bank
www.seniorjobbank.com/

Senior Success
www.seniorsuccess.net/

REPORTS

Workforce Investment Act: Issues Related to Allocation Formula for Youths, Adults, and Dislocated Workers (April 2003)
(U.S. General Accounting Office)
www.gao.gov/cgi-bin/getrpt?GAO-03-636

Older Workers: Policies of Other Nations to Increase Labor Force Participation (February 2003)
(U. S. General Accounting Office)
www.gao.gov/new.items/d03307.pdf

Workforce Training: Employed Worker Programs Focus on Business Needs, but Revised Performance Measures Could Improve Access for Some Workers (February 2003)
www.gao.gov/cgi-bin/getrpt?GAO-03-353
www.gao.gov/highlights/d03353high.pdf Highlights

Older Workers: Employment Assistance Focuses on Subsidized Jobs and Job Search, But Revised Performance Measures Could Improve Access to Other Services (January 2003)
(U.S. General Accounting Office)
www.gao.gov/new.items/d03350.pdf

Voices of Experience: Mature Workers in the Future Workforce (2002)
(U.S. Conference Board)
www.conference-board.org/publications/describe.cfm?id=604

Aging Baby Boomers in a New Workforce Development System
(U.S. Department of Labor)
http://wdsc.doleta.gov/seniors/other_docs/Aging_Baby_Boomers.doc

Work, Retirement and Pensions (Chapter) (2001)
Preparing for an Aging World: The Case for Cross-National Research
(National Academy Press)
books.nap.edu/books/0309074215/html/66.html—pagetop

Workers and Chronic Conditions (2000)
(National Academy on an Aging Society
www.georgetown.edu/research/ihcrp/agingsociety/pdfs/Workers.pdf

New Opportunities for Older Workers (1999)
(Committee for Economic Development)
www.ced.org/projects/older.shtml

A Century of Progress . . . A Century of Change (1999)
(Employment Policy Foundation)
www.epf.org/labor99/getpdfs99.html

Ageing and Labour Markets for Older Workers (1999)
(International Labour Organization)
www.ilo.org/public/english/employment/strat/publ/etp33.htm

STATISTICS

Civilian Labor Force Participation Ratios by Sex, Age, Race and Hispanic Origin, 1980, 1990, 2000, and Projected 2010
(Bureau of Labor Statistics, U.S. Department of Labor)
pdf: www.bls.gov/emp/emplab2000-03.pdf
text: ftp://ftp.bls.gov/pub/special.requests/ep/labor.force/mlrtab2000-03.txt

Distribution of the Population and Labor Force by Age and Sex, 1980, 1990, 2000, and Projected 2010
(Bureau of Labor Statistics, U.S. Department of Labor)
pdf: www.bls.gov/emp/emplab2000-11.pdf
text: ftp://ftp.bls.gov/pub/special.requests/ep/labor.force/mlrtab2000-11.txt

Age Adjusted Labor Force Participation Rates, 1960–2045
(Bureau of Labor Statistics, U.S. Department of Labor)
www.bls.gov/opub/mlr/2002/09/art3full.pdf

Persons Not in the Labor Force by Desire and Availability for Work
(Bureau of Labor Statistics, U.S. Department of Labor)
ftp://ftp.bls.gov/pub/special.requests/lf/aat35.txt

Persons at Work in Nonagricultural Industries by Age, Sex, Race, Marital Status, and Usual Full- or Part-Time Status
(Bureau of Labor Statistics, U.S. Department of Labor)
ftp://ftp.bls.gov/pub/special.requests/lf/aat22.txt

Employed Persons in Agriculture and Nonagricultural Industries by Age, Sex, and Class of Worker
(Bureau of Labor Statistics, U.S. Department of Labor)
ftp://ftp.bls.gov/pub/special.requests/lf/aat15.txt

Work Experience and Mean Earnings in 1999—Work Disability Status of Civilians 16 to 74 Years Old, by Sex: 2000
(U.S. Census Bureau)
www.census.gov/hhes/www/disable/cps/cps300.html

Farmers Have Highest Percentage of Older Workers
(U.S. Bureau of Labor Statistics)
stat.bls.gov/opub/ted/2000/Sept/wk2/art01.htm

Demographic Trends Pose Challenges for Employers and Work—November, 2001
(U.S. General Accounting Office)
www.gao.gov/new.items/d0285.pdf

Older Workers, Retirement and Pensions (1995, revised 1999)
(U.S. Census Bureau)
www.census.gov/ipc/www/ipc95_2.html

OLDER WORKER PROFESSIONAL ORGANIZATIONS

National Association of Older Worker Employment Services
http://206.112.84.147/content.cfm?sectionID=38

Interest Group on Older Workers and Retirement
(University of North Carolina)
www.aging.unc.edu/groups/work/resources.html

ARTICLES ON EDUCATION AND TRAINING

Integrating Work and Learning: A Key to Older Employee Success
(American Society for Aging)
www.asaging.org/networks/bfa/networker-087.html

U.S. Department of Labor—Employment and Training Administration Supervisors Guide: Managing Older Workers
http://wdsc.doleta.gov/seniors/other_docs/SupervisorGuide.doc

An Employer's Guide to Older Workers: How to Win Them Back and Convince Them to Stay
http://wdsc.doleta.gov/seniors/other_docs/EmplGuide.doc

Development Systems: Benchmarks for Mature and Older Workers
http://wdsc.doleta.gov/seniors/html_docs/docs/Benchmarks1999.cfm

Changing Workforce in America: Training Older Workers for the Future
(Radcliffe Pubic Policy Center)
www.radcliffe.edu/pubpol/cwia_cc.html

ARTICLES ON EMPLOYMENT AND BENEFITS

AARP—Public Policy Institute

Staying Ahead of the Curve: The AARP Work and Career Study (2002)
www.aarp.org/stayingahead

Update on the Older Worker (2002)
(Public Policy Institute, AARP)
http://research.aarp.org/econ/dd88_worker.html

Update on the Older Worker (2001)
http://research.aarp.org/econ/dd69_worker.html

American Business and Older Employees: A Summary of Findings (2000)
http://research.aarp.org/econ/amer_bus_findings.html

Update on the Older Worker—Employment Gains Continue (1998)
http://research.aarp.org/econ/dd42_worker98.html

Bureau of Labor Statistics

Older Workers in the 21st Century: Active and Educated, a Case Study
http://stats.bls.gov/opub/mlr/1996/06/art3abs.htm

Work After Early Retirement: An Increasing Trend Among Men
http://stats.bls.gov/opub/mlr/1995/04/art2abs.htm

Changing Retirement Age: Ups and Downs—(2001)
http://stats.bls.gov/opub/mlr/2001/04/art1full.pdf

Center for Retirement Research, Boston College

Job Search Behavior at the End of the Life Cycle (2002)
www.bc.edu/centers/crr/wp_2002-10.shtml

Is Working Longer the Answer for an Aging Workforce? (2002)
www.bc.edu/centers/crr/issues/ib_11.pdf

Are Older Workers Responding to the Bear Market? (2002)
www.bc.edu/centers/crr/jtf_5.shtml

Elderly Labor Supply: Work or Play? (2001)
www.bc.edu/bc_org/avp/csom/executive/crr/papers/wp_2001-04.pdf

Employment Benefit Research Institute (EBRI)

The 1999 Small Employer Retirement Survey: Building a Better Mousetrap Is Not Enough
www.ebri.org/ibex/ib212.htm

Social Security, Retirement Incentives, and Retirement Behavior: An International Perspective
www.ebri.org/ibex/ib209.htm

Retirement Patterns and Bridge Jobs in the 1990s
www.ebri.org/ibex/ib206.htm

Contingent Workers and Workers in Alternative Work Arrangements
www.ebri.org/ibex/ib207.htm

Employee Benefits, Retirement Patterns, and Implications for Increased Work Life
www.ebri.org/ibex/ib184.htm

Urban Institute

Letting Older Workers Work: Rethinking Retirement Policies (2002)
www.urban.org/Template.cfm?Section=ByTopic&NavMenuID=62&
template=/TaggedContent/ViewPublication.cfm&PublicationID=8050

Legal and Institutional Impediments to Partial Retirement and Part-Time Work by Older Workers (2002)
www.urban.org/Template.cfm?NavMenuID=24&template=/
TaggedContent/ViewPublication.cfm&PublicationID=7991

Incentives for Early Retirement Private and Health Insurance Plans (ND)
www.urban.org/retirement/briefs/3/brief_3.html

The Effects of Changes in State SSI Supplements on Pre-Retirement Labor Supply (July 2003)
(National Bureau of Economic Research)
http://papers.nber.org/papers/W9851

Lifetime Labor Supply in a Search Model of Unemployment (2003)
(Tinbergen Institute)
www.tinbergen.nl/discussionpapers/03032.pdf

Age and Individual Productivity: A Literature Survey (2003) Abstract
(Max Planck Institute for Demographic Research)
www.demogr.mpg.de/papers/working/wp-2003-028.pdf

Early for Delayed Retirement Age Under Social Security
(U.S. Social Security Administration)
www.ssa.gov/OACT/ProgData/nra.html

An Older and Wiser Future (UK)
(The Guardian)
http://society.guardian.co.uk/comment/column/0,7882,921564,00.html

Work Support—Information, Resources and Research on Work and Disabilities Issues
(Work Support.com)
www.worksupport.com

Young Retirees and Older Workers (2002)
(Center on an Aging Society)
www.georgetown.edu/research/ihcrp/agingsociety/profiles.html—retirees

Elderly Labor Supply: Work or Play? (2001)
(RAND)
www.rand.org/labor/DRU/DRU2582.pdf

Economic Downturn Could Hurt Older Worker (2001)
(USA Today)
http://cgi.usatoday.com/careers/news/2001-02-22-olderworkers.htm

Productive Lives: Paid and Unpaid Activities of Older Americans (2000)
(International Longevity Center)
www.ilcusa.org/_lib/pdf/product1.pdf

The Incidence of Job Loss: The Shift from Younger to Older Workers, 1981-1996 (2000)
(International Longevity Center)
www.ilcusa.org/_lib/pdf/job_loss.pdf

From the Phonograph to the Hip Shake: Older Workers Sound Like the Future
(College Recruiter)
www.collegerecruiter.com/pages/articles/article365.html

Out to Pasture, Greener Pasture: Older Workers Are Thriving in Tight Job Market
(Global Action on Aging)
www.globalaging.org/elderrights/us/olderworkers.htm

Older Workers Are Thriving in Tight Job Market
(Gustavus Adolphus College)
www.gac.edu/~dick/classes/adult/older-workers.html

Unprotected Until Forty: The Limited Scope of the Age Discrimination in Employment Act of 1967
(Indiana School of Law)
www.law.indiana.edu/ilj/v73/no4/07.html

Unemployment Compensation and Older Workers
Christopher O'Leary and Steven Wandner
(WoPEe)
http://netec.mcc.ac.uk/WoPEc/data/Papers/upjweupjo00-61.html

Older Workers and Employers' Attitudes and Practices
(University of Bradford)
http://nitrogen.cen.brad.ac.uk/admin/conted/guidance/leaflets/employment
.html

The Changing Face of the 21st Century Workforce: Trends in Ethnicity, Race, Age, & Gender
(Employment Policy Foundation)
http://epf.org/racegend.htm

Has the Early Retirement Trend Reversed?
(Boston College of Economics)
http://econpapers.hhs.se/paper/bocbocoec/424.htm

Insuring Older Workers
(National Center for Policy Analysis)
www.ncpa.org/health/pdh99.html

Older Workers and On-the-Job Deaths
(National Center for Policy Analysis)
www.ncpa.org/pd/affirm/pdaa/pdaa10.html

BMC 08/27/03
Center for Communication and Customer Services
Tel. 202-619-0724
FAX 202-357-3523
Internet: www.aoa.gov/
E-mail: aoainfo@aoa.gov

NOTES

CHAPTER 1

1. National Older Worker Career Center, Inc. www.nowcc.org/aging

2. Harvey L. Sterns and Linda M. Subich, "Career development in midcareer," in *Work Careers*, ed. Daniel C. Feldman (San Francisco: Jossey-Bass, 2002), pp. 186–213.

3. Harvey L. Sterns and Margaret H. Huyck, "The role of work in midlife," in *Handbook of Midlife Development*, ed. Margie E. Lachman (New York: John Wiley and Sons, Inc., 2001), pp. 447–486.

4. Mitra Toossi, "Labor force projections to 2012: The graying of the U.S. workforce." *Monthly Labor Review* 127,(2) (2004): 37–57, www.bls.gov/opub/mlr/2004/02/art3full.pdf

5. Wharton School, www.pensionresearchcouncil.org

6. American Federation of State, County and Municipal Employees, "Aging workforce," AFSCME, www.afscme.org/publications/2228.cfm

7. American Federation of State, County and Municipal Employees, "Baby boomers," AFSCME, www.afscme.org/publications/2227.cfm

8. National Public Radio, "Line workers retiring at fast clip," 22 March 2005, www.npr.org/templates/story/story.php?storyId=4554625

9. David Delong, *Lost Knowledge: Confronting the Threat of an Aging Workforce* (New York: Oxford University Press, 2004).

10. SHRM Survey Program, *2003 SHRM/NOWCC/CED Older Workers Survey* (Alexandria, VA: SHRM Research, 2003).

11. Administration on Aging, "2005 White House Conference on Aging Speakers," U.S. Department of Health and Human Services, www.whcoa.gov/press/speakers/speakers.asp

12. Harvey L. Sterns and Dennis Doverspike, "Aging and the training and learning process in organizations," in *Training and Development in Work Organiza-*

tion, eds. I. Goldstein and R. Katzell (San Francisco: Jossey-Bass, 1989), pp. 299–332.

13. Harvey L. Sterns, Dennis Doverspike, and Greta A. Lax, "The age discrimination in employment act," in *Employment Discrimination Litigation: Behavioral Quantative and Legal Perspectives*, ed. Frank S. Landy (San Francisco: Jossey-Bass, 2005), pp. 256–293.

14. Paul B. Baltes, Hayne W. Reese, and Lewis P. Lipsitt, "Life-span development psychology," *Annual Review of Psychology*, 31 (1980): 65–110.

15. Douglas T. Hall and Associates, *The Career Is Dead: Long Live the Career* (San Francisco, CA: Jossey-Bass, 1996).

16. Harvey L. Sterns and Jennifer H. Gray, "Work, leisure, and retirement," in *Gerontology*, eds. John Cavanaugh and Susan Whitbourne (New York: Oxford University Press, 1999), pp. 355–390.

17. Sterns and Huyck, op. cit.

18. Ibid.

19. Sherry L. Willis and Samuel S. Dubin, "Maintaining professional competence: Directions and possibilities," in *Maintaining Professional Competence*, eds. Sherry L. Willis and Samuel S. Dubin (San Francisco, CA: Jossey-Bass, 1990), pp. 306–314.

20. Committee for Economic Development, *New Opportunities for Older Workers* (New York: CED, 1999), www.ced.org/docs/report/report_older.pdf

21. Sterns and Gray, op. cit.

22. Harvey L. Sterns, "Commentary: The decision to retire or to work," in *Impact of Work on Older Adults*, eds. K. Warner Schaie and C. Schooler (New York: Springer, 1998), pp. 131–142.

23. Harvey L. Sterns and Anthony A. Sterns, "Past and future directions for career development theory," in *Thriving on an Aging Workforce: Strategies for Organizational and Systematic Change*, eds. Paulette B. Beatty and Roemer M. Visser (Malabar, FL: Krieger, 2005).

24. Harvey L. Sterns and Jerome Kaplan, "Self-management of career and retirement," in *Retirement: Current Research and Future Directions*, eds. Gary A. Adams and Terry A. Beehr (New York: Springer Publishing Co., 2003), pp. 188–213.

25. Ron Zemke, Claire Raines, and Bob Filipczak, *Generations at Work* (New York: American Management Association, 2000).

26. Sterns and Sterns, op. cit.

27. Harvey L. Sterns, "Training and retraining adult and older worker," in *Age, Health, and Employment*, eds. J. E. Birren and J. Livingston (Englewood Cliffs, NJ: Prentice Hall, 1986), pp. 93–113.

28. Sterns and Huyck, op. cit.

29. Harvey L. Sterns and Ralph A. Alexander, "Industrial gerontology: The aging individual and work," in *Annual Review of Geriatric Medicine and Gerontology, Vol. 7*, ed. K. Warner Schaie (New York: Springer, 1987), pp. 243–264.

30. Harvey L. Sterns and Linda M. Subich, "Counseling for retirement," in *Career Development and Counseling: Putting Theory and Research to Work*, eds. Steven D. Brown and Robert W. Lent (Hoboken, NJ: Wiley, 2005), pp. 506–521.

31. Ibid.

32. Sterns, Doverspike, and Lax, op. cit.

33. Sterns and Huyck, op. cit.

34. Ibid.

35. Ibid.

36. Gary A. Adams, "Career-related variables and planned retirement age: An extension of Beehr's model," *Journal of Vocational Behavior*, 55 (1999): 221–235.

37. Ibid.

38. Harvey L. Sterns and Anthony A. Sterns, "Health and employment capability of older Americans," in *Older and Active*, ed. Scott Bass (New Haven, CT: Yale University Press, 1995), pp. 10–34.

39. Ibid.

40. Ibid.

41. Ken Dychtwald, *Age Power: How the 21st Century Will Be Ruled by the New Old* (New York, Tarcher/Putnam, 2000).

42. Sterns and Huyck, op. cit.

43. Sterns and Alexander, op. cit.

44. Sterns and Huyck, op. cit.

45. Sterns and Gray, op. cit.

46. Ibid.

47. Lydia Bronte, *The Longevity Factor: The New Reality of Long Careers and How It Can Lead to Richer Lives* (New York: HarperCollins, 1993).

48. Sterns and Subich, op. cit.

49. Sterns and Gray, op. cit.

50. Sterns and Subich, op. cit.

51. Sterns and Huyck, op. cit.

52. Ibid.

53. Ibid.

54. Gail Sheehy, *New Passages: Mapping Your Life Across Time* (New York: Random House, 1995).

55. Erik H. Erikson, *Childhood and Society,* 2nd ed. (New York: Norton, 1963).

56. Sterns and Gray, op. cit.

CHAPTER 2

1. Joel Reaser, Diane M. Spokus, Harvey L. Sterns, and William J. Rothwell, *A Survey of Employers.* Unpublished survey results (Arlington, VA: National Older Worker Career Center [NOWCC], 2007. All rights reserved).

2. *Alabama Survey of Employers' Practices for Managing an Aging Workforce* (Washington, DC: AARP, 2006).

3. Ibid.

4. U.S. Bureau of Census, *Current Population Reports* (Washington, DC: U.S. Government Printing Office, 2000).

5. J. R. Graham, "Getting older is getting better," *USA Today: The Magazine of the American Scene, 120* (January 26–27, 1992).

6. U.S. Department of Labor, Bureau of Labor Statistics, Employment and Earnings, January 2005, retrieved January 23, 2007 from www.dol.gov/wb/factsheets/Qf-olderworkers55.htm

7. Ibid.

8. American Association of Retired People, "Staying ahead of the curve," in *The Work and Career Study* (Washington, DC: American Association of Retired People, 2002).

9. National Academy on an Aging Society, *Who Are Young Retirees and Older Workers?* (Washington, DC: National Academy on an Aging Society, June 2000).

10. Jill Quadagno, *Aging and the Life Course,* 3rd ed. (New York: McGraw-Hill, 2005), p. 127.

11. Ibid.

12. James M. Raymo, Jersey Liang, Hidehiro Sugiasawa, Erika Kobayashi, and Yoko Sugihara, "Work at older ages in Japan: Variation by gender and employment status," *Journals of Gerontology: Series B: Psychological Sciences on Social Sciences, 59*(B) (2004): S154–S163.

13. Deborah D. Newquist, "Health and extended work life," in *Older and Active,* ed. Scott A. Bass (Chelsea: Yale University Press, 1986), p. 17.

14. William J. Evans and Irwin H. Rosenberg, M.D., *Biomarkers: The 10 Determinants of Aging You Can Control* (New York: Simon and Schuster, 1991).

15. Waneen W. Spirduso, Karen L. Francis, and Priscilla G. MacRae, *Physical Dimensions of Aging,* 2nd ed. (Champaign, IL: Human Kinetics, 2005), p. 17.

16. Evans and Rosenberg, op. cit.

17. Quadagno, op. cit.

18. Evans and Rosenberg, op. cit.

19. Ibid.

20. AARP, *American Business and Older Employees* (Washington, DC: Bureau of Labor Statistics).

21. Arthur D. Fisk, Wendy A. Rogers, Neil Charness, Sara J. Czaja, and Joseph Sharit, *Designing for Older Adults: Principles and Creative Human Factors Approaches* (Malabar, FL: CRC Press, 2004), pp. 49–59.

22. Spirduso, Francis, and MacRae, op. cit.

23. Fisk et al. op. cit.

24. Ibid.

25. Ibid, p. 18.

26. AT and Older Workers from ATWiki. Downloaded 31 January 2007 from http://atwiki.assistivetech.net/AT_andOlder_Workers

27. Fisk et al. op. cit.

28. Reaser, Spokus, Sterns, and Rothwell, op. cit.

29. AT and Older Workers from ATWiki, op. cit.

30. Karl H. E. Kroemer, *Ergonomics in Design* (Santa Monica, CA: Human Factors and Ergonomics Society, 2006).

31. Ibid.

32. Ibid.

33. AT and Older Workers from ATWiki, op. cit.

34. Neil Charness, C. Kelley, E. Bosman, and M. Mottram, "Word processing training and retraining: Effects of adult age, experience, and interface," *Psychology and Aging, 16* (2001): 110–127.

35. Neil Charness and Sara J.Czaja, "Adaptation to new technologies," in *Cambridge Handbook on Age and Ageing,* ed. M. L. Johnson (Cambridge, UK: Cambridge Press, 2005), pp. 662–666.

36. *Resource Guide for Individuals with Visual Difficulties and Impairments.* Downloaded 31 January 2007 from www.microsoft.com/enable/guides/vision.aspx

37. Reaser, Spokus, Sterns, and Rothwell, op. cit.

38. Kroemer, op. cit.

39. James Bond, Ellen Galinsky, C. Thompson, and D. Prottas, *Highlights of the National Study of the Changing Workforce* (New York: Families and Work Institute, 2003).

40. Lisa M. Finkelstein, Intergenerational Issues Inside the Organization, *Thriving on an Aging Workforce: Strategies for Organizational and Systemic Change* (Malabar, FL: Krieger, 2005).

41. Rosalind C. Barnett, "Home to work spillover revisited: A study of full-time employed women in dual-earner couples," *Journal of Marriage and the Family, 56*(3) (1994): 647–656.

42. B. Gottlieb, E. Kevin Kelloway, and M. Fraboni, "Aspects of eldercare that place employees at risk," *The Gerontologist, 34*(6) (1994): 815–821.

43. Sabine A. E. Geurts, Toon W. Taris, Michiel A. J. Kompier, Josje S. E. Dikkers, Madelon L. M. Van Hooff, and Ulla M. Kinnunen, "Work-home interaction from a work psychological perspective: Development and validation of a new questionnaire, the SWING," *Work & Stress*, Radboud University, Nijmegen. The Netherlands University of Jyvaskyia, Finland. Downloaded March 11, 2007 from http://dx.doi.org/10.1080/02678370500410208

44. *Older Americans 2000: Key Indicators of Well-being, a Report by the Federal Interagency Forum on Aging Related Statistics* (Washington, DC: The Data Dissemination Branch of the National Center on Health Statistics). Available: www.agingstats.gov

45. John R. Katzenbach and Douglas K. Smith, *The Wisdom of Teams* (New York: Harper Press, 1999), p. 25.

46. Celeste Brotheridge and Raymond T. Lee, "Impact of work-family interference on general well-being: A replication and extension," *International Journal of Stress Management, 12*(3) (2005): 203–221.

47. Ibid.

48. Harry R. Moody, *Aging: Concepts and Controversies*, 5th ed. (Thousand Oaks, CA: Pine Forge Press, 2006).

49. Ibid.

50. Harry M. Bobonich, *Seeing Around Corners: How Creative People Think* (Pittsburgh, PA: Dorrance Publishers, 2002).

51. Reaser, Spokus, Sterns, and Rothwell, op. cit.

52. Helen Dennis, "Management training," in *Fourteen Steps in Managing an Aging Workforce*, ed. Helen Dennis (Lexington, MA: Lexington Books, 1988), pp. 141–154.

53. K. Warner Schaie and Sherry L. Willis, *Adult Development and Aging*, 5th ed. (Upper Saddle River, NJ: Prentice Hall, 2002), p. 19.

54. *Global Aging Report, A Global View of Aging and Productivity, 3*(3) (May/June, 1998).

55. Ibid.

56. Ibid.

57. *Americans With Disabilities Act*, downloaded January 29, 2007, from http://en.wikipedia.org/wiki/Americans_with_Disabilities_Act_of_1990.

58. Ibid.

59. Kroemer, op. cit.

60. Harvey L. Sterns and Anthony A. Sterns, "Health and employment capability," in *Older and Active*, ed. Scott A. Bass (New Haven, CT: Yale University, 1995), p. 21.

61. *Understanding the Americans with Disabilities Act*, downloaded on January 28, 2007, from www.allbusiness.com/government/employment-regulations -americans/1316-1.html

62. *O*NET*, downloaded January 28, 2007, from www.occupationalinfo.org/ onet/about.html

63. Ibid.

64. Ibid.

65. Fraser, "Productivity and functional limitations," in *Handbook of Employment and the Elderly*, ed. William H. Crown (Westport, CT: Greenwood Press, 1996), p. 281.

66. Deborah D. Newquist and Pauline K. Robinson, "Health and extended work-life," in *Health and Employment Capability: Older and Active*, ed. Scott A. Bass (New Haven, CT: Yale University, 1995), p. 18.

67. William H. Crown, ed., *Handbook on Employment and the Elderly* (Westport, CT: Greenwood Press, 1996), pp. 278–302.

68. Kroemer, op. cit.

69. U.S. Bureau of Labor Statistics, downloaded on January 28, 2007, from www.bls.gov

70. Hobbs and Stoops (2002), in Quadagno, op. cit.

71. Chenoa Flippen and Marta Tienda, "Pathways to retirement: Patterns of labor force participation and labor market exit among the pre-retirement population by race, Hispanic, origin, and sex," *Journal of Gerontology*, *55B*(1) (2000): S14–27.

72. U.S. Department of Labor, *America's Most Dangerous Jobs*, downloaded from http://money.cnn.com/2005/08/26/pf/jobs_jeopardy

73. Elizabeth Rogers and William J. Wiatrowski, *Injuries, Illnesses, and Fatalities Among Older Workers*, *128* (10) (October 2005), downloaded January 30, 2007, from www.bls.gov/opub/mlr/2005/10/art3exc.htm

74. Vicki L. Hanson, Andi Snow-Weaver, and Shari Trewin, "Software personal-ization to meet the needs of the older adults," *Journal of the International Society for Gerotechnology*, *5*(3) (September, 2006): 161.

75. Neil Charness and Sara J. Czaja, "Adaptation to new technologies," in *Cambridge Handbook on Age and Ageing*, ed. M. L. Johnson (Cambridge, UK, Cambridge Press, 2005), pp. 662–666.

76. Herman Bouma, "Gerontechnology: Making technology relevant for the elderly," in *Gerontechnology*, eds. Herman Bouma and J. A. M. Graafmans (Amsterdam: IOS Press, 1992), pp. 1–5.

77. Sally J. Weaver, *Musculoskeletal Pain in University Workers: Age and Gender Effects.* Unpublished master's thesis, Florida State University, 2006.

CHAPTER 3

1. Lydia Bronte, *The Longevity Factor* (New York: HarperCollins Publishers, 1993), p. 58.

2. K. Warner Schaie and Sherry L. Willis, *Adult Development and Aging*, 5th ed. (Upper Saddle River, NJ: Prentice Hall, 2002), p. 381.

3. J. H. Howard and D. V. Howard, "Learning and memory," in *Handbook of Human Factors and the Older Adult,* eds. A. D. Fisk and W. A. Rogers (San Diego: Academic Press), pp. 2–26.

4. Schaie and Willis, op. cit., p. 316.

5. Ibid, p. 319.

6. Ibid, p. 320.

7. *Memory Improvement Tools*, downloaded March 13 2007 from www.mindtools.com/memory.html

8. D. F. Hultsch, C. Hertzog, R. A. Dixon, and B. J. Small (1998). "Memory changes in the aged," in *Adult Development and Aging* 5th ed, eds. K. Warner Schaie and Sherry L. Willis (Upper Saddle River, NJ: Prentice Hall, 2002), p. 321.

9. Schaie and Willis, op. cit., pp. 321–322.

10. Harvey L. Sterns and Dennis Doverspike, "Aging and the training and learning process," in *Training and Development in Organizations,* eds. Irwin L. Goldstein and Associates (San Francisco, CA: Jossey-Bass Publishers, 1989).

11. Schaie and Willis, op. cit.

12. Ibid., p. 362.

13. *Fluid Intelligence*, downloaded March 13, 2007, from penta.ufrgs.br/edu/telelab/3/fluid_in.htm

14. Schaie and Willis, op. cit.

15. Ibid., p. 363.

16. Arthur D. Fisk and Wendy A. Rogers, "Influence of training and experience on skill acquisition and maintenance in older adults," *Journal of Aging and Physical Activity,* 8 (2000): 373–378.

17. L. W. Poon, "Differences in human memory with aging: Nature, causes, and clinical implications," in *Handbook of the Psychology of Aging*, eds. J. E. Birren and K. W. Schaie (New York: Van Nostrand Reinhold, 1985), pp. 427–455.

18. Schaie and Willis, op. cit., p. 339.

19. F. I. M. Craik and J. M. Jennings, "Human memory," in *Adult Development and Aging*, 5th ed., eds. K.Warner Schaie and Sherry L. Willis (Upper Saddle River, NJ: Prentice Hall, 2002), p. 339.

20. A. D. Smith, "Memory," in *Handbook of the Psychology of Aging*, 4th ed., eds. J. E. Birren and K. W. Schaie (San Diego, CA: Academic Press, 1996).

CHAPTER 4

1. William J. Rothwell and H. C. Kazanas, *Mastering the Instructional Design Process*, 3rd ed. (San Francisco: Pfeiffer, 2003).

2. David D. Dubois and William J. Rothwell, *The Competency Toolkit*, 2 vols. (Amherst, MA: HRD Press, 2000).

3. David D. Dubois and William J. Rothwell, *Competency-Based Human Resource Management* (Palo Alto, CA: Davies-Black, 2004).

4. William J. Rothwell and H. C. Kazanas, *Improving On-the-Job Training: How to Establish and Operate a Comprehensive OJT Program*, 2nd ed. (San Francisco: Pfeiffer, 2004).

5. William J. Rothwell, Marilynn Butler, Cecilia Maldonado, Daryl Hunt, Karen Peters, Jessica Li, and Jo King Stern, *Handbook of Training Technology: An Introductory Guide to Facilitating Learning with Technology: From Planning Through Evaluation* (San Francisco: Pfeiffer, 2006).

6. Neil Charness and Sara Czaja, *Older Worker Training: What We Know and Don't Know*. No. 2006-22 (Washington: AARP Public Policy Institute, 2006).

7. Ibid., p. vi.

8. Harvey L. Sterns and Dennis D. Doverspike, "Aging and the training and learning process," in *Training and Development in Organizations*, ed. Irwin L. Goldstein (San Francisco: Jossey-Bass, 1988), pp. 299–332.

9. Ibid.

10. Stephen D. Brookfield, *Becoming a Critically Reflective Teacher* (San Francisco: Jossey-Bass, 1995).

11. Ibid., p. 114.

12. Ibid., p. 132.

13. Gary J. Conti and Rita C. Kolody, "Guidelines for selecting methods and techniques," in *Adult Learning Methods*, 2nd ed., ed. Michael W. Galbraith (Malabar, FL: Krieger, 1998), p. 132.

14. William J. Rothwell, Harvey L. Sterns, Diane M. Spokus, and Joel Reaser, *Working Longer: New Strategies for Managing, Training, and Retaining Older Employees* (New York: AMACOM, 2008).

15. Arthur D. Fisk, Wendy A. Rogers, Neil Charness, Sara J. Czaja, and Joseph Sharit, *Designing for Older Adults: Principles and Creative Human Factors Approaches* (Malabar, FL: CRC Press, 2004).

16. Steve Kozlowski and B. Hults, "An exploration of climates for technical updating and performance," *Personnel Psychology*, 40(3) (1987): 539–563.

17. Rothwell and Kazanas, op. cit.

18. Rothwell, Sterns, Spokus, and Reaser, op. cit.

19. Ibid.

20. D. T. Hall and P. H. Mirvis, "Careers as lifelong learning," in *Training for a Rapidly Changing Workforce*, eds. M. A. Quinones and A. Ehrenstein (Washington DC: American Psychological Association, 1995), p. 18.

21. Rothwell, Sterns, Spokus, and Reaser, op. cit.

22. V. H. Vroom, *Work and Motivation* (New York: Wiley, 1964).

23. Eunice Belbin and R. Meredith Belbin, *Problems in Adult Retraining* (London: Heinemann, 1972).

24. David Kolb, *Experiential Learning* (Englewood Cliffs, NJ: Prentice Hall, 1984).

25. John Elias and Sharan Merriam, *Philosophical Foundations of Adult Education*, 2nd ed. (Malabar, FL: Krieger, 1995).

26. P. J. Batsakes and Arthur D. Fisk, "Age and dual-task performance: Are performance gains retained?" *Journal of Gerontology: Psychological Sciences, 55B* (2000): 332–342.

27. B. J. Avolio, D. A. Waldman, and M. A. McDanile, "Age and work performance in nonmanagerial jobs: The effects of experience and occupational type," *Academy of Management Journal, 32* (1990): 407–422.

28. Wendy A. Rogers, B. Meyer, N. Walker, and Arthur D. Fisk, "Functional limitations to daily living tasks in the aged: A focus group analysis," *Human Factors, 40* (1998): 111–125.

29. Sara J. Czaja and Joseph Sharit, "Age differences in attitudes toward computers," *Journal of Gerontology: Psychological Sciences, 53B* (1998): 329–340.

30. Ibid.

31. Lorraine M. Zinn. "Philosophy of Adult Education Learning Inventory (PAEI)," in *Adult Learning Methods: A Guide for Effective Instruction*, 2nd ed., ed. Michael W. Galbraith (Malabar, FL: Krieger, 1998), pp. 57–71.

32. Adapted from John Elias and Sharan Merriam, "Philosophical foundations of adult education," in *Adult Learning Methods*, 2nd ed., ed. Michael W. Galbraith (Malabar, FL: Krieger, 1995), pp. 70–71.

33. Sharan B. Merriam and Phyllis M. Cunningham (Eds.), *Handbook of Adult Education* (San Francisco: Jossey-Bass, 1989), p. 192.

34. Ibid.

35. Arthur D. Fisk, Wendy A. Rogers, Neil Charness, Sara J. Czaja, and Joseph Sharit, *Designing for Older Adults: Principles and Creative Human Factors Approaches* (Malabar, FL: CRC Press, 2004).

36. Mary L. Broad and John W. Newstrom, *Transfer of Training: Action Packaged Strategies to Ensure High Payoff from Training Investments* (Reading, MA: Addison-Wesley, 1992).

37. Vivian W. Mott, *The Promise—and Peril—of Web-Based Course Delivery in Adult Continuing Education*. Paper presented at the 41st meeting of the Adult Education Research Conference, Vancouver, BC, Canada, (2000).

38. K. Warner Schaie and Sherry L. Willis, *Adult Development and Aging*, 5th ed. (Upper Saddle River, NJ: Prentice Hall, 2002).

39. Harry R. Moody, "Philosophical presuppositions of education for old age," *Educational Gerontology, 1* (1976): 1–16.

40. Ibid.

41. *Older Americans 2000: Key Indicators of Well-Being: A Report by the Federal Interagency Forum on Aging-Related Statistics,* (Washington, DC: The Data Dissemination Branch of the National Center on Health Statistics. Available: www.agingstats.gov).

42. N. Cutler, B. Whitelaw, and B. Beattie, *American Perception of Aging in the 21st Century: A Myths and Realities of Aging Chartbook* (Washington, DC: National Council on Aging, 2002).

43. American Association of Retired Persons. "Staying ahead of the curve," *The Work and Career Study* (AARP, 2002). Downloaded February 2, 2007, from www.aarp.org/stayingahead

44. Patricia Simpson, "Academic perspectives on training older workers," in *Thriving on an Aging Workforce* (Malabar, FL: Krieger, 2004), p. 65.

45. Moody, op. cit.

46. Ibid.

47. Abraham Maslow, *Motivation and Personality* (New York: Harper and Row, 1954).

48. Moody, op. cit.

49. Suzanne Dunn, "Effective strategies for training older workers," in *Thriving on an Aging Workforce*, eds. Paulette T. Beatty and Roemer M. S. Visser (Malabar, FL: Kreiger), p. 72.

50. Ron Zemke, Claire Raines, and Bob Filipczak, *Generations at Work: Managing the Clash of Veterans, Boomers, Xers and Nexters in Your Workplace* (New York: AMACOM, 2000).

trueNotes 225

true51. Bruce Klatt, "The ultimate training workshop handbook," in *An Employer's Guide to Older Workers: How to Win Them Back and Convince Them to Stay*, ed. Barbara McIntosh (New York: McGraw-Hill, 1999); downloaded March 9, 2007, from www.doleta.gov/Seniors/other_docs/EmplGuide.pdf

52. George A. Wendt, "Training notebook," *Business and Management Practices*, *152*(5) (May 1999): 30–40.

53. Barbara McIntosh, *An Employer's Guide to Older Workers: How to Win Them Back and Convince Them to Stay* (Washington, DC: U.S. Department of Labor, Employment and Training Administration, 2001). Downloaded March 9, 2007, from www.doleta.gov/Seniors/other_docs/EmplGuide.pdf

54. Administration on Aging, *Workforce and Aging*. Downloaded March 9, 2007, from www.aoa.gov/prof/notes/Docs/Workforce.doc#_Articles_on_Education

CHAPTER 5

1. Alvin Toffler, *Powershift: Knowledge, Wealth, and Violence at the Edge of the 21st Century* (New York: Bantam Books, 1994).

2. Michael Lombardo and Robert Eichinger, "High potentials as high learners," *Human Resource Management, 39*(4) (2000): 321.

3. See, for instance, William J. Rothwell, Ethan Sanders, and Jeffrey G. Soper, *ASTD Models for Workplace Learning and Performance* (Alexandria, VA: ASTD, 1999).

4. William J. Rothwell, *The Workplace Learner: How to Align Training Initiatives with Individual Learning Competencies* (New York: AMACOM, 2002).

5. See, for instance, L. Bennington and P. Tharenou, "Older workers: Myths, evidence and implications for Australian managers," *Asia Pacific Journal of Human Resources, 34*(3) (1996): 63–76; G. Boulton-Lewis, L. Buys, and J. Lovie-Kitchin, "Learning and active aging," *Educational Gerontology, 32*(4) (2006): 271–282; D. Duays and V. Bryan, "Senior adults' perceptions of successful aging," *Educational Gerontology, 32*(6) (2006): 423–445; J. Guthrie and C. Schwoerer, "Older dogs and new tricks: Career stage and self-assessed need for training," *Public Personnel Management, 25*(1) (1996): 59–72; J. Hedge, W. Borman, and S. Lammlein, *Aging Workforce: Realities, Myths, and Implications for Organizations* (Washington, DC: American Psychological Association, 2006); S. Johnson and K. Taylor, eds. *Neuroscience of Adult Learning* (San Francisco: Jossey-Bass, 2006); T. Maurer and N. Rafuse, "Learning, not litigating: managing employee development and avoiding claims of age discrimination," *Academy of Management Executive, 15*:(4) (2001): 110–121; G. Odums, "A New Year's resolution: Optimize older workers," *T + D, 60*(1) (2006): 34–36; F. Rothstein and D. Ratte, *Training and Older Workers: Implications for*

U.S. Competitiveness. Eric Document No. ED 336608, (Columbus, OH: Eric Clearinghouse, 1990).

6. David D. Dubois and William J. Rothwell. *Competency-Based Human Resource Management* (Palo Alto, CA: Davies-Black, 2004).

7. Ibid.

8. John Stanard, *Information Explosion Yields Data Nightmare*, 1998. Downloaded December 26, 2006, from www.govtech.net/publications/gt/1998/June/story2/story2.htm

9. William J. Rothwell, *The Workplace Learner: How to Align Training Initiatives With Individual Learning Competencies* (New York: AMACOM, 2002).

10. See, for instance, the classic article Ron Zemke and Susan Zemke, "Adult learning: What do we know for sure?" *Training, 32*(6) (1995): 31–40.

11. K. O'Donnell and C. Chapman, *Adult Education Participation in 2004–2005* (Washington, DC: U.S. Dept. of Education, 2006).

12. Neil Charness and Sara Czaja, *Older Worker Training: What We Know and Don't Know*. No. 2006-22 (Washington, DC: AARP Public Policy Institute, 2006); F. Rothstein and D. Ratte, *Training and Older Workers: Implications for U.S. Competitiveness*. Eric Document No. ED 336608 (Columbus, OH: Eric Clearinghouse, 1990).

13. William J. Rothwell, *The Action Learning Guidebook: A Real-Time Strategy for Problem-Solving, Training Design, and Employee Development* (San Francisco: Jossey-Bass/Pfeiffer, 1999).

14. William J. Rothwell and Stanley Poduch, "Introducing technical (not managerial) succession planning," *Public Personnel Management, 33*(4) (2004): 405–420; William J. Rothwell, "Knowledge transfer: 12 strategies for succession management," *IPMA-HR News* (2004): 10–12.

CHAPTER 6

1. Harvey L. Sterns and Dennis Doverspike, "Aging and the training and learning process in organizations," in *Training and Development in Work Organization,* eds. I. Goldstein and R. Katzell (San Francisco: Jossey-Bass, 1989), pp. 299–332.

2. Harvey L. Sterns and Jerome Kaplan, "Self-management of career and retirement," in *Retirement: Current Research and Future Directions,* eds. Gary A. Adams and Terry A. Beehr (New York: Springer, 2003), pp. 188–213.

3. Harvey L. Sterns, and Linda M. Subich, "Career development in midcareer," in *Work Careers: A Developmental Perspective,* ed. D. C. Feldman (San Francisco: John Wiley and Sons, 2002), pp. 186–213.

4. Douglas T. Hall and P. H. Mirvis, "Career as lifelong learning," in *The Changing Nature of Work,* ed. A. Howard (San Francisco: Jossey-Bass, 1995a), pp. 323–361.

5. Douglas T. Hall and P. H. Mirvis, "The new career contract: Developing the whole person at midlife and beyond," *Journal of Vocational Behavior,* 47 (1995b): 269–289.

6. Douglas T. Hall and Associates, *The Career Is Dead: Long Live the Career* (San Francisco, CA: Jossey-Bass, 1996).

7. Harvey L. Sterns and Jennifer H. Gray, "Work, leisure, and retirement," in *Gerontology,* eds. John Cavanaugh and Susan Whitbourne (New York: Oxford University Press, 1999), pp. 355–390.

8. James L. Farr, Paul E. Tesluk, and Stephanie R. Klein, "Organizational structure of the workplace and the older worker," in *The Impact of Work on Older Adults,* eds. K. Warner Schaie and Carmi Schooler (New York: Springer, 1998), pp. 143–185.

9. Harvey L. Sterns and Suzanne Miklos, "The aging worker in a changing environment: Organizational and individual issues," *Journal of Vocational Behavior,* 47 (1995): 248–268.

10. Douglas T. Hall and P. H. Mirvis, "The new protean career: Psychological success and the path with a heart," in *The Career Is Dead: Long Live the Career,* eds. Douglas T. Hall and Associates (San Francisco: Jossey-Bass, 1996).

11. Ibid.

12. Donald Super, "A lifespan, life-space approach to career development," *Journal of Vocational Behavior,* 18 (1980): 282–298

13. Timothy Salthouse and Todd Maurer, "Aging, job performance, and career development," in *Handbook of the Psychology of Aging,* 4th ed., eds. J. E. Birren and K. W. Schaie (San Diego: Academic Press, 1996), pp. 353–364.

14. E. M. Brady, R. H. Fortinsky, S. Norland, and D. Eichar, *Predictors of Success Among Older Workers in New Jobs: Final Report* (Portland, ME: Human Services Development Institute, University of Southern Maine, 1989).

15. Mildred Doering, Susan R. Rhodes, and Michael Schuster, *The Aging Worker: Research and Recommendations* (Beverly Hills, CA: Sage Publications, 1983).

16. Janet L. Barnes-Farrell, "Contextual variables that enhance/inhibit career development opportunities for older adults: The case of supervisor-subordinate age disparity," in *Development in the Workplace,* eds. J. Demick and P. M. Miller (Hillsdale, NJ: Lawrence Erlbaum, 1993), pp. 141–175.

17. E. Kim Jungmeen and Phyllis Moen, "Moving into retirement: Preparation and transitions in late midlife," in *Handbook of Midlife Development,* ed. Margie Lachman (New York: John Wiley, 2002), pp. 487–527.

18. Harvey L. Sterns, "Training and retraining adult and older adult workers," in *Age, Health, and Employment,* eds. J. E. Birren, P. K. Robinson, and J. E. Livingston (Englewood Cliffs, NJ: Prentice Hall, 1986).

19. Margaret Clark-Plaskie and Margie Lachman, "The sense of control in Midlife," in *Life in the Middle: Psychological and Social Development in Middle*

Age, eds. Sherry L. Willis and James D. Reid (San Diego: Academic Pess,1999), pp. 234–246.

20. Ursula M. Staudinger, "Social cognition and a psychological approach to an art of life," in *Social Cognition and Aging,* eds. T. M. Hess and F. Blanchard-Fields (San Diego: Academic Press, 1999), pp. 343–375.

21. Jacquie Smith, "Planning about life: A social-interactive and life-span perspective," in *Interactive Minds: Life Span Perspectives on the Social Foundation of Cognition,* eds. P. B. Baltes and U. M. Staudinger (Hillsdale, NJ: Lawrence Erlbaum, 1996), pp. 242–275.

22. Douglas T. Hall and P. H. Mirvis, op. cit.

23. Mark L. Savickas, "Career adaptability: An integrative construct for life span, life-space theory," *Career Development Quarterly,* 45(3) (1997): 247–259.

24. Ibid.

25. Paul B. Baltes and Margaret M. Baltes, "Psychological perspectives on successful aging: The model of selective optimization with compensation," in *Successful Aging: Perspectives from the Behavioral Sciences* (New York: Cambridge University Press, 1990), pp. 1–34.

26. Staudinger, op. cit.

27. Todd Maurer and B. Tarulli, "Perceived environment, perceived outcome, and person variables in relationship to voluntary development activity by employees," *Journal of Applied Psychology,* 70, (1996): 3–14.

28. Sterns and Gray, op. cit.

29. Lawrence L. Bailey and Robert O. Hansson, "Psychological obstacles to job or career change in late life," *Journals of Gerontology: Series B: Psychological Sciences and Social Sciences,* 50B(6) (1995): 280–288.

30. Harvey L. Sterns and Jerome Kaplan, "Self-management of career and retirement," in *Retirement: Current Research and Future Directions,* eds. Gary A. Adams and Terry A. Beehr (New York: Springer Publishing Co., 2003), pp. 188–213.

31. Ibid.

32. Harvey L. Sterns and Margaret H. Huyck, "The role of work in midlife," in *Handbook of Midlife Development,* ed. Margie E. Lachman (New York: John Wiley and Sons, Inc., 2001), pp. 447–486.

33. Daniel C. Feldman, *Managing Careers in Organizations* (Boston, MA: Scott, Foresman, 2002).

34. Manuel London, "Organizational assistance in career development," in *Work Careers: A Developmental Perspective,* ed. D. C. Feldman (San Francisco: John Wiley, 2002), pp. 323–345.

35. Harvey L. Sterns and Anthony A. Sterns, *Training and Careers: Growth and Development over Fifty Years*. Paper presented at the 48th Annual Scientific Meeting of the Gerontological Society, 1995.

36. Sterns and Huyck, op. cit.

37. Daniel C. Feldman, "Stability in the midst of change: A developmental perspective on the study of careers," in *Work Careers: A Developmental Perspective*, ed. D. C. Feldman (San Francisco: Jossey-Bass, 2002), pp. 3–26.

38. Harvey L. Sterns and Anthony A. Sterns, "Past and future directions for career development theory," in *Thriving on an Aging Workforce: Strategies for Organizational and Systematic Change*, eds. Paulette B. Beatty and Roemer M. Visser (Malabar, FL: Krieger, 2005).

39. E. H. Schein, "The individual, the organization, and the career: A conceptual scheme," *Journal of Applied Behavioral Science*, 7 (1971): 401–426.

40. Douglas T. Hall, "Potential for career growth," *Personnel Administration*, 34 (1971): 12–35.

41. Daniel J. Levinson, C. N. Darrow, E. B. Klein, M. L. Levinson, and B. McKee, *The Seasons of a Man's Life* (New York: Knopf, 1978).

42. Gail Sheehy, *Passages* (New York: Dutton, 1976).

43. Paul B. Baltes, Haynes W. Reese, and Lewis P. Lipsett, "Life-span developmental psychology," *Annual Review of Psychology*, 31 (1980): 65–110.

44. R. Katz, The influence of job longevity on employee reactions to task characteristics," *Human Relations*, 31 (1980): 703–725.

45. Donald E. Super, "Career and life development," in *Career Choice and Development*, eds. D. Brown, L. Brooks, and Associates (San Francisco: Jossey-Bass, 1984), pp. 192–234 .

46. Sterns and Sterns, op. cit.

47. J. Neapolitan, "Occupational change in mid-career: An exploratory investigation," *Journal of Vocational Behavior*, 16 (1980): 212–225.

48. S. Gould, "Characteristics of career planners in upwardly mobile occupations," *Academy of Management Journal*, 22 (1979): 539–550.

49. T. A. Beehr, T. D. Taber, and J. T. Walsh, "Perceived mobility channels: Criteria for intraorganizational job mobility." *Organizational Behavior and Human Performance*, 26 (1980): 250–264.

50. J. F. Veiga, "Mobility influences during managerial career stages," *Academy of Management Journal*, 26 (1983): 64–85

51. J. Sonnenfeld and J. P. Kotter, "The maturation of career theory," *Human Relations*, 35 (1982): 19–46.

52. Harvey L. Sterns and Meg Patchett, "Technology and the aging adult: Career development and training," in *Aging and Technical Advances*, eds. Pauline. K. Robinson, Judy E. Livingston, and James E. Birren (New York: Plenum Press, 1984).

53. Meg B. Patchett and Harvey L. Sterns, *Career Progression in Middle and Later Adulthood*. Paper presented as part of the symposium "Industrial Gerontological Psychology: Current Issues for the Curriculum and Research," at Tenth Annual Meeting of the Association for Gerontology in Higher Education, Indianapolis, February, 1984.

54. Jungmeen and Moen, op. cit.

55. Douglas T. Hall, "Potential for career growth," *Personnel Administration, 34* (1971): 12–35.

56. Hall and Mirvis, op. cit.

57. Sterns and Gray, op. cit.

58. Sterns and Sterns, op. cit.

59. James L. Farr and Carolyn L. Middlebrooks, "Enhancing motivation to participate in professional development," in *Maintaining Professional Competence*, eds. Sherry L.Willis and Samuel S. Dubin (San Francisco: Jossey-Bass, 1990), pp. 195–213.

60. James L. Farr, Paul E. Tesluk, and Stephanie R. Klein, "Organizational structure of the workplace and the older worker," in *Impact of Work on Older Adults*, eds. K. Warner Schaie and Carmi Schooler (New York: Springer 1998), pp. 143–185.

61. J. A. Fossom and Richard D. Arvey, "Market place and organizational factors that contribute to obsolescence," in *Maintaining Professional Competence*, eds. Sherry L. Willis and Samuel S. Dubin (San Francisco: Jossey-Bass, 1990).

62. James C. Vortuba, "Strengthening confidence and vitality in midcareer faculty," in *Maintaining Professional Competence*, eds. Sherry L.Willis and Samuel S. Dubin (San Francisco: Jossey-Bass, 1990), pp. 214–232.

63. Sherry L.Willis and Samuel S. Dubin, eds., *Maintaining Professional Competence* (San Francisco: Jossey-Bass, 1990).

64. J. H. Lawrence, "Developmental needs as intrinsic incentives," in *Incentives for Faculty Vitality*, ed. R. G. Baldwin (San Francisco: Jossey-Bass, 1985).

65. Vortuba, op. cit.

66. A. E. Reichers, "A review and reconceptualization of organizational commitment," *Academy of Management Review, 10* (1985): 465–476.

67. D. M. Randall, "Commitment and the organization: The organization man revisited," *Academy of Management Review, 12* (1987): 460–471.

68. J. P. Meyer and N. J. Allen, "Testing the 'side bet' theory of organizational commitment: Some methodological considerations," *Journal of Applied Psychology*, 69 (1984): 372–378.

69. H.S. Becker, "Notes on the concept of commitment," *American Journal of Sociology*, 66 (1960): 32–42.

70. Harvey L. Sterns and Michael McDaniel, "Job performance and the older worker," in *Older Workers: How Do They Measure Up? An Overview of Age Differences In Employee Costs and Performances*, ed. Sara Rix. Paper prepared for Public Policy Institute of the American Association of Retired Persons, Washington, DC, 1994.

71. Nancy S. Matheson, *"The Influence of Organizational-Based Self-Esteem on Organizational Commitment: An Analysis of Age Differences,"* Ph.D. Dissertation, The University of Akron, 1991.

72. Sterns and Sterns, op. cit.

73. Patricia A. Simson and Linda K. Stroh, "Revisiting gender variation in training," *Feminist Economics*, 8(3) (2002): 21–53.

CHAPTER 7

1. Jessica Collison, *Older Workers Survey* (Alexandria, VA: SHRM Research, 2003).

2. David Walker, *A Look at Our Future When Baby Boomers Retire*, downloaded March 13, 2007, from www.whcoa.gov/press/speakers/Walker_WhiteHouseCOA12-12-12-g.ppt#640,1,Slide 1

3. Martin Sicker, *The Political Economy of Work in the 21st Century: Implications of an Aging American Workforce* (Westport, CT: Quorum Books, 2002).

4. W. McNaught, and M. C. Barth, "Are older workers 'good buys'? A case study of Days Inn of America," *Sloan Management Review Spring* (1992): 53–63.

5. The Media Audit, *Internet Use Continues Growing; Most New Growth Driven by Older Age Groups* (Houston, TX: Author, 2004).

6. SeniorNet, *Growing Number of Seniors Use the Web for News and Searches According to SeniorNet*, downloaded March 13, 2007, from www.todaysseniorsnetwork.com/seniors_and_the_web.htm

7. AARP, *Best Employers Program Honorees*, downloaded February 26, 2008, from www.aarp.org/money/careers/employerresourcecenter/bestemployers/winners/volkswagen_of_america_inc.html

8. Linda Barrington, *Demographic Trends and the Aging Workforce* (Philadelphia, PA: AARP Global Aging Conference: Maximizing Your Workforce: Employees Over 50 in Today's Global Economy, 2004).

9. Michael Hay, "Strategies for survival in the war on talent," *Career Development International* (February 2002): 52–55.

10. Barbara McIntosh, *An Employer's Guide to Older Workers: How to Win Them Back and Convince Them to Stay* (Washington, DC: U.S. Department of Labor, Employment and Training Administration, 2001). Downloaded March 9, 2007, from www.doleta.gov/Seniors/other_docs/EmplGuide.pdf

11. William Rothwell, *Effective Succession Planning: Ensuring Leadership Continuity and Building Talent from Within*, 2nd ed. (New York: AMACOM, 2000).

12. William Rothwell and Stan Poduch, "Introducing technical (not managerial) succession planning," *Public Personnel Management*, 33(4) (Winter 2004): 405–419.

13. David W. DeLong, *Lost Knowledge: Confronting the Threat of an Aging Workforce* (New York: Oxford University Press, 2004).

14. Society for Human Resource Management, testimony before U.S. Senate Special Committee on Aging, September 3, 2003, downloaded from aging.senate.gov/events/fr108dc.pdf

15. David Newman, "A landmark supreme court decision is being hailed as 'the Emancipation Proclamation' for older workers," *AARP Bulletin* (May 2005) (Washington, DC: AARP). www.aarp.org/bulletin/yourlife/breakthrough.html

16. Committee for Economic Development, *New Opportunities for Older Workers* (Washington, DC: Author, 1999).

17. McIntosh, op. cit.

18. Janemarie Mulvey and Steven Nyce, *Strategies to Retain Older Workers* (Philadelphia, PA: The Wharton School, University of Pennsylvania, April 26–27, 2004).

19. Federal Deposit Insurance Corporation, Downloaded March 13, 2005, from www.fdic.gov/about/workforce_act/

20. AARP Press Center, *AARP Honors 35 Best Employers for Workers Over 50* (Washington, DC: AARP, August 31, 2004).

21. More information available at www.microsoft.com/enable/centers

22. Watson Wyatt, *Phased Retirement: Aligning Employer Programs with Worker Preferences - 2004 Survey Report* (Washington, DC: Author, 2004).

23. More information available at solutions.3m.com/wps/portal/3M/en_US/global/sustainability/s/performance-indicators/community/volunteerism

24. The act is available at www.eeoc.gov/policy/adea.html

25. More information available at www.askmecorp.com/services/methodology.asp

26. Dr. Yogesh Malhotra, Founder of the BRINT Institute, New Hartford, New York. More information available at www.brint.com/casestudies.html

27. Computer World, *Using IT to Tap Experts' Know-How* (March 15, 2004).

28. William J. Rothwell and Stan Poduch, "Introducing technical (not managerial) succession planning," *Public Personnel Management, 33* (4) (Winter 2004).

29. McIntosh, Barbara (2000). "An employer's guide to older workers: How to win them back and convince them to stay," www.doleta.gov / seniors / other_docs / emplguide.pdf

30. National Older Worker Career Center, *How to Recruit, Manage, Train, and Retain the New Older Worker* (Arlington, VA: Author).

31. David W. DeLong, *Lost Knowledge: Confronting the Threat of an Aging Workforce.* (New York: Oxford University Press, 2004). Through www.lostknowledge. com / pages / book.html

32. Good, Vicki S. (2002). "Baylor preventing generational collisions," Baylor All Saints Medical Center, Fort Worth, TX. At www.aacn.org / AACN / chapters.nsf / Files / Generation / $file / Generation.ppt

33. Committee for Economic Development, *New Opportunities For Older Workers* (1999). At www.ced.org / docs / report / report_older.pdf

34. AARP (2004). *Staying Ahead of the Curve 2004: Employer Best Practices for Mature Workers.* At assets.aarp.org/www.aarp.org_/build/templates/money/ BE_stayingahead.pdf

35. A list of online survey services is available at www.surveymonkey.com / Pricing.asp

36. www.microsoft.com / enable / cd

37. A. D. Fisk, W. A. Rogers, N. Charness, S. J. Czaja, and J. Sharit, *Designing for Older Adults: Principles and Creative Human Factors Approaches.* Boca Raton, FL: CRC Press, 2004).

ABOUT THE AUTHORS

William J. Rothwell, Ph.D., SPHR, is Professor of Workforce Education and Development in the Department of Learning and Performance Systems on the University Park campus of The Pennsylvania State University. In that capacity, he leads a graduate specialty in Workplace Learning and Performance within the Workforce Education and Development program. He is also President of his own consulting company, Rothwell & Associates, Inc. (see www.rothwell-associates.com).

He completed a B. A. in English from Illinois State University, an M.A. (and all courses for the doctorate) in English at the University of Illinois at Urbana-Champaign, an M.B.A. with a specialty in Human Resource Management at Sangamon State University (now called the University of Illinois at Springfield), and a Ph.D. in Education/Training at the University of Illinois at Urbana-Champaign. He has also earned life accreditation as a Senior Professional in Human Resources (SPHR) through the Human Resource Certification Institute as well as the Registered Organization Development Consultant (RODC) designation through the Organization Development Institute.

Before entering academe, Dr. Rothwell was a Director of Human Resource Development in the public and private sectors from 1979 to 1993. He managed, planned, designed, and evaluated countless learning and performance programs.

Dr. Rothwell has authored, co-authored, edited, or co-edited more than 275 books, book chapters, and articles. His recent books include:

Bernthal, P., Colteryahn, K., Davis, P., Naughton, J., Rothwell, W., & Wellins, R. (2004). *Mapping the future: Shaping new workplace learning and performance competencies*. Alexandria, VA: The American Society for Training and Development.

Cecil, R., & Rothwell, W. (2007). *Next generation management development: The complete guide and resource.* San Francisco: Pfeiffer & Co.

Dubois, D., & Rothwell, W. (2007). *Competency-based human resource management.* Chinese translation. Beijing: The People's University Press.

Powers, B., & Rothwell, W. (2007). *Instructor excellence: Mastering the delivery of training,* 2nd ed. San Francisco: Pfeiffer.

Rothwell, W. (2005). *Beyond training and development: The groundbreaking classic,* 2nd ed. New York: AMACOM.

Rothwell, W. (2005). *Effective succession planning: Ensuring leadership continuity and building talent from within,* 3rd ed. New York: AMACOM.

Rothwell, W., Butler, M., Maldonado, C., Hunt, D., Peters, K., Li, J., & Stern, J. (2006). *Handbook of training technology: An introductory guide to facilitating learning with technology—from planning through evaluation.* San Francisco: Pfeiffer & Co.

Rothwell, W., Donahue, W., & Park, J. (2005). *Creating in-house sales training and development programs.* [Translation.] Beijing: Publishing House of the Electronics Industry.

Rothwell, W., Gerity, G., and Gaertner, E. (Eds.). (2004). *Linking training to performance: A guide for workforce developers.* Washington: American Association of Community Colleges.

Rothwell, W., Hohne, C., & King, S. (2007). *Human performance improvement: Building practitioner performance,* 2nd ed. Boston: Butterworth-Heineman (an imprint of Elsevier).

Rothwell, W., Jackson, R., Knight, S., Lindholm, J. with Wang, A., & Payne, T. (2005). *Career planning and succession management: Developing your organization's talent—for today and tomorrow.* Westport, CT: Greenwood Press.

Rothwell, W., & Kazanas, H. (2004). *Improving on-the-job training: How to establish and operate a comprehensive OJT program,* 2nd ed. San Francisco: Pfeiffer & Co.

Rothwell, W., & Kazanas, H. (2005). *Strategic planning for human resources.* Mumbai, India: Jaico Publishing House.

Rothwell, W., Lindholm, J., & Wallick, W. (2007). *What CEOs expect from corporate training.* Korean translation. Seoul.

Rothwell, W., Prescott, R., & Taylor, M. (2005). *Strategic human resource leader: How to prepare your organization for the six key trends shaping the future*. Mumbai: Jaico Publishing House.

Rothwell, W., & Sullivan, R. (Eds.). (2005). *Practicing organization development: A guide for consultants*, 2nd ed. San Francisco: Pfeiffer & Co.

He may be reached at 814-863-2581 or by email at wjr9@psu.edu.

Harvey L. Sterns, Ph.D., is Professor of Psychology and Director of the Institute for Life-Span Development and Gerontology at The University of Akron. He is also a Research Professor of Gerontology at the Northeastern Ohio Universities College of Medicine and Pharmacy. He is a faculty member in the Applied Cognitive Aging and Industrial/Organizational Psychology graduate programs and chairs the specialization in Industrial Gerontological Psychology. He has published extensively on cognitive intervention, work and retirement, career development, training and retraining, and maintaining professional competence. He has published over 100 book chapters and articles in professional journals. He is co editor or co-author of five books, most recently Papalia, D. E., Sterns, H. L., Feldman, R. D. & Camp, C. J. (2007). *Adult development and aging*, 3rd ed. New York: McGraw Hill.

He is a licensed psychologist in Ohio and is a Fellow of the Gerontological Society of America, the American Psychological Association, American Psychological Society, Association for Gerontology in Higher Education, and the Ohio Academy of Science. He has served as president of Division 20 Adult Development and Aging of the American Psychological Association, Association for Gerontology in Higher Education, Sigma Phi Omega National Academic and Professional Society in Gerontology, Ohio Network of Educational Consultants in the Field Of Aging, Jewish Family Service, Akron, and served as Chair of the City of Akron Commission on Aging to the Mayor and City Council. He is a current Board of Trustee Member of the American Society on Aging, Ohio Association of Gerontology and Education, and Immediate Past Chair, Board of Trustees of Mature Services, Inc., Akron. He is Vice President of Business Development for Creative Action, LLC., a consulting practice with his wife and son.

He has three decades of experience in teaching undergraduate and graduate students lifespan development and adult development and aging. He received his bachelor's degree from Bard College with a double major in biology and psychology, his master's degree in experimental psychology from the State University of New York at Buffalo, and a Ph.D. in lifespan developmental psychology from West Virginia University. Additional training in gerontology was received at the University of Southern California and the Pennsylvania State University.

He may be reached at sternsh@uakron.edu or 330-972-6724.

Diane Spokus, Ph.D., CHES, is an adjunct instructor of Human Resource Management in Healthcare and Aging at The Pennsylvania State University, teaches undergraduate Biobehavioral Health courses and is, concurrently, a Health Educator for the Pennsylvania Area Health Education Center, where she has worked in community-based diabetes Train-the-Trainer programs. She was also a Research Assistant in the Penn State School of Nursing. Her areas of research interest are older workers' training, retention, the influences of organizational incentive structures, health, job satisfaction, job demands unretirement, and re-careering. She has had experience in career development counseling, having worked with the Freshman Testing and Counseling program through the Division of Undergraduate Studies.

Diane holds a B.S. degree in Human Development and Family Studies and a Minor in Gerontology from The Pennsylvania State University. Diane has also earned a M.S. degree in Adult Education from The Pennsylvania State University, where she is also presently a Ph.D Candidate in Workforce Education, Training, and Development. In addition, she is also an adjunct instructor, having taught Adult Development and Aging and Biobehavioral Health courses. Prior to her doctoral program, she also worked on various research projects where older adults were tested in cognitive and physiological factors affecting independence. In addition, Diane has also worked in outreach units as a project assistant for Continuing Education at the university. She has also served the past four years as a member of the Allied Health Care Steering Committee of the Workforce Investment Board. She is a member of the Society for Human Resource Development (SHRM), the American Society for Training and Development (ASTD), the Penn State Workforce Development Society, the Pennsylvania Department of Aging Prime Time Health Advisory Council, the Gerontological Society of America, the American Psychological Association, the National Council on Aging, the American Society on Aging, the MaturityWorks Alliance, The American Association of University Women (AAUW), the Geriatric Interest Network, the Human Factors and Ergonomics

Society, the International Society of Gerotechnologists and served as a graduate student representative on the Geriatric Education Center Committee of the American Gerontologists in Higher Education.

Diane may be contacted at www.personal.psu.edu/dms201 or at 717-994-1798.

Joel M. Reaser, Ph.D., is Senior Vice President at the National Older Worker Career Center (NOWCC) in Arlington, Virginia. In that capacity, he directs strategic planning and management activities, including NOWCC's IT initiatives. He also coordinates information and education activities for the Senior Environment Employment (SEE) Program, which NOWCC administers for the U.S. Environmental Protection Agency, and serves as Program Manager for the ACES older worker program for the NRCS in the U.S. Department of Agriculture. He was instrumental in the planning and implementation of the National Academy for Public Administration (NAPA) forum on the aging of the federal workforce. He is the principal author of *Graying and still growing: Removing barriers to older worker utilization and boosting the economy*, published by NAPA in fall 2004. He also served as a reviewer on 2003 Older Worker Survey on which NOWCC collaborated with the Society for Human Resource Management. Prior to joining NOWCC, he served as Associate Director for Research at AARP where he contributed to, and oversaw, numerous internal research studies on the needs and attitudes of older Americans, and directed programs on the strategic use of technology by, and for, AARP's 35 million members. Prior to joining AARP, he was with the U.S. Army, IBM, and the Human Resources Research Organization and consulted with IBM, the U.S. Army Research Institute, the National Recreation and Park Association, Science Applications Inc., the Financial Executives Institute, and the American Management Association.

He completed his A.B. degree in psychology at Gettysburg College and his M.A. and Ph.D. degrees in Industrial/Organizational Psychology at the Southern Illinois University at Carbondale with a focus on organizational leadership. He also served as Visiting Professor at the George Washington University School of Engineering and Applied Sciences where he taught graduate courses in information management and served on a number of dissertation committees for candidates doing research on information management, collaborative technologies, and decision making.

He may be reached at jreaser@nowcc.org or 703-558-4200.

INDEX

401K plans, 19

A

Absenteeism
  caregiving responsibilities and, 52
  decreased, 28
Accommodation, 60, 61
  psychological, 142
Active participation, training and, 77
Activities of daily living (ADL), 42, 59
Acute illness, 57
ADDIE model, 85–98
Adult education, participation in, 118, 120
Adult workers, defining, 6–9
Advance organizer, xxv–xxvii
  scoring and interpreting, xxvi–xxvii
Aerospace industry, worker shortfall in, 4
Affective commitment, 22, 154
African Americans, in workplace, 66
Age
  biological, 41
  chronological, 7, 9, 17
  distributions, 17
  functional, 7
  norms, 17, 20
Age Discrimination in Employment Act (ADEA), 7, 16, 72, 144, 189
  amendments to, 28
Age-graded determinants, 9
Ageism, 11, 56

Age-related changes, 62–63
Aging
  biological, 40–50
  cognitive tasks and, 69–81
  global view on, 40
  hearing and, 45–47
  maintaining strength, 41–44
  physical changes and, 44–47
  psychological, 50–52
  psychometric skills and, 47–50
  social, 52–53
  stereotypes about, 56–57
  variability in, 41
  vision and, 44–45
Agriculture Conservationist
  Enrollee / Seniors (ACES) project, 187
American Association of Retired People (AARP), 38
Americans with Disabilities Act (ADA), 57–63
Analysis, 86
  instructional setting, 87
  job, 88
  learner, 86
  performance, 86
  results of, 90
  task, 89
  for training older workers, 90–91
  work, 87
  work setting, 87
Anthropometry, changes in, 62

239

Assessment procedures, 10
Assistive listening device (ALD), 46

B
Baby boomers, 108, xiv
  retirement of, xvii
  training, 99
Behavioral change, factors affecting, 9
Benefits, employment, 19
Biological age, 41
Biological aging, 40–50
Biological changes, 16
Biological determinants, 9
Biomarkers of vitality, 42
Bureau of Labor Statistics, 5
Burnout, 105
Buyouts, 18, 29, 127

C
Career development, 127–66
  future of, 151–55
  models of, 12, 27, 146–51
Careers, for older workers, 23–29
Caregiving
  absenteeism and, 52
  issues, 15
CARES program, 187, 188
Chronic illness, 57
Chronological age, 9, 17
Chronological/legal approach to
    defining older workers, 6–7
Cochlear implants, 47
Cognition, 67
Cognitive tasks, aging and, 69–81
Cohorts. *See* Generations, differences in
Commitment
  affective, 22, 154
  continuance, 22
  organizational, 155
Committee for Economic Development
    (CED), 6
Communication, hearing and, 45
Continuance commitment, 22

Cost/benefit ratios, 30
Crystallized intelligence, 78, 107

D
Decision making, by older adults, 32–33
Defense industry, worker shortfall in, 4
Demographics
  changing, xv
  workforce, 3
Disabilities, age-related, 59
Diversity training, 109–10
Downsizing, 9

E
Education industry, worker shortfall
    in, 4
Empirical research, 12
Employers
  maintaining ties with retirees, 30
  planning for aging workforce, 169–200
  practices for training older workers,
    95
  support for older workers, 29–32
  survey of, xxi–xxiv
Employment
  benefits, 19
  crisis, xvii
  extending, 6
  issues, xx
  life-long, 18
  practices, 161–62
Energy industry, worker shortfall in, 4
Environment, work, 143
  older workers and, 16–18
Environmental determinants, 9
Episodic memory, 70
Expectancy theory, 102
Experience sharing, fostering, 166
Explorers, 27

F
Familiarity, training and, 76
Family interference with work (FIW),
    53

Federal civil service, worker shortfall in, 4
Fluid intelligence, 79
Full-time work, 28
Functional age, 7
Functional approach to defining older workers, 7
Functional capacity, 61

G
Gender norms, 20
Generations, differences in, 30
Global Aging Report, 59
Government Accountability Office (GAO), 3, 170
Grandchildren, caring for, 50
Gross domestic product (GDP), 3
spending as share of, 171

H
Healthcare industry, worker shortfall in, 4
Health insurance, 19
Hearing, 45–47
changes in, 63
High potentials, 112
Hispanic Americans, in workplace, 66
Homesteaders, 23
Human Factors and Ergonomics Society, 67
Human factors designs, 64–65
Human resource management (HRM), xvi

I
Incentives, for older workers, 37
Instructional setting analysis, 87
Instructional systems design (ISD) model, xvii
ADDIE model, 85–98
for training older workers, 85–111
Intelligence
crystallized, 78, 107

fluid, 79
maintenance of abilities, 79
International Society for Gerontechnology, 67

J
Job
analysis, 88
characteristics, 10
displacement, 29
security, 18
Job satisfaction, 23
research, 129
Job Training Partnership Act, 7, 29
Joint stiffness, 48

K
Knowledge networks, 190

L
Large business initiatives, 184–96
Layoffs, 18, 29
Learner analysis, 86
Learner characteristics, of older *versus* younger adults, 116–17
Learning competence
defined, 113
workplace, 112–15
Learning performance, improving, 112–26
Learning principles, for training, 117–26
Learning strategies, training and, 77–80
Learning styles, 98, 104–5
Licensure, 11
Life-cycle theories, 32
Life expectancy, trends in, 38
Life-long employment, 18
Life-span approach to defining older workers, 8–9
Life-stage theories, 32
Long-term memory, 49, 70
Lost knowledge issue, 5

M

Management
  of older workers, 134
  practices, 137
Mandatory retirement age, abolishment
  of, 22
Manufacturing industry, worker
  shortfall in, 4
McDonald's, example, 24–27
Memory
  changes in, 70
  episodic, 70
  long-term, 49, 70
  primary, 70
  procedural, 70
  prospective, 70
  semantic, 70
  short-term, 49
  three-stage model of, 71
  working, 70
Mental capability, 30
Microsoft Accessibility Resources
  Centers, 186
Middle-aged workers
  increase in, 3
  perception of, 17
Mid-level management, 9
Midlife changes, 33–35
Mid-size business initiatives, 178–84
Mini-cycles, 148
Minorities, in workplace, 63–66
Mnemonics, 70
Mortality rates, 40
Motivation, 73–76
Myths, about older workers, 43

N

National Older Worker Career Center
  (NOWCC), 6, 187
Natural Resources Conservation
  Service (NRCS), 187
Normative determinants, 9
Nursing, worker shortfall in, 5

O

Occupations, age-typing of, 7
Older Americans Act, 7
  Title V, 29
Older workers
  active, 66–67
  adapting workplace for, 36–68
  career development for, 127–66
  careers for, 23–29
  challenges facing, 18–21
  changing jobs and, 21–23
  chronological/legal approach to
    defining, 6–7
  decision making and work
    opportunities for, 32–33
  defining, 6–9
  functional approach to defining, 7
  future of, 151–55
  as human resource, 6
  incentives for, 37
  increase in, 3
  instructional design for training,
    85–111
  issues for, 66
  learner characteristics of, 116–17
  learning styles, 104–5, 107–9
  life-span approach to defining, 8–9
  managing, 134
  midlife changes and, 33–35
  myths about, 43
  organizational issues, 13–15
  organizational view of, 8
  perceptions about, 57, 58
  physical changes affecting, 44–47
  psychosocial approach to defining, 7
  recommendations for, 155–57
  recruiting, 139, 174–75, 180–81, 185
  self-management, 9–13
  strengths of, 101–2
  support from employers for, 29–32
  technology and, 48
  training for, 69–81, 124–25
  unemployment rate of, 29

work environment changes and, 16–18
working longer, 15–16
workplace and, 54–56
Older Workers Benefit Protection Act (OWBPA), 11
Organization, training and, 76–77
Organizational-based self-esteem (OBSE), 131
Organizational commitment, 155
Organizational view of older workers, 8
Osteoporosis, 55

P
Parents, caring for, 50
Part-time work, 28
Performance analysis, 86
Personality variables, 13
Physical capability, 30
Physical changes, in midlife, 33
Population, shift in, 3
Primary memory, 70
Procedural memory, 70
Processing, speed of, 47
Productivity, increase in, 4
Professional competence, 10
Prospective memory, 70
Protean career, 10
Psychological accommodation, 142
Psychological aging, 50–52
Psychometric skills, 47–50
Psychomotor abilities, 67
Psychosocial approach to defining older workers, 7

R
Recertification, 11
Recruiting
older workers, 139, 174–75, 180–81, 185
overcoming barriers in, 160
practices, xvii
Resources, 201–13

Restructuring, 9
Retirement
of baby boomers, xv
benefits, 19
decision about, 15
notions of, xvii
policies, 30
postponing, 20
self-management and, 127–43
Reward systems, 153, 157

S
Sandwich Generation, 50–51
Sarcopenia, 42
Self-concept, 138
Self-management, 9–13, 127–43, 157
obstacles to, 144–46
Semantic memory, 70
Senior Community Service Employment Program, 29
Senior Environmental Employment (SEE) Program, 187
Short-term memory, 49
Small business initiatives, 174–78
Social aging, 52–53
Social role model, 21
Society for Human Resource Management (SHRM), 5
Speed of processing, 47
State civil service, worker shortfall in, 4
Stereotypes
about aging, 56–57
negative aging, 144
Stock portfolios, 19
Structure, training for, 76
Success, individual factors in, 142–43

T
Tardiness, decreased, 28
Task analysis, 89
Technology
impact on workplace, 177
older adults and, 48

Time, training for, 77
Training, 12, 36
  ADDIE model, 85–98
  diversity, 109–10
  formats, 97
  guidelines, 105
  improving, 126
  individual differences in, 98–99
  instructional systems design for,
    85–111
  modalities, 106–7
  for older workers, 69–81, 124–25
  opportunities, 152
  principles, 74–75
  transferring results, 105–6
  value of, 101–4
Transformers, 27
Turnover, decreased, 28

U
Unemployment rate, of older adults, 29

V
Vision, 44–45
  changes in, 62–63
Vitality, biomarkers of, 42

W
When Actually Employed (WAE)
    program, 187

White House Conference on Aging, 16
Work analysis, 87
Work environment, older workers and,
    16–18
Workforce
  decline in, 170
  demographics, 3
  older adult workers in, 3–35
  outlook, 4
  preparing for future, 197–200
Work influences, 132
Working memory, 70
Work interference with family (WIF),
    53
Work opportunities, for older adults,
    32–33
Workplace
  adapting for older adults, 36–68,
    67–68
  designing for older workers, 54–56
  evolving, 169–72
  learning climate, 113–15
  learning competence, 112–15
  minorities in, 63–66
Workplace learning and performance
    (WLP), xvi
Work setting analysis, 87

www.ingramcontent.com/pod-product-compliance
Ingram Content Group UK Ltd.
Pitfield, Milton Keynes, MK11 3LW, UK
UKHW020135190625
459827UK00001BA/198

9 780814 473924